D0595930

JASPER COUNTY MIDDLE/HIGH SCHOOL
1289 College Street
Monticello, GA 31064

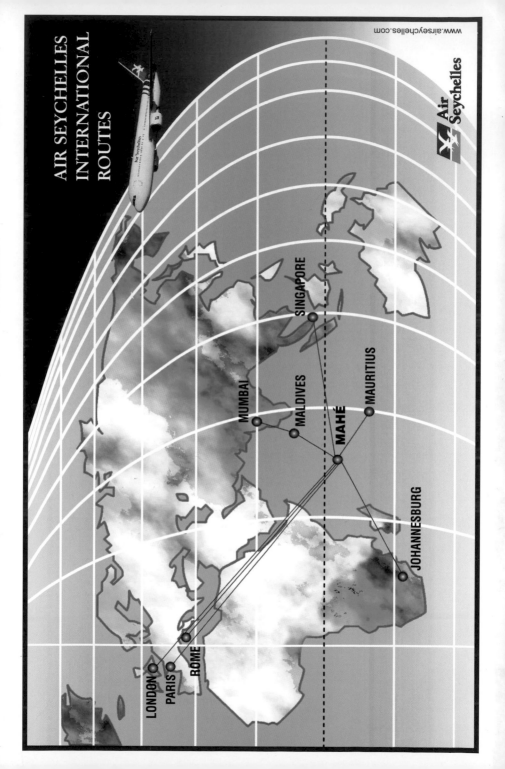

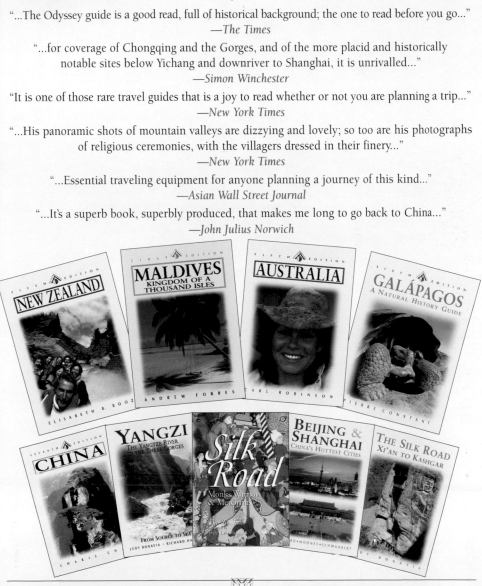

North Island Resort blends in beautifully with its natural surroundings
(left) *Vallée de mai*

(above) *The crystal clear seas around Seychelles are at their best between October and May*
(right) *A trip on Helicopter Seychelles reveals deserted, pristine beaches, far from the beaten track*

(below) *Fly fishing in the shallows of St Francois lagoon, near Alphonse*
(right) *Sooty terns in flight.* (lower right) *If fish are not destined for the dinner table, they are tagged and released*

Sooty terns live most of their life on the wing over the ocean, but return in their thousands each year to the northern corner of Bird Island, to hatch their young in a vast noisy colony

North Island Resort offers massage and beauty treatments both indoors and out

(clockwise from top right) *Grilled seafood, fresh from the ocean; sprays of white orchids and brightly-coloured ginger; the lagoon at sunset; sundown cocktails*

Total relaxation amid the back-to-nature setting of North Island Resort

Published by Odyssey Books & Guides, an imprint of
Airphoto International Ltd., 903 Seaview Commercial Building,
21–24 Connaught Road West, Sheung Wan, Hong Kong
Tel: (852)2856 3896; Fax: (852)2565 8004; E-mail: sales@odysseypublications.com
www.odysseypublications.com

Distributed in the United States of America by
W.W. Norton & Company, Inc.,
500 Fifth Avenue, New York, NY 10110, USA
Tel: 800-233-4830; Fax: 800-458-6515
www.wwnorton.com

Distributed in the United Kingdom and Europe by
Cordee Books and Maps,
3a De Montfort Street, Leicester, LE1 7HD, UK,
Tel: 0116-254-3579; Fax: 0116-247-1176
www.cordee.co.uk

Library of Congress Catalog Card Number has been requested.

ISBN: 962-217-752-2

Grateful acknowledgment is made to the following authors and publishers:

Kew Royal Botanical Gardens for *A Vision of Eden* by Marianne North

Cambridge University Library for *Pursuit of an Island* by J A Mockford

The Site of the Garden of Eden by General Gordon

Managing Editors: Helen Northey, Neil Art
Design: Au Yeung Chui Kwai
Maps: Mark Stroud
Index: Don Brech

Photography by Paul Turcotte
Additional photography/illustrations courtesy of Banyan Tree Seychelles 200–1, 201; Bibliothèque Municipale
of Caen 27 (bottom); Bibliothèque Nationale, Paris 27 (top), 167; Richard Bradbury 96 (top), 138; Andrew
Carpin 69, 89, 264; Jacques Fauquet 92, 98, 99, 103, 249 (bottom); Nature Seychelles 96 (bottom); David
Rowatt 288; Royal Commonwealth Society Collection 294; Tally & Lionel Pozzoli—Seychelles Tourism
Marketing Authority 269, 298, 299; Taj Denis Island Resort 226–7; Rosemary Wise 120, 131

Production by Twin Age Ltd, Hong Kong
E-mail: twinage@netvigator.com
Manufactured in Hong Kong

(front cover) *Yacht mooring at Grande Soeur Island (Big Sister Island), north east of La Digue*
(previous page) *Fly fishing as the sun quickly sets over the Indian Ocean:*
this is bound to be the last catch before darkness falls

SEYCHELLES

Sarah Carpin
Photography by Paul Turcotte

(above) *Basking in the pool of the Banyan Tree*
(left) *Intendance Beach is hailed by many as the finest beach in Seychelles*

Contents

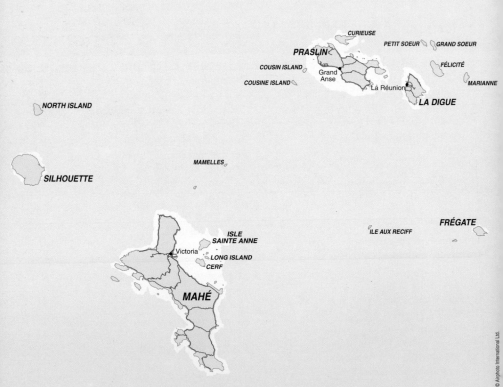

THE SEYCHELLES GROUP

INNER
ISLANDS

AMIRANTES
GROUP   ● Desroches

Indian Ocean

ALPHONSE
GROUP

N
↑

0   100   200 kms
0   50   100 miles

ALDABRA GROUP

FARQUHAR GROUP

© Airphoto International Ltd.

Treasure Islands

The old corsair stood on the scaffold, the noose around his neck. With a final flourish he produced a small scrap of parchment from his cloak and flung it to the crowd below. "My treasure," he bellowed, "to he who can understand."

Thus the hunt began for the buried treasure of the most infamous of pirates to sail the Indian Ocean, Frenchman Olivier le Vasseur, known as 'La Buze' (the buzzard). In the 1720s he joined forces with another pirate, Englishman John Taylor, to terrorise shipping throughout the Indian Ocean. In 1730 Le Vasseur was captured by the French and, on the 7th July of that year, hanged on Isle de France (now Mauritius). Many still believe his priceless booty remains hidden on one of the small islands of Seychelles, long used as pirate bases. Modern day treasure-seekers come to Seychelles for very different reasons: the lure of golden beaches and the elusive ideal of a tropical paradise.

In their 'dream holiday' promotion, British Airways maintain that Seychelles is their customers' top choice. So does Seychelles live up to its paradise hype? In a word—yes. On the hundred or so islands in Seychelles, scattered over an area of 400,000 square kilometres of ocean, you can discover primeval mistforests, huge flocks of sea birds and giant tortoises, black parrots and the flightless white-throated rail bird (related to the extinct Dodo). There are old plantation houses, ruins of leper hospitals, pirate graves and legends of buried treasure. Then, of course, there are the famous beaches— miles of deserted powdery white sands, surrounded by coral reefs and sparkling lagoons.

The archipelago of Seychelles lies four degrees south of the Equator and 'a thousand miles from anywhere,' as the tourist board slogan reminds visitors. The inner granite islands were created from a splinter of India when it tore away from Africa over 650 million years ago and were subsequently protected from the outside world by a thousand mile moat of ocean. The outer islands, many of which are uninhabited, are flat and coralline.

Seychelles is one of those few places in the world that has no real natural hazards or dangers. There is no malaria or serious disease. It lies outside the cyclone and hurricane belts, so the weather is mild, hot and humid all year round. The local people enjoy a good standard of living and there are no beggars or hawkers on the streets or beaches. There is little crime, and the country has that laid back tropical atmosphere guaranteed to make even the most nervous of travellers relax. Tourist numbers are modest: even at the height of the tourist season (July to August and December) you can easily find a deserted beach. There are no high-rise hotels and the airport is considered busy if two flights arrive around the same time.

The Seychelles Government is considered to be one of the world's most environmentally-conscious administrations. It has limited the number of tourist beds available on the islands and kept airline ticket prices high, in order to stop over-commercialisation. Because Seychelles came late to the tourist industry—the international airport was not built until 1971—it has learned from the mistakes of many other tropical holiday destinations.

Island-hopping holidays are deservedly popular. Most visitors spend at least part of their holiday on the main island of **Mahé**, which has the International Airport and capital town of Victoria. Although the most densely populated, with less than 68,000 people living here, it is hardly crowded. Mahé has the most beaches and hotels together with a wide range of restaurants and water sports facilities. **Praslin** is the next largest island, with a good range of hotels from exclusive resorts to small family run guesthouses. It is also home to the Valleé de Mai—a primeval rainforest containing the famous coco de mer palms, which have the largest, heaviest and most suggestively shaped nuts in the world.

For tropical charm, **La Digue** has it all—tumbledown plantation houses, dusty roads used by slow-moving bicycles and ox carts and a working coconut plantation open to visitors. The beaches of La Digue are supposedly the most photographed in the world, distinguished by the weathered granite boulders that resemble modern art pieces. Many other smaller islands have been turned into discreet hideaways for the rich and famous or nature reserves for the many examples of rare species found nowhere else on earth. Pet tortoises amble around on most of the small islands, but the wild population lives exclusively on **Aldabra**, the far flung atoll which has been designated a World Heritage Site by UNESCO. For many years this 'Galapagos of the Indian Ocean' was only accessible to the scientists who work there, but now the government is beginning to open it up to a limited number of visitors each year. Prices will be kept high in order to attract committed botanists and zoologists and keep the merely curious at bay.

The government is beginning to realise that money can be made from its green stance—a new conference centre on Mahé has been opened to encourage academics to use Seychelles as a base for environmental conferences. Wildlife holidays are also being developed. Seychelles has a unique array of flora and fauna. Every other bird or animal is likely to be prefixed by one superlative or another—the smallest (frog), largest and heaviest (tortoise) and rarest (almost all the endemic trees and birds seem to fall into this category). Ornithologists visit Seychelles to view the thousands of seabirds that nest on the islands each year or to catch a glimpse of local rarities, like the black parrot, Seychelles brush warbler and the toc toc bird.

Diving holidays are increasing in popularity; a new dive centre has recently opened on the outlying island of Desroches, part of the Amirante Islands, an hour's flight from Mahé. The 'Desroches Drop' is a site renowned for the best diving in Seychelles, if not the Indian Ocean. There are also well run diving centres on the main islands of Mahé and Praslin, which provide PADI courses and supervised dives. Even if you are no diver, a snorkel on the reefs around the islands is almost as amazing: if the birds are sometimes lacking in colour, the fish make up for it in a vivid living kaleidoscope. Many of the best sites lie in the national marine parks around Mahé and Praslin. Diving and snorkelling is strictly controlled—spear guns are prohibited and it is illegal to pick up any coral or shells. As a result the reefs remain intact and the fish are so tame they are likely to be as curious about you as you are about them.

Edouard Ernesta and his ox cart

The main islands have only been settled for about 200 years. The Possession Stone was erected by Frenchman Captain Morphey on the first of November 1756, signifying that he had taken possession of Mahé and several other nearby islands on behalf of the King of France. It was Morphey that named these islands Seychelles, thought to have been in honour of Vicomte Moreau de Sechelle who was controller-general of France at the time. The stone was almost lost in 1894, removed by a visiting French general wanting to take it back to the Paris Museum. However, on his way back to France he was intercepted with a telegram demanding its immediate return to Mahé. During the Napoleonic Wars the islands passed from French to English rule then back again several times over, before the English finally took over as colonial masters in 1811. The English never really settled on the islands and the French influence remains strong. Many African slaves were also brought in to work the land. After the abolition of slavery many of them were liberated in Seychelles, when illegal slaving ships were captured by the English in the Indian Ocean.

It was the slaves that introduced the musical traditions of the Sega and the Moutia. The Sega, similar to the music and dance of neighbouring Mauritius, is a calypso-like rhythm with a shuffling, hip-swaying dance. The Moutia is much more African—usually played by the light of a beach bonfire. It is a primitive sounding beat played on a heated goatskin drum and helped along with large doses of bacca or calou—both locally brewed liqueurs made from sugar cane and coconut palm sap.

Besides the African slaves and the French landowners, other nationalities came to Seychelles—Arabs, Chinese and Indians have stayed and settled and the Seychellois population today is a wonderful mixture of all these influences, resulting in a complete lack of racial tension. Seychellois women, in particular, are famed throughout Africa for their beauty and elegance. They are sometimes described as 'French enough to have good shapes, English enough to have good manners, Asian enough to have the touch of the exotic about them, and African enough to have a call of the wild in them!'

Does it all sound too good to be true? Perhaps I am biased, having fallen in love with the islands while living there several years ago and marrying a Seychellois into the bargain. I agree with Victorian explorer General Gordon that paradise on earth can be found here—a pirate's treasure trove waiting to be discovered.

Anse Lazio, Praslin

The History of Seychelles

The islands of Seychelles remained uninhabited until only about 200 years ago and their existence was not even properly documented until the 17th century. The granite islands were isolated from the outside world by a thousand mile moat of ocean. Although the history of this country is brief, it is remarkably colourful. Many of the documents in the Seychelles National Archives reveal the frictions of the early settlers' lives against the backdrop of the Napoleonic Wars: the arguments that arose from living in such a small and remote community; the heartbreak of being so far from civilisation when disease and disaster broke out; and the stories, still told today, of notorious corsairs and sea battles.

Discovery

Seychelles remained largely undiscovered by early navigators. Some believe that the islands were first discovered by Arab sailors in the 12th century. Arab manuscripts from this period talk of 'high islands' beyond the Maldives. Later, in the 16th century, Portuguese navigators referred vaguely to a group of islands as the 'seven sisters'. Vasco de Gama took a short cut from Mozambique to India and, in so doing, sailed past previously unrecorded islands. These were later referred to on Portuguese maps as 'Almirante'—the Admiral's islands. Today they are still called the Amirantes.

It was not until 1609 that we have the first recorded discovery and landing of islands in the main Seychelles group. The expedition, the fourth voyage of the East India Company, led by Englishman Alexander Sharpeigh in the ship *Ascension*, came across a group of mountainous islands which, based on their inadequate charts, they thought must be the Amirantes. It is clear from their descriptions, however, that these islands were part of the granitic Seychelles group. On board the Ascension was one John Jourdain, whose account of the voyage was later published. The sailors spent ten days in Seychelles, where they found fresh water, fish and fruit. Jourdain's own account refers to the islands as 'some earthly Paradise', describing the dense dark forests with floors of guano a foot deep and an abundance of sea and bird life.

After the ships left, Seychelles remained almost unvisited for a further 130 years. It was not until November 1742 that the *Charles* and the *Elisabeth*, French ships under the command of Lazare Picault, sailed into the waters of a small bay on the southwest of Mahé. The ships were a thousand miles off course, on a voyage of discovery for the French colonies of Isle de France (now called Mauritius) and Bourbon (Reunion). They anchored in the bay and the sailors went in search of fresh water and food.

Picault later remarked that Mahé should be called the 'Island of Plenty', for they found an abundance of fruit, fish and birds. After four days of exploration the ships sailed on, laden down with 33 tortoises and 600 coconuts. Tortoises were traditionally collected and stored in the ships as edible ballast. The legs are the only edible parts of tortoises and these were usually cut off, one at a time, while the tortoise was alive.

On their return to Isle de France the governor there, Mahé de La Bourdonnais, expressed interest in these newly discovered islands. Rumours were rife that the European war of 1740, between the English and the French, could spread to India. If this were to happen, then the new islands could be of strategic importance. Late in 1743 Lazare Picault was sent out in the *Elisabeth* to find these islands again, to properly chart where they were and whether they were suitable for settlement. In May 1744 Picault anchored off the northeast coast, in the area that was to become the first French settlement. He named it Port Royale.

Picault spent two weeks on Mahé—which he had named in honour of his governor—writing a report on the suitability of the land for farming. He concluded that sugar cane and rice could be grown there and estimated that up to 300 large farms could be established on the island. Picault also sailed to the second largest island (Praslin), which he named Isle de Palme.

But if Mahé de la Bourdonnais had immediate plans for establishing a settlement in Seychelles, they were not to be. In 1744 the war had reached India. De la Bourdonnais sailed to India, where he successfully fought the English and captured Madras. However, he was later charged with corruption and, although a trial eventually vindicated him, he died in 1753 in the Paris Bastille. He never visited the island named after him or authorised the establishment of a new colony.

Seychelles once more was left undisturbed and half forgotten, while the war with England dragged on throughout the Colonies. In 1756 the new governor of Isle de France, René Magon de la Villebague, decided the time was right to send another expedition to lay formal claim to the islands, in case the English got there first. Company Officer Corneille Nicolas Morphey was despatched aboard *Le Cerf*, arriving at the northeast coast of Mahé on the 6 September 1756. The ship anchored close to a small island off Mahé. Being the feast day of Saint Anne, Morphey named it after her.

Men were sent out in several parties to explore the main island, to ascertain if the soil was suitable for farming and discover what fruit and timber could be found. After receiving their reports, Morphey concluded that the island was not suitable for settlement, being too steep and rugged. But he did decide that the islands were in a strategic enough position to be useful to France. On 1 November 1756 the French Tricolour was raised, a stone of possession laid, cannons fired and the island claimed for France. Then it was promptly forgotten for another 12 years.

'The Journal of John Jourdain, 1608–1617'

Jan 19 1609.

Aboute nine in the morninge wee descryed heigh land, which bare of us East by South. At three in the afternoone wee sawe other ilands, which wee made to bee four ilands, and in the eveninge they bare of us North by East some five leagues of. And wee stoode with a slacke sail all night untill towards the morninge, and then wee stoode in for the land to seeke water and other refreshinge.

North Island, much as expedition leader Alexander Sharpeigh, John Jourdain and the rest of the crew of the Ascension *may have first seen it*

Jan 20.

In the morninge, beeinge neere the land, wee slacked our sail and tooke our skiffe to goe sowndinge before the shipp, and to seeke a good place to anker in. Soe they came to a small iland (NORTH ISLAND) beeing nearest to us, which lyeth about twoe leagues to the north of the heigh island (SILHOUETTE), where they landed in a faire sandy cove, where wee might have ankered very well, butt because our men made no sight of any water wee ankored not. Soe the boat retourned and brought soe many land tortells as they could well carrie. Soe we stoode alonge towards the other islands. The tortells were good meate, as good as fresh beefe, but after twoe or three meals our men would not eate them, because they did looke so uglie before they were boyled; and so greate that eight of them did almost lade our skiffe.

Published in 1905 by *The Hakluyt Society*, London.

In 1768 another expedition was sent out from Isle de France to Mahé, under the command of Jean Duchemin, with orders to cut the fine timber that previous expeditions had noted for shipbuilding. Duchemin sailed to Mahé in his ship, the *Digue*, and remained on the main islands for three months. A journal of the expedition gives a vivid account of the islands and in particular the dangers that were faced by the French from the large population of crocodiles.

They were sleeping in tents and one unfortunate sailor woke to find a small crocodile eating his hand. Happily he was able to escape without too much damage being done. Hammocks were then erected for greater safety, but even this did not provide total immunity from danger. The journal describes an evening when the camp was attacked by no less than seven angry crocodiles:

> One bit at a hammock and severed the rope. Someone fetched it several blows with an axe and it retreated, but without us being able to catch it or any of the others. We have been seeing greater numbers of these animals lately, and especially of an enormous size, since they are some 19 to 21 feet in length.

It was this expedition that re-named the Isle de Palmes—Praslin—in honour of the French Minister of Marine, the Duc de Praslin. Many other smaller islands were also named at this time: La Digue, Félicité, Marianne, Ronde, Aride, Cousin and Cousine. At the end of his stay Duchemin raised the French flag over the stone of possession on Mahé once more and declared the whole group of islands 'within sight, and out of sight' to be French property.

Settlement: Disaster and Disorder

The first settlers to arrive in Seychelles landed on the island of Sainte Anne in 1770, three years after the end of the Seven Years War. Journals note that they arrived in the ship *Thélemaque* from Isle de France on the 27th August, under the command of one Major Delaunay. Aboard were 27 men and one woman. They included a doctor, a carpenter and seven slaves, including a woman by the name of Marie. Arriving in Seychelles, Delaunay decided the most suitable spot for the new settlement was on the island of Sainte Anne, close to Mahé, with the idea of transferring to the main island once more men arrived.

The aim of this new colony, financed by the unscrupulous Henri François Charles Brayer du Barre, who was based on Isle de France, was to exploit the resources of timber and tortoises and to use the islands as a staging post for shipping slaves between Africa and Isle de France. But then another enterprise, this time growing spices, was initiated by Pierre Poivre, who was also based on Isle de France.

The different aims of these two men and their two separate colonies on Mahé—one under the control of du Barre's commander Delaunay, the other centred around the Jardin du Roi spice gardens at Anse Royale on the southeastern coast—was, as one historian noted, a recipe for disaster.

Delaunay seems to have been a man with plenty of ideas and vision for the potential of the settlement, but with little practical sense to carry them through. Although the first crops planted on Sainte Anne flourished, later reports reveal that the settlers had lost heart in farming and did little else but hunt the tortoises.

Poivre entrusted the command of his half of the colony to former soldier Antoine Nicolas Benoit Gillôt, who was chosen to supervise the spice garden. Another notable settler in this camp was old soldier and former slaver Pierre Hangard. The new arrivals on the scene were not welcome. Delaunay and Gillôt seemed to irritate each other at first sight, while du Barre tried unsuccessfully to bar Hangard from even setting foot on the islands.

Arriving in Seychelles, Gillôt and Hangard were shocked at the state of Delaunay's settlers. The second year's harvest had failed and most of the men had left Sainte Anne to live on Mahé, constantly squabbling with each other. Delaunay had effectively lost control and, according to du Barre, spent his days collecting shells from the beaches.

Hangard moved to Sainte Anne, while Gillôt searched for a suitable site for his spice garden, eventually choosing Anse Royale. The report they later sent back to Isle de France on the disarray of the first arrivals led to a quick evacuation of the malnourished settlers, including Delaunay, but leaving behind just 20 men to make sure the islands stayed French. The new governor general of Isle de France remarked dolefully: 'It could have been wished, no doubt, that one had never discovered these islands.'

Hangard also decided to stay on, quickly seizing Delaunay's possessions in lieu of payment for his crops, and Gillôt returned to create the spice gardens. It is Hangard who is regarded as the first true settler in Seychelles, living and working on the islands for longer than anyone else at that time and choosing to retire and die on Mahé in 1807. A street in Victoria is now named after him.

It was at this time that another ship was dispatched to the islands and discovered the last main island of the Seychelles group, claiming it for France. Denis de Trobriand found a small coral island northeast of Mahé in 1773, which he named Denis, burying a bottle containing an act of possession in the sand.

Gillôt's colony fared no better than du Barre's. Poivre's efforts to grow spices on Isle de France had also failed and he returned home to France in disgust. His successors showed no interest in the spice garden project on Mahé. Gillôt remained on Mahé for two and a half years, but his slaves escaped and for a year he was forced to live off nothing but maize. The grandly named Jardin du Roi was nothing more than one clove bush, five nutmeg trees, four cinnamon bushes and a handful of green pepper plants.

To cap it all he developed painful haemorrhoids and in 1775 returned to Isle de France for treatment. The authorities on Isle de France were not pleased to see him; to give up the spice garden project so quickly would be an embarrassment. Much to his displeasure, Gillôt was sent back to Seychelles to continue tending the garden.

Du Barre's fortunes collapsed with his colony. Bankrupt, he turned to fraud, spreading erroneous reports that a large quantity of silver had been discovered in Seychelles and could be mined profitably. The trick failed, but, after much letter writing and pleading with the French authorities, he managed to get a passage to Seychelles from Isle de France, to try to redeem his investments.

No sooner had he arrived in Seychelles, in 1776, than du Barre met with more problems. Isle de France's governor had decreed that no more tortoises should be taken from Mahé by passing ships, because their numbers were declining so fast. Du Barre was unable to enforce this law. It is not certain if du Barre was forced to leave Seychelles or if he left of his own accord, but leave he did, in May 1777 for India, where he promptly died. His departure and death was a great relief to all concerned with Seychelles, because it meant the colony could finally be administered by the French crown.

Most of the settlers arriving at this time were from previously well-to-do families, who had fled France because of financial difficulties or political problems, and came to Seychelles via Isle de France or Bourbon. Others had come to Mahé from India, deciding to leave after the collapse of French supremacy there in 1761. Most of the settlers appear to have been men, but some did bring families with them. On arriving their role seems to have been that of farmers, although most were simply looking to the new colony as a means of restoring their fortunes as quickly as possible. The quickest way of making money was to hunt and sell tortoises for food or deal in timber. Unfortunately, both resources were soon exhausted. It has been estimated that between 1784 and 1789 some 13,000 giant tortoises were shipped from Mahé.

(left) *Sauzier Falls, Mahé*; (above) *Le Jardin du Roi*

In 1777 France once more declared war on England, forming an alliance with American rebels, Spain and Austria. With the possibility of war spreading to the Indian Ocean colonies, it was decided to send a small contingent of troops to Mahé, to stop the islands falling into enemy hands. Under the command of Lieutenant Charles Routier de Romainville, a force of 15 soldier-tradesmen arrived in 1778. Romainville also had the task of restoring order to the colony and distributing land to new settlers, who were expected to arrive from Bourbon. The soldiers immediately set about constructing living quarters on the banks of the St Louis River, a settlement which was to be called L'Établissement—the beginnings of what would evolve into the capital, Victoria.

Romainville noted with dismay that the tortoise population on Mahé had been decimated by the settlers. It was now necessary to travel to other islands in order to collect the tortoises required by the ships dispatched from Isle de France. Smaller ships patrolled the seas around Mahé to make sure the settlers did not sail out to plunder the tortoises for themselves. While most of Romainville's efforts to restore order to Seychelles were commendable, the Jardin du Roi project ended in fiasco. In May 1780 a ship was sighted from Mahé. Believing it to be English, Romainville ordered the gardens to be burnt, rather than fall into enemy hands. When the ship sailed closer it was discovered to be French after all. But by then it was too late: the gardens and the spices, save a cinnamon tree or two, were completely destroyed. A year later Romainville was ordered back to Isle de France, suffering from a liver complaint apparently brought on through overwork. With Romainville's departure the colony was once more plunged into argument and disarray.

Gillôt, the failed spice gardener with haemorrhoids, was to become the acting commander—much to the dismay of the other colonists. The soldiers paid him little respect and soon became a scruffy ill-disciplined force. But the biggest opposition Gillôt faced was from his former ally Hangard, who was now the most wealthy and powerful man on the island. He had moved to Mahé from Sainte Anne and purchased a vast estate on the northwestern coast. He owned 90 personal slaves and paid scant attention to Gillôt's new authority. Gillôt naturally resented Hangard's success and complained about his many slave-mistresses.

For months Gillôt was confined to bed with his embarrassing ailment. He complained strongly that he had no cows to provide milk and a lack of vegetables was causing severe constipation. It was Gillôt's haemorrhoids that were to bring about his downfall: a heated argument with a ship's surgeon about his treatment led to the surgeon's imprisonment. The doctor later died, his possessions mysteriously disappearing. Other settlers complained to the authorities on Isle de France that Gillôt was an untrustworthy incompetent. Gillôt, realising he was about to be the subject of an inquiry, resigned to avoid disgrace and later returned to Isle de France.

The next notable commandant of Seychelles was a much-needed sober and hardworking engineer; Jean-Baptiste de Malavois was sent out by the governor general of Isle de France with orders to bring some control to the colony. The hunting of tortoises and turtles was again banned, together with the collection of coconuts and timber. Cultivation of the land was strongly encouraged and large landowners, like Hangard, were told that they could keep only the land they were living on—other properties to be made available to Malavois to transfer to new arrivals. Anyone who did not accept these new conditions would simply have to leave. The settlers listened to the new regulations with dismay and naturally there was a great deal of resistance. Malavois did his best to enforce the regulations, but was soon in conflict with his charges, who by now were too accustomed to getting their own way.

The year 1789 saw the start of the French Revolution. The colony in Seychelles at this time consisted of 69 French, including three soldiers, 32 free 'coloureds' and 487 slaves. Although the number of fully enfranchised French citizens only amounted to 20, the colony was quick to adapt the revolutionary theory to the advantage of the island community. In 1790 they set up their own Assembly and Committee to administer the island, announcing independence from Isle de France, whose governors they considered did not always understand or recognise the needs of the Seychelles inhabitants.

Establishing independence from Isle de France, Seychelles for the first time laid claim to all the islands which now make up the archipelago. But the newly independent colony was not to last long. One by one the great declarations of independence were dropped and the revolutionary theory toned down; especially the radical ideas about the Rights of Man and the abolition of slavery, which were not at all popular with the colonists. Eventually it was agreed that the powers of the committee, which only met once a year, should be given over to a new commandant, who would be able to govern more effectively.

The Age of de Quinssy

Seychelles new commandant was a popular choice: Captain Queau de Quinssy (later spelled Quincy) was not only the longest serving governor of the colony, but also achieved the most during the long troubled years of the Napoleonic Wars between England and France. His contemporaries described his 'frankness, good manners and helpfulness'; qualities which were to serve him well during his 18 years in charge of an often unruly colony.

During the wars the settlers were concerned to protect their property against English invasion. It was de Quinssy who again and again negotiated sensible terms of capitulation, avoiding any conflict or plunder. Some later criticised de Quinssy for his lack of patriotism and courage; but, looking at the facts, any other option but capitulation would have been suicidal. There were now no troops at all posted on Mahé and to defend the colony de Quinssy would have had to rely on only about 40 Frenchmen with any aptitude for soldiering and a handful of slaves or free 'coloureds' who could be trusted with arms. In the armoury there were just eight small cannons, about 60 muskets and some pistols. With such an army he would stand no chance against even one shipload of trained English soldiers.

The first encounter with the enemy, on the 16 May 1794, was a sighting of not one but five ships approaching Mahé from the south. That same morning the *Olivette*, a brig captained by French corsair Jean François Hodoul, had sailed into port at Mahé ahead of the British ships. Hodoul had 400 slaves aboard. He decided to run his ship aground to avoid capture, but before he could do so English sailors boarded and captured his vessel.

Meanwhile the settlers gathered at the Établissement and were issued with guns in readiness: a cannon was fired and the French flag raised, but the enemy ships did not respond. After a tense period of waiting, during which time most of the settlers had dropped their muskets and fled into the hills, de Quinssy sent out a surgeon to see

Queau de Quinssy's grave at the State House

State House

what the enemy ships wanted. Shortly afterwards a boat was lowered from one of the ships and a party came ashore. The leader introduced himself as Lieutenant William Goate, under the command of Captain Henry Newcome, commodore of the squadron which had been blockading Isle de France. Goate requested water and provisions for his men and the prisoners aboard the ships. This posed a dilemma for de Quinssy: should he agree, or refuse and risk a fight?

De Quinssy took the problem to the few settlers who had not fled. Together they agreed that the most sensible option would be to refuse to help the enemy voluntarily, but to offer formal terms of surrender with as much dignity as they could muster. The terms of capitulation were drawn up. The following morning the French flag was lowered and the Union Jack raised.

After the triumphant English had departed, de Quinssy was left with a major problem: what was to be done with the Union Jack? Should the settlers fly their national flag again and risk conflict with the English, who could return at any time, or continue to fly the despised English banner? After a general meeting it was decided to fly no flag at all until clear instructions were received from the authorities on Isle de France. This agreed, it was soon accepted by all that Seychelles was to become a neutral open port to the English and the French alike. In so doing the islanders did not have to face the conflicts or blockades that other Indian Ocean ports suffered.

However sensible this course of action was, it did not meet with the approval of the governors on Isle de France. De Quinssy was soon given orders to re-hoist the French flag. This he did, but cannily removed it at the first sight of an enemy ship. As other English ships visited Mahé during the wars, de Quinssy renewed his capitulation in order to gain further advantages for the colony, such as the right for the settlers' own ships to sail under a flag of capitulation to avoid attack.

The Age of the Corsairs

De Quinssy's clever capitulations ensured a time of peace and prosperity for Seychelles while all other colonies were under attack. Remaining neutral, the settlers could profit by supplying ships from both England and France and provide a convenient port of call for French corsairs, who were making their own profits by plundering enemy ships throughout the Indian Ocean.

Corsairs considered themselves on a higher plane than mere pirates. In effect, the French corsairs used a form of legalised piracy to benefit France. They had government licences, known as *lettres des marques*, which gave them permission to plunder English merchant ships. Any booty taken was supposed to be shared with the authorities. The corsairs also supplemented their income by trading slaves.

The most notorious of these Corsairs was Robert Surcouf, infamous for his raids on English ships off the coast of India. He was well known for his audacity in attack, but also for his chivalry towards prisoners—especially women. Surcouf visited Seychelles several times during the heyday of his exploits in the Indian Ocean. He recruited some of his crew from amongst the islanders and used Mahé as a stop-over on several missions. In 1801 Surcouf returned to France to be honoured by Napoleon. He refused to take the naval command offered to him and returned to the Indian Ocean to continue his plundering. He retired in 1808, uncaptured by the British, who had offered a 250,000 rupee reward for his head.

The corsair most closely associated with Seychelles was Jean François Hodoul, who made a successful living as a privateer from Mahé itself. After losing his brig *Olivette* to the English in 1794, he commanded the much larger 16 gun *Apollon* on a successful expedition off the Malabar coast, taking many prizes from the English. He sailed on to Isle de France a wealthy man and purchased the *Uni*. It was in this ship that he captured the English privateer *Henriette*. It has been rumoured that *Henriette* had treasure aboard and Hodoul, having seized it, later buried it somewhere in Seychelles.

At the age of 29 Hodoul married the daughter of a Seychelles settler, Olivette Jorre de St Jorre. The days of the corsairs were numbered, as the English asserted their dominance in the Indian Ocean. Hodoul lived out the rest of his life in Seychelles as a prosperous and highly respected member of the community.

Unwelcome Visitors

De Quinssy's policy of capitulation and neutrality for Seychelles paid off during most of the war, but inevitably there came a time when his duplicity was exposed. In 1801 the British ship Sybille arrived at Mahé to find the French frigate *Chiffonne* already anchored and flying the French Tricolor. The *Chiffonne* had arrived in Seychelles with a number of French deportees aboard, exiled to Mahé for an alleged conspiracy to assassinate Napoleon.

After a brief battle the *Chiffonne* was taken by the British, with 35 men killed and 50 wounded. Some guns were fired from Mahé itself and naturally the British commander, Captain Adam, was not amused. The wily commandant however, yet again, managed to talk his way out of a sticky situation and renewed the capitulation of Seychelles to his own advantage.

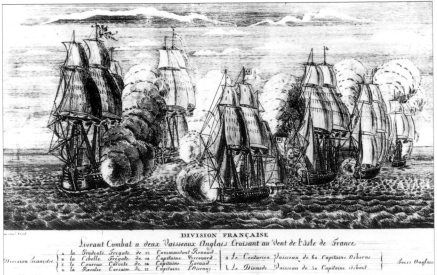

Battle off Isle de France in 1794

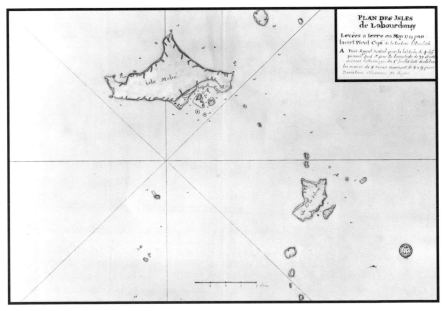

Map of Seychelles by Lazare Picault

Once the *Sybille* had sailed off another French ship, *La Flèche*, arrived with more deportees. Seventy men landed on Mahé, all of them charged with terrible deeds done during the Revolution. Reluctantly de Quinssy allowed them to disembark, but heard with dismay that *La Flèche* was being chased by another British sloop. The 21-gun *Victor* soon arrived and a fierce sea battle commenced. *La Flèche* came under heavy fire and began to sink. Realising this, Captain Bonamy ran her onto a reef and burnt her. Later, celebrating his victory in a gentlemanly manner over drinks at de Quinssy's house, the British commander, Captain Collier, shook hands with Bonamy and praised him for his valiant efforts. De Quinssy did his best to persuade Captain Collier to take the deportees away—all to no avail. The British ship was soon gone, leaving the 70 exiles behind with the frightened settlers.

The deportees caused great problems for de Quinssy. Aside from their violent reputations, the settlers' greatest fear was that, with their new code of liberty and common property, they might incite the slaves to revolt. One of the detainees, Louis François Serpolet, did indeed begin preaching the principles of revolution to the slave population and encouraged them to seize their freedom by taking over the colony. Greatly alarmed by the prospect of insurrection, de Quinssy quickly banished the more fervent revolutionaries to Frégate Island and sent a petition to Isle de France demanding that the deportees be removed from Seychelles.

The episode had a sad ending for the deportees, most of whom had been rounded up with little evidence against them. A group of 33, including Serpolet, were transported to Anjouan in the Comoros, where they were poisoned to death by the ruling sultan. Most of the remaining deportees did not remain on Mahé for much longer—some escaped on passing boats, heading for Africa or the Americas, others returning to France. By 1807 only eight out of the original 70 remained, resuming their former trades. Out of these was a baker called Joseph Quinon, who was the only deportee to leave descendants who still live on the islands.

Seychelles as a British Colony

The British fought for Seychelles and Isle de France, because they were strategic points in the route between India and the Cape and because the corsairs were a menace to the British East India Company ships returning from India. Britain assumed control of Isle de France in 1810, after a long blockade, renaming it Mauritius. That Seychelles would automatically become British property was now guaranteed, but the transfer of the islands was not formalised until the Treaty of Paris in 1814.

Quincy (he had now anglicised his name) remained in office. For several years life under the British was no different from during the wars. Under the latest capitulation terms French laws, customs and land rights all remained as they were. The attitude of

The Dauban family, owners of a coconut plantation on Silhouette from 1860 to 1960, built this impressive mausoleum after the death of Auguste Dauban's two-year-old daughter, Eve, in 1864

the time was summed up by one planter who remarked: 'I do not hate Britain, but I would die for France.' Lieutenant Sullivan, who was left behind by HMS *Nisus* to monitor the island, had to turn a blind eye as Quincy continued to offer his port to passing French ships and slavers; although in British eyes slavery had now been outlawed.

In June 1812 Sullivan received news that a cargo of slaves had just arrived on Praslin. He rowed through the night from Mahé to seize them, but despite such efforts the settlers' lives remained largely untouched by his presence and he resigned out of sheer frustration. The next Civil Agent was much more Quincy's sort of man: Lieutenant Bibye Lesage was more sympathetic to the settlers' claim to need slaves and happily turned a blind eye when required. Between 1810 and 1815 the slave population of Seychelles doubled from 3,015 to 6,950.

In 1814 a new Civil Agent, Captain Madge, arrived in Seychelles. His relationship with Quincy was less affable. After arresting one of the leading slave-traders on the island, Madge suspected Quincy of helping the man escape. Quincy was arrested and sent to Mauritius for trial, but again his silver tongue meant he emerged unscathed. He returned to Seychelles—outlasting Captain Madge, who was removed in 1826, having been unable to stop the slave trading.

Quincy died in 1827 at the age of 79. He was buried with full honours near Government House, where his impressive grave can still be seen today.

The End of Slavery

The slaves in Seychelles were from four main areas. Firstly there were the **Creoles**— those of mixed African and European blood, who had been born in Seychelles and who were regarded as more intelligent than the rest. Those that were slaves were usually employed as foremen. Many Creoles were, in fact, free and even had slaves of their own. The second group were the **Malagaches**—people from Madagascar who were noted for their ferocious pride and regarded plantation work as fit only for women. The Malagaches were often employed as carpenters or blacksmiths. The third group was a small population of Indians and Malays, known as **Malabars**, and they were usually employed as domestic servants.

The fourth and largest group were the Africans or **Mozambiques**. Few came from Mozambique itself, but were brought to the Mozambique coast from the African interior for shipping out to plantations. These people found it hard to settle into their slave lives. Contemporary reports express shock at their continued preference for nakedness and their inability to learn the most basic of French commands. The 'Mozambiques' were looked down upon by all: indeed the modern Kreol word *Mazambik* is still used as an insult.

The Anti-Slavery movement, led by William Wilberforce, became increasingly powerful in the early 19th century. For a time, even though slave-trading was outlawed, the settlers in Seychelles were allowed to keep slaves, until the number of slaves outnumbered the white settlers by about ten to one. In 1827 it was recorded that the population consisted of 685 'free men' and 6,638 slaves. In 1835 slavery was finally abolished. The new civil agent, Mylius, mentions in his despatches that Emancipation Day (11th February) was celebrated in certain quarters with 'peaceable demonstrations of joy'.

The plantocracy, or **Grands Blancs**, were of course less enthusiastic. After emancipation their former slaves could not be induced back to work on the plantations. They asked Mylius to impose a poll tax, so that former slaves would need to work to raise money to pay it. They introduced the *moitie* system, whereby workers were given land to live on and farm in return for three days work a week.

After a few years of uncertainty over labour, more arrivals led to greater numbers of workers. Ships arrived with hundreds of liberated Africans, rescued from Arab slave traders operating out of Zanzibar. Seychelles was a favoured place of emancipation and the new arrivals were quickly hired as labourers on the many coconut plantations.

Marianne North

Another famous visitor to Seychelles was Marianne North. She was a middle-aged Victorian spinster of comfortable means, who set off in 1871 to travel the tropics and paint unusual flora in its native habitat. She arrived in Seychelles in 1883, having already travelled to Jamaica, Brazil, Indonesia, South Africa and India. Marianne's observations on Seychelles were published after her death, using the journals she kept of her travels, *Recollections of a Happy Life*, which became a best seller at the time.

Marianne arrived on Mahé at daybreak on 13 October 1883 and her first reaction was to scream with delight when she spied a crab on the shore line with a turquoise body and red legs. Her Seychellois porters remarked coolly that the crabs were not good to eat. Marianne marvelled at the luxuriance of the foliage in Seychelles, much of which was not native to the islands, but introduced from elsewhere. She noted that it grew more abundantly here than anywhere else she had seen.

After spending a week at Government House, Marianne was pleased to leave Mahé, a 'land of squabbles and how not to do it', for Praslin. A British couple who lived on the island took her to see the main object for her visit to Seychelles, the coco de mer:

> Above were the deep purple-red, stony topped hills, with forests between, the famous coco de mer palms shining like golden stars among them. At last we ran into the valley of the coco de mer: a valley as big as old Hastings, quite filled with the huge straight stems and golden shiny stars of the giant palm; it seemed almost too good to believe that I had really reached it.

'Voyage in the Indian Seas'

At length a breeze sprang up and carried the ship to anchor in the principal harbour of the island of Mahé. . . . . At the bottom of the bay, directly in front, is a large white mansion, the residence of a medical gentleman, formerly the surgeon of the Chiffon French frigate, captured here in 1801 by the English frigate Sybille. . . . . To the right . . . . is the governor's house, attached to which is a small battery. A few other habitations, including that of the first settler on the island, who is now old, infirm and blind, appear on the same side indistinctly through trees. Still farther on is the village . . . . The situation, like its habitations and people, appears to be very retired and rural. . . .

The appearance of the village is of such a description that an enthusiast might be tempted to exclaim—'here I may take up my abode, secure of being exempted from the cares of the busy world'. It is placed in a small and shady glen, sheltered by the higher grounds rising on either side, and strewed here and there with a cottage: while at the upper end runs a brook, overhung with shrubs bearing fruits and flowers and gently murmuring over a bed of pebbles.

The structure of the cottages corresponds with the outline. Several are neat and well built; others sufficiently rustic to shew that their owners care little for external decoration; some framed merely by huddling together the rough and unshaped materials for building. Gardens are attached to the majority, with tamarind, plantain, banana, and cocoa-nut trees shade the doors and windows. I was charmed by this picture of rural life, for it seemed one of those calm, contented and charming scenes of seclusion, familiar in the pages of romance, and often strongly pictured in the vivid imaginations of youth.

The people, in the meantime, crowded their doors to examine the strangers. We in return gazed as eagerly at a little isolated community, *removed to so vast a distance from the general haunts of men; shut up within themselves, dependent not only for comforts but, I may add almost for society, on the quadrupeds, the shrubs, fruits and flowers that surrounded their simple abode.*

In passing a rustic habitation, a jolly looking man gave us an invitation to enter. Our attention had been previously excited by hearing that he had been once an officer of the dragoons in the republican army in Europe, but exiled hither, with many others, after the discovery of a conspiracy (that of the infernal machine I believe) in which he was suspected to have been concerned. We did not hesitate to accept the invitation. He seemed chatty, lively, bustling and good humoured. In appearance he was about 50 years of age, with a full round face and robust person, clothed with vestments of blue dungaree; he might have sitten for the picture of John Bull, and therefore not very like the figure we usually associate with the idea of an assassin.

Observing our eyes wander over his abode, the son of Mars began to apologise for its homely appearance: and at the same time eyeing a thread bare portion of his own dress. 'Tis all', said he, with a smile 'my friends in France have left me; but it is enough—I am content.' The good humour of the man left us with no reason to doubt it. He insisted on regaling us with a pleasant drink made of citrons; the addition of rum was proffered, which we declined, our host remarking with a laugh, it was an unusual refusal from Englishmen. . . .

On the 24th we took formal possession of the islands, by landing the marines and hoisting the British ensign under a salute from the ship. Lieutenant Sullivan, of the marine corps, who came with us from Mauritius, remained as resident, having been appointed to this situation by Governor Farquar as a slight compensation for the severe wound received in the unfortunate action at Grand Port.

James Prior aboard the HMS *Nisus* during the years 1810 and 1811 (published 1820)

Vallée de Mai, Praslin (left) has changed little in essence since Marianne North's depiction; (above) painted in the 1880s

Observations of Life in Seychelles

Hospitality and strong parental and filial affection are amongst their leading virtues, whilst a want of all public spirit, indolence and ignorance constitute the weaker points of their character. They profess the Roman Catholic religion but their conformity to this or any other faith is very lax. In society there is very little or no distinction of class, beyond that of colour, but those who are the most wealthy or intelligent are regarded with the most attention and respect. Cards, billiards and dancing are their chief amusement. . . .

The inhabitants have numerous canoes built and fitted with much skill and neatness. In these they pay their visits from island to island, and at the close of a party it sounds rather novel to a stranger to hear 'Madame Chose's canoe!' instead of carriage announced as in waiting; torches are at hand, they are lighted at the water, where some stout negroes, almost in a state of nudity, await to transport the ladies and gentlemen.

Captain Owen 1824

More coco de mer palms were seen on the island of Curieuse and, in great excitement, Marianne wrote to a friend in England about the experience of painting these strange trees. She enclosed a pen and ink sketch, depicting her perched precariously on a pile of boulders, built specially to enable a good view of a male and a female tree growing closely together. '*I know if cramp had seized me you would have seen little more of your friend,*' she wrote.

Of the many islands she visited, Marianne preferred Praslin, '*the most perfect situation I ever was in*'. She even took her shoes and stockings off for a paddle in the sea—something quite unheard of for a lady to do in those days. Marianne took her work seriously, spending many weeks painting all sorts of fruit trees and shrubs she found on the islands. She made a study of one tree, known locally as the capucin, which afterwards was declared to be a new genus and was named *Northea sechellana* after her.

Unfortunately, while she was waiting to travel back home, Marianne became ill with what she termed her 'nerves'. She was 53 years old and suffered from deafness and rheumatism. While she was in smallpox quarantine on Long Island, she began hearing voices and became paranoid that the other people on the island were playing tricks on her. She thought they had let rats loose in her room and, believing they were going to rob or murder her, barricaded herself in and stitched all her money into her clothes.

Marianne recovered her senses on the long journey back to England. On her return she mounted the many paintings from Seychelles in the gallery she had built especially for her work at the Royal Botanical Gardens in Kew. The gallery is still open today, where 832 closely hung paintings bear testament to her life and work.

There are also plans to open a Marianne North Gallery on Mahé, at new botanical gardens at Barbarons, in the south of the island. The Marianne North Gallery will display a collection of her works, including the many she painted while she visited Seychelles, and is planned to open to the public soon.

La Grande Avalasse

Seychelles has had few natural disasters. It is outside the cyclone belt and severe storms are rare. But, in October 1862, torrential rains and hurricane-force winds struck Mahé, causing a devastating landslide. The centre of the storm was above the hills overlooking Victoria and the deluge caused a major landslip. The worst of the storm was late in the evening, when most of the inhabitants were in bed. They were woken with a start by the sound of water and huge granite boulders being swept towards them, like a huge roar of thunder crashing down the hills, demolishing houses and trees in its path. One survivor said the flood carried houses torn from their foundations 'like ships tossed about in the sea'.

In all 75 people were killed, many of them sheltering with the nuns of St Joseph de Cluny, when their house was crushed and collapsed in the water. Other residents listened helplessly to the cries of people being washed out to sea by the flood, screaming 'sauve moi, sauve moi!' Sadly, many of those who died were children, too small and weak to withstand the torrents.

Victoria, by this time a thriving little harbour town, was devastated. Fortunately, immediate help was given by HMS *Orestes*, which was in port at the time; later a large gang of Indian prisoners from Mauritius were sent to help rebuild the settlement.

Thirty years later another disaster was to hit the small community. In 1883 a ship from Zanzibar docked at Mahé and landed a sick Seychellois, who was diagnosed as having chicken pox. The man was sent home to be cared for by his family, but it was not until they had all died that doctors realised this was not chicken pox, but the deadly smallpox. An epidemic quickly swept through the colony, killing hundreds and disfiguring thousands. Many people abandoned their work and fled to the hills. The island of Mahé was quarantined, which meant no essential food supplies arrived from Mauritius for two years.

June of the same year saw the eruption of Krakatoa. Although Krakatoa is thousands of miles away from Seychelles, its effects caused a tidal wave of two and a half feet above the usual spring tide. It receded again in about 15 minutes, leaving boats high and dry on the beaches. In three hours the sea ebbed and flowed 17 times and all the residents marvelled at the strange vivid sunset.

A New Crown Colony

Victoria and the rest of Mahé soon recovered from the disasters of the late 19th century. Gravel roads were laid and schools, churches and a hospital were built. By now the population of Seychelles was around 7,000, the majority of these being Creoles, but the land and the power still rested with the French Grands Blancs.

In 1903 Seychelles became a crown colony in its own right, separate at last from Mauritius. The new British governor, Mr Sweet-Escott, commemorated the event by erecting a clock tower in the centre of Victoria, modelled on the Vauxhall Bridge Road Clock Tower outside Victoria Railway Station in London.

Although now a British colony, the culture of Seychelles remained steadfastly French. A British woman writing in 1893 complained that: 'The islands are but English in name—indeed they are as much French as they were a hundred years ago. The language, manner and customs are emphatically French; French is spoken in the law courts, where French law is also pre-eminent, and in the Government-aided schools English is taught only as a subject.'

Governor Sweet-Escott made efforts to anglicise Seychelles, encouraging the schools to teach more English, but the colony had been French for too long and customs and language did not alter much during the British colonial era.

Court and Treasury Building, Mahé, Seychelles

This clock tower was erected in the centre of Victoria by Seychelles British governor, Mr Sweet-Escott, in 1903 to commemorate Seychelles newfound Crown colony status. Photo circa 1930

Exiles

During the British colonial period, Seychelles was largely forgotten by London, apart from being a suitably far-flung place to send undesirables from the Empire into exile. The first of these was the Sultan of the Malay state of Perak, who was implicated in the murder of the first resident British Consul in 1875. The Sultan and three of his chiefs were deported to Seychelles in 1877, accompanied by their wives and children and a large retinue of servants. They were kept in strict confinement on Mahé for several months, before being transferred to the small island of Félicité, where they lived for just over a year, before returning to Mahé until 1895.

Exile in Seychelles does not seem to have been unduly harsh. Records show that the Sultan was allowed to visit Mauritius, where he enjoyed watching sporting events, and he was even allowed a brief visit to Britain. Despite his confinement, he was a regular visitor to Government House and kept society with all the best families on Mahé. His children were educated at the best schools on the island and were even sent to Britain for 'finishing'. On leaving Seychelles in 1895 to return to Perak, the Sultan discovered in Singapore that he alone was not to be allowed to return to his former country. It is not surprising that he at once applied to return to Seychelles, but was denied.

King Prempeh, of Ashanti in Ghana, was the next to be banished to Seychelles. Arriving in 1900, his exile was to last 24 years. During his captivity he was treated with the utmost respect and was housed in a luxurious bungalow (all provided by the British). He learnt to read and write English from the police sergeant sent to guard him, held meetings regularly with his chiefs and became a Christian. The King seemed to have borne no bitterness towards the British. He chose to join the Church of England because he said 'it was the church of kings' and, when he decided to take up a Christian name, he chose Edward after the reigning King of England. His children were also baptised into the Anglican church and one of his sons later became a priest. One English writer to visit Seychelles, Alec Waugh (the elder brother of Evelyn), remarked on King Prempeh that: 'He arrived clad in a leopard skin, but after 25 years exile he returned to his throne in spongebag trousers, a cutaway morning coat and a silk hat. Half the colony came to the wharf to see him off. He had made himself popular and respected. He was greatly missed.'

Other African kings that the British found troublesome were also sent to Seychelles, including the King of Buganda and the King of Bunyoro, both regions of what is now Uganda. In the 1920s three members of a religious sect, who preached the coming of a second messiah, were also sent to Seychelles from Nyasaland and the same decade saw numerous political detainees arrive in Mahé from Africa, Zanzibar, Egypt and Aden. During the 1930s Britain became involved with policing Palestine and a number of Arab terrorists were also sent to Seychelles. These 'terrorists' apparently soon gained the sympathy of most of the islanders and, like all the other exiles, were well treated.

The Two World Wars

In the early 20th century the economy of Seychelles was in a bad way. Vanilla production fell to an unprecedented low, due to bad harvests and a collapse in the world market. The economy relied on exporting coconuts for copra and harvesting guano from the outlying islands, but World War I intensified hardship in Seychelles, as commercial links with Europe were virtually cut off.

During the First World War a labour corps from Seychelles was formed and sent to East Africa. The governor of Seychelles was happy to send men away to war—there was little work to be had on the islands and, with the increase in food prices, the crime rate was rising. In replying to a military request for porters he wrote:

I think the departure of these men will be an excellent thing for the country.
There should now be enough work for those that remain and those who do not
want to work at any price will be unable to plead that they cannot obtain

work. Further, those who go will probably learn some much needed lessons of discipline and industry, which should have a good effect when they return.

Sadly, many of these men did not return. Arriving in East Africa, the Seychellois quickly fell victim to tropical diseases unknown back home. By May 1917, five months after landing, 250 men had died of dysentery or malaria and many more were sick. It was then decided to repatriate the majority of those that were left. Dr Bradley, one of the colony's medical officers at the time, wrote about the condition of those who had returned:

The number who arrived was 359, their general health was deplorable in the extreme. Apart from the acute cases they were all practically infected with malaria, large numbers were suffering from foul septic ulcers of the feet and legs and, with few exceptions, they had some degree of bronchitis.

In all there were 335 deaths, a mortality rate of almost 50 per cent. All killed not by the bullet but by disease and the mistaken belief that colonial troops would be more resistant to tropical disease than Europeans.

World War II had even more of an impact on Seychelles. With the introduction, in 1926, of electricity and the telephone communications with the outside world greatly improved, Seychelles became an important refuelling base for 'flying boats' and British ships. A seaplane depot was built, a battery constructed to protect the harbour and a small garrison established. Despite such precautions, Seychelles did not come under enemy attack during the war and it was only the enlisted men that saw any action. Over 2,000 men were recruited for the 'Pioneer Companies'.

As early as 1941 pioneer officers went to many parts of the world enlisting and training volunteer native pioneers. There were Swazis, Basutos and Bachuanas from the High Commissioner Territories of South Africa, who volunteered to fight for Queen Victoria's great grandson; East and West Africans; Mauritians, Rodriques and Seychellois; Indians of all classes, some traditional soldiers and others making good as soldiers for the first time; Singalese; Syrians; Cypriots; Palestinians; Maltese and Arabs. Most of this cross section of the Empire descended on the Pioneer Corps Dept, Quassassin, Egypt, from mid June 1941 onwards. The work was arduous and the tasks varied. At all stages pioneers were in demand. It was in Italy that pioneer versatility was first recognised. And the slogan was born; 'No Labour: No Battle'.

The first contingent of Seychellois troops left for Suez in 1941 with no uniforms or equipment, as none had been sent. Apparently, on arriving in Egypt, the men were mistaken for a gang of prisoners. Most Seychellois saw action at Tobruk, but left the town shortly before it was taken by Rommel; it was a Mauritian Company that was captured by the Germans there. After Tobruk a new unit was formed for all pioneers with trades—the Seychelles Artisan Works Company, which spent the rest of the war building airfields in Palestine and Egypt. Those without trades joined up with the second Seychelles Pioneer Company, who landed in Egypt in 1942. After the El Alamein breakthrough in November 1942, the unit followed the advance on to Tobruk, where it was assigned to the docks. In February 1943 the Company moved up to Buerat, where aviation fuel was being shipped urgently to the Navy. A British Army Journal records the incident:

> Old Desert Rats may remember how Seychellois Pioneers saved the day for the armour by swimming 40 gallon petrol drums ashore in 1942 during the December pursuit. The Seychellois are almost amphibious, and were kept active in the cold seas by a reward of a tot of rum for each petrol drum recovered.

Later the Company moved on through Tunisia, where they received commendation for their work in erecting three miles of telegraph poles in two days. The rest of the war was spent mainly in North Africa. In 1946 two further companies of Seychellois were recruited for post-war service overseas in Kenya, Egypt and Palestine. The pioneers also landed in Italy at Salerno on D-Day and served throughout the Italian campaign. In 1953 the Company was demobbed and returned to Seychelles.

The Road to Independence and Revolution

During World War II the beginnings of political change in Seychelles were stirring. In 1939 the Taxpayers' Association was formed, representing the employers and landowners. Its aims were to preserve the high status of the Grands Blancs. The British governor, Sir Arthur Grimble, complained that it was, 'the embodiment of every reactionary force in Seychelles'. A previous governor had already noted that the plantocracy 'expect as a right champagne standards on a ginger beer income'.

After the war the new governor, Selwyn Clarke, acknowledged that self-rule was inevitable and began the process of political change, eventually achieving adult suffrage. Until then the vote was given only to literate property owners, who had to pass a written test in order to be enfranchised (a total of 2,000 voters out of a population of 36,000).

In 1952 two political parties were formed under the leadership of two lawyers. The Seychelles People's United Party (SPUP), led by France Albert René, campaigned strongly for independence, while the Seychelles Democratic Party (SDP), under James Mancham, pressed for close integration with Britain.

In 1965 the British Secretary of State for the Colonies, Anthony Greenwood, proposed that a constitutional adviser visit Seychelles to consider constitutional development and the wishes of the local people. The following year Sir Colville Deverell visited the islands and recommended the vote for all adults, the forming of electoral divisions and the establishment of a single governing council. The recommendations were agreed and a new constitution was drawn up, expanding the electorate to 17,900. An election followed. Each party gained three seats, with Mancham claiming a majority through the support of an independent candidate—a position Mancham kept in subsequent elections.

In 1975, at a constitutional conference held in London, the SDP and the SPUP formed a coalition government. The date was set for independence from Britain: 29 June 1976. James Mancham became President of the new nation of Seychelles and Albert René his Prime Minister.

Wind and waves sculpt the rocks at Anse Marron, La Digue

The coalition was always a fragile one, given the different standpoints of the two parties. The SPUP was a progressive socialist party. James Mancham's Democratic Party on the other hand looked more towards Western capitalist democracies as its role models. On 5 June 1977, while Mancham was in London attending a Commonwealth Heads of State Conference, he was overthrown by a political coup and René was installed as the new president.

A new constitution was adopted and the SPUP changed its name to the Seychelles People's Progressive Front (SPPF). Many of Mancham's supporters joined him in exile.

During the late 1970s and 1980s a large army was created. The new President was worried that his exiled political opponents might attempt to regain power by force. These worries were not unfounded, as rumours of countercoups abounded. In 1981 a group of South African mercenaries led by 'Mad' Mike Hoare arrived at the airport, disguised as businessmen with presents for the orphanage. Automatic weapons were hidden beneath the toys in secret compartments of their suitcases, but they were exposed by a diligent customs officer and their surprise attack was thwarted before they could leave the airport. They were later arrested and imprisoned in Seychelles and South Africa.

The press in Europe, fuelled by reports from disillusioned Seychellois exiles, were quick to denounce President René as a tyrant. But in reality President René has achieved a great deal for Seychelles; probably more than any past ruler. After the airport was opened in 1971, tourism took off as the country's main currency earner. The fishing industry was also expanded and many countries fished for tuna under licence in the Seychelles' huge national waters. Seychelles, for the first time, was realising its dream of self-determination and prosperity. Health care, education and a welfare state were all developed; the proclaimed rights of every Seychellois to have a job and a house were largely realised. As a result poverty diminished and the crime rate was negligible. The new government also took care not to spoil the environment at the expense of economic progress. High-rise hotel development was prohibited and much of the pristine environment, above and below the sea, turned into national parks.

In international politics René was a shrewd customer (reminiscent of his predecessor de Quinssy), happily adopting a non-aligned position to play off one superpower against the other. Russian ships were allowed to use the port, while there was a large American presence on Mahé at the satellite tracking station. The Chinese built a large embassy and close links were formed with North Korea and Cuba.

All this changed, however, with the ending of the Cold War. A new wind of democratic change swept across Africa and Seychelles was not to escape untouched. On 4 December 1991 President René announced that, after 15 years of one-party rule, Seychelles was to be transformed into a 'pluralist democratic system'. He set out a transition process: the election of a commission which would be responsible for the drafting of a new constitution and the holding of a new general election. René's old antagonist, James Mancham, returned to Seychelles and Seychellois who for years had lived in exile were encouraged to return and cast their vote.

The general election was held in July 1993. President René and his SPPF party was elected back into power. This was not surprising, as many ordinary Seychellois had grown to respect him and had benefitted from his changes, while many of those who might have been expected to vote against the ruling party were now living abroad. Further elections were held in 1998. Once again, the ruling SPPF gained an overwhelming majority. James Mancham's Democratic Party experienced the heaviest losses, becoming the smallest party in the Seychelles parliament, the National Assembly.

The return to a full democracy continued with Presidential elections in September 2000 once again peacefully returning the 67 year old incumbent, but with a significantly decreased majority, for his final term of office during troubled economic times for the small island state. The main opposition party since the 1998 elections, the Seychelles National Party, led by Anglican priest Wavel Ramkalawan, continues to grow in strength as it campaigns against corruption and for greater transparency within government. In April 2004 following persistent bad health, President René retired from office at the age of 69, handing over the presidency to his long-serving Vice President, James Michel.

As the third president of Seychelles, President Michel has inherited a country saddled with a debt, with huge economic problems and uncertainties. He has just two years before the next presidential elections, due in 2006, to prove his leadership capabilities and introduce much needed fiscal reform, although he is still, like his predecessor, baulking at suggestions of any devaluation of the Seychelles rupee, which has been recommended as part of an economic reform programme by the IMF and World Bank.

Meanwhile, the opposition SNP wait in the wings for their first feasible chance of defeating the ruling party in almost thirty years. Political change on these far flung islands may be as slow moving as their tortoises, but the islands remain stable and peaceful as democratic changes amble along.

Culture and Folklore

The Seychellois are a blend of different nationalities, all of whom have brought their own customs and culture to the islands. The result is a country steeped in folklore and legends from many continents. From France came Roman Catholicism and, of course, the language; from Britain a variety of ghost stories and Scottish dancing; from Africa and Madagascar the mysterious black magic that the first slaves brought to the islands and the music and dance of the Moutia and Sega.

It cannot be said that the Seychellois are a fast-living race. From the earliest settlement, the people who have lived on these islands have been characterised by their happy-go-lucky nature. One story is told of a visitor to Seychelles who, remarking on the large quantities of seaweed washed up on the beach, said to a fisherman standing by, 'Do you make good use of all this seaweed?' To which the fisherman replied, 'Of course not—why should we? God didn't give seaweed legs.'

Language

Kreol is the lingua franca of the islands, but most Seychellois will speak at least three languages fluently: Kreol, English and French. Until recently, Kreol was looked down upon as an inferior language. It was not written down in any standardised form, and, because its origins lie in a slave adaptation of French, it was considered a 'lower class' language—all the best families spoke pure French. But since independence Kreol has been recognised as a language to be proud of and an institute called 'Lenstiti Kreol' has been founded to promote it.

At one time people wrote down the language in any spelling that seemed right to them. Now a new dictionary has been published and the language has been written phonetically, with K and Z replacing the C and S in the French words and no accents—hence 'Kreol', rather than 'Creole', and it is this spelling that is taught in schools. However, many of the older generation complain that they cannot understand the new spelling, so they stick to the old ways of writing that more closely resemble French.

Anyone who can speak a little French will be able to largely understand Kreol, which is much simpler to learn, as there is no gender and the verb endings remain constant. Sometimes, to emphasise a word, it is said twice—so for 'very slowly', the Kreol version is *dousman dousman*. The key to understanding the written version is to read it aloud. Although the basis of Kreol is French, there are some English words used: *Ayskrim* for instance (say it out aloud and you will realise this means ice cream).

A Praslin woman offers a warm smile freely

An oriental-looking Rasta illustrates the great racial mix of the Seychellois people

English-Kreol

Hello/Good morning	—	Bonzour
How are you?	—	Konman sava?
Very well thank you-	—	Byen mersi
Thank you	—	Mersi
Goodbye	—	Orevwar
Today	—	Ozordi
Tomorrow	—	Demen
Come here	—	Vini
Over there	—	Laba
Go away	—	Ale
I	—	Mon
You	—	Ou
He, she	—	Li
They	—	Zot
What?	—	Kwa?/Ki?
Who?	—	Ki?/Lekel?
Where?	—	Kote?

Although Kreol has been dismissed in the past as a rough language for the uneducated, it is an extremely expressive language and the many sayings and proverbs that exist prove this. Many sayings are, unfortunately, quite unprintable, but a selection of the less vulgar follow:

Napa kitouz ki pa trouv son brenzel. The literal translation of this saying is, 'You always find aubergine to cook the salted turtle with'. A traditional Kreol dish is a curry made of salted turtle with aubergines and the saying means something along the lines of 'every man will find his girl'— just as an aubergine can always be found when you have some salted turtle to eat, so a man—whatever his looks or character—will always be able to find his perfect match in a woman.

Labou pe riye lanmar. The mud laughs at the swamp. A version of 'the pot calling the kettle black'.

Vye marmite i fer bon kari. An old pot makes good curry. 'The longer you live with a woman, the sweeter the love gets.' Often said to married men who are being tempted to stray with a younger woman!

Lakord ki anmar bef nwar i osi anmar bef rouz. Literally, 'The rope that ties the black cow, also ties the brown cow'. What happens to the poor can also happen to the rich.

Victoria market is a good place to catch up on the local kankan, or gossip!

Religion

The majority of Seychellois would consider themselves to be Roman Catholic (89 per cent), but historically religion has never taken a strong hold in Seychelles. When the islands were first colonised it was some time before a church was built or a priest installed. Early observers remarked on the lack of any religious sensibilities in the new colony. In the late 18th century one visitor wrote: 'The people of these islands live without moral instructions, and are buried like the flesh of animals.'

The first Catholic missionary arrived in 1851. Father Leon des Avanchers was a Capucin priest from France and was greeted with great enthusiasm by the colonists and a small wooden chapel was built in Victoria. It is said that as many as 200 baptisms were carried out in one day. In 1862 the present cathedral of Victoria was built and three sisters from St Joseph de Cluny arrived from Réunion to start a boarding school and small orphanage. The Roman Catholic church continued to grow on the islands throughout the 19th century, despite the change of colonial rule. Swiss Capucin priests were sent to Seychelles after the First World War, because of a shortage of French missionaries, and it was not until 1975 that the first Seychellois bishop was appointed. Even after this, many of the priests continued to be elderly Swiss Capucins: in 1989 three young Seychellois were ordained—the first for 20 years.

When Britain took over as colonial master, priests from the Anglican church tried to win the people over, but with little success. There are a good number of small Anglican churches on Mahé and Praslin, but comparing the impressive Roman Catholic Cathedral in Victoria with the smaller and much humbler Anglican cathedral, it is easy to see which church has greatest influence.

Today, however, the fastest growing churches are Protestant, particularly the Pentecostal Assembly Church. This was formed in the early 1980s as the first evangelical church on Mahé and it now boasts a modern building on the outskirts of Victoria, which seats some 700 people. The services here are loud and joyous, with songs of praise sung in a Sega tempo. Other Protestant churches include the Seventh Day Adventists and some smaller evangelical 'house churches'. There is also a Hindu temple and a Muslim mosque in Victoria. Whatever the denomination, it is usual to be dressed in splendid 'Sunday best'—this is particularly noticeable in the congregation at the Roman Catholic Cathedral. Shorts and beachwear are not considered at all respectable.

Gris Gris and Herbalism

For many years **gris gris**, the blend of black magic and herbalism brought to Seychelles by the African and Malagasy slaves, would have had just as much influence on people's day to day lives as the Roman Catholic Church and the two beliefs often sat side by side, with no apparent contradiction, in people's minds.

Gris gris has now largely died out. Britain banned all sorcery, fortune-telling and the possession of amulets and charms in 1958, which drove gris gris underground for a time. There are still some men and women who profess to be adept in its arts. They are known as **Ti-Albert** or **Grand-Albert**—a black magician. **Bonhom** or **Bonfem du Bois**—meaning man or woman of the woods, more often mix superstition with a genuine herbalist craft. Their power and influence is now greatly diminished, although some traditions have lingered on. For example, when a death in the family occurs it remains the custom to hold an all night vigil over the open coffin the night before the funeral (which takes place the day after death). This practice began in the belief that a Ti-Albert could steal the body to turn into a *dandotia* or zombie.

One of the most famous Bonhoms du Bois was one Charles Zialor, who lived until he was 92 years old (dying in 1962). The British authorities at the time were sufficiently upset by his influence that they sought to have him banned from practising his art of herbal-healing and enchanting. But a botanist, who made scientific tests of the types of plants and potions he used, claimed that many of them do indeed have valid medicinal properties. A great respect for herbal medicines exists independently of the Bonhoms du Bois: for example many homes will have a shrub of Madagascar periwinkle growing in their garden, which is used to cure minor illnesses. The healing properties of the plant are now recognised by the scientific community and extracts from it are being used internationally as a treatment for childhood leukaemia.

Bel Ombre Church & Beau Vallon Bay beach, Mahé

Victoria, as seen from the air a decade ago

*The British and French flags still fly over Francis Rachel Street in Victoria,
from the offices of the British High Commission and the French Embassy*

Superstitions

The Seychellois are notoriously superstitious and there are numerous sayings linked with good or bad luck, with warding off evil spirits and the *dandotia*. Today most people would not admit to being superstitious, blaming it on the ignorance of their forebears. Nevertheless, many of the old superstitions are still followed, just in case.

> If a cock crows in the day, visitors are on their way.
>
> If a fork falls during a meal, it will be a male visitor—but if a spoon falls, a woman will soon be knocking on your door.
>
> If you eat from the cooking pot it will rain on your wedding day.
>
> Do not sweep the house after sunset—if you do you will bring bad luck.
>
> If you sweep your yard after sunset the *dandotia* (zombies) will come and dance there at night.
>
> To eat sweets after sunset drives away wealth.
>
> Never sell a black hen—it may be used in black magic against you.
>
> Do not jump over a toddler—it will stop her from growing properly.
>
> If a teething baby sees her reflection in the mirror, it will stop her teeth from growing.
>
> Never answer to an unknown voice in the dark—it could be a *dandotia* (zombie).
>
> If someone admires your hair, it is later bound to fall out.
>
> If you keep pigeons and there is a death in the family, you will have to tie a black flag to their roost or they will never fly back.
>
> If a kestrel nests in your roof, someone in your family will die.

Ghosts, Apparitions and a Giant

Stories of ghosts and strange apparitions abound in Seychelles. Some tales are linked to buried treasure: it is thought that some pirates would kill a slave and bury him with their treasure, so his spirit would guard their booty until they returned. Brendan Grimshaw, the Yorkshire-born owner of Moyenne island, is a firm believer that treasure is buried on his island and that a ghost does indeed guard it; several strange near 'accidents' occurred when he was digging for treasure. Other ghost stories revolve around the tormented spirits of old slaves or of those who died during the smallpox epidemic of the late 19th century and were hastily buried in a mass grave in Victoria.

The small island of Sainte Anne, close to Mahé, is believed to be haunted by an ill-tempered French woman, infamous in the early 19th century for her cruelty to slaves. The story goes that this woman had one slave girl beaten to death: she sat on the verandah of her house to watch and even ordered her dinner to be served there while the execution was taking place. Although little is left of the old plantation house now, the ghost of the woman is supposed to have haunted the area since her death.

At the end of the last century a British governor's wife, Fanny Barkly, wrote of her experience of seeing the ghost of a young woman when she stayed for a few days on Long Island.

On Mahé the oldest graveyard, at the bottom of the Bel Air Road to the west of Victoria, is reputed to be haunted by a giant. In the middle of the cemetery stands a large stone pillar, which marks the grave of an early settler who was almost nine feet tall. According to legend he was poisoned by other settlers, who were frightened by his great strength. He is believed to have haunted the area since his death. Many people have told stories of walking up the road by the cemetery and of hearing heavy footsteps behind them; others of seeing a tall man lurking by his shadowy grave.

Buried Treasure

Because many of the islands in the Seychelles group were used as pirate hideaways, stories of buried treasure have always fuelled the imagination of Seychellois and some have made it their life's quest. Actual evidence of discovering great treasures is rare, but the stories make interesting reading. One tale is told of a discovery of a huge treasure trove in a mountain cave on north Mahé. The British governor at the time wanted to take the treasure to Britain secretly and came up with a plan to involve the British Navy, who happened to be in port at the time. He circulated a story that a smallpox epidemic had broken out in the area where the treasure was and had the whole region quarantined. The Navy then went into the cave and brought back the treasure in

The Ghost

After a few days on Long Island, we begin to feel quite settled, and enjoy the tropical beauty of the place. On this particular day, my husband and I have taken a long walk round the Island, explored the groves of cocoa-nut palms, and come back laden with wild flowers, fruits and curious shells. We have dined among the rocks by moonlight. My husband, the children and the servants, excepting one only, are asleep. The maid is sitting outside also, with my little girl; we only remain there, the heat being too great for me to sleep or stay indoors, and Dolly feels the same.

I go and sit on the rocks close by the sea, and as I glance around me, I am enchanted by the weird and unearthly beauty of the scene. The moonlight is so brilliant, that it sheds a silvery light over everything, with an effect quite indescribable. It touches the great rocks and flowers, glances over the white sands and large shells, sparkles over the phosphorescent waves, sheds a wide pathway over the sea, and shines also on me and my white transparent dress, and the little child with her golden hair and white dress, and little delicate face. Everything seems to be, as it were, glorified by the silvery light. No more beautiful effect could possibly be imagined. One could easily fancy fairies, holding high revel, and dancing on these sparkling sands, or mermaids disporting themselves in those transparent waters.

When lo! what is this I see; it is neither fairy nor mermaid; but a young and beautiful Creole girl, dressed in the usual costume of these islands, a white turban round her pretty head, white embroidered Indian jacket, and blue cotton skirt. She has large soft brown eyes, silky black hair, small hands and feet, and light brown skin. She appears to rise from the sea, at a distance from the shore. She walks right up the pathway of light on the sea, to the landing place. As she glides quickly across, she mutters fearfully, and keeps looking round, as if to see that no one is near, and throws a shawl over her shoulders in great haste.

She does not walk up the path which leads to our house, but glides right over walls, through rocks, in a slanting direction, until she comes to a grove of trees, where she vanishes. As I know that there is not a soul on the island, but the guardian, no one being allowed to land, or approach it without permission, what I see therefore, is no human form, but the spirit of a Creole girl. Being convinced of this, I am for the moment completely paralysed with a sort of awe; but as soon as I am able, I go into the house and awake my husband, who, being most anxious to see the apparition, gets up and goes towards the trees, where she disappeared, and finds there, on pushing away the branches which overshadow it, the moon shining brightly—a grave!

Next morning we interviewed the guardian, and after some trouble we persuaded him to tell us that the spirit of a young girl, named 'Anais', walks at times as we describe.

She is supposed to have been 'unfortunate', as it is termed, and to have drowned her child close to the landing place, but her spirit still haunts the place where she committed the dreadful deed.

My Indian nurse comes and falls down on her knees before me, her hands clasped and her eyes streaming with tears, as she implores me to intercede with 'Monsieur le Gouverneur to send for the boats and let us leave this place!' as she also had seen the apparition from a distance. The other servants join in her entreaties, being very superstitious and much alarmed. So at last my husband consents, and sends for the yacht and galley, and we pack up and leave the enchanted island, and I never had the courage to revisit it!

Fanny A Barkly 'From the Tropics to the North Sea' 1883

coffins—supposedly the people who had died from smallpox. The treasure was then loaded onto the ship and safely sent back to Britain. As with all treasure stories, this tale should be taken with a large pinch of salt!

One man who made it his life's mission to search for buried treasure was Englishman Reginald Herbert Cruise-Wilkins, a former sentry at Buckingham Palace. He visited Seychelles in 1949 and was given what was supposed to be a cryptogram revealing the whereabouts of the treasure trove buried on Mahé by the French pirate Olivier le Vasseur, La Buze.

La Buze plundered the Indian Ocean during the late 18th century and it was believed part of his treasure trove included a priceless diamond cross, taken from the Bishop of Goa as he was sailing to India in a Royal Portuguese Papal vessel *Le Cap de Ver*. Certainly the cross and other valuable church ornaments were taken by the pirate and their whereabouts have never been officially documented. It was his cryptogram that Cruise-Wilkins believed he had in his possession and would lead him to the treasure trove of his dreams.

Cruise-Wilkins studied the cryptogram, which made references to Greek mythology. He then looked at the site which some people believed to contain the treasure and found similar symbols carved into the rocks. In anticipation, he purchased the site and began to dig. The first finds were of the bones of an ox and the skeleton of a horse, which he believed were important clues leading to the ultimate symbol of the Golden Fleece, which would contain the treasure. Later two coffins were unearthed, containing two skeletons still wearing gold earrings and a further skeleton buried without a coffin. Between 1949 and 1955 Cruise-Wilkins and his mother spent nearly £7,000 looking for the treasure, after which he decided to go to the public in search of more funds. The prospectus he wrote in 1955 is full of optimism that the treasure would soon be discovered:

> *Extreme caution is now needed and suitable pumping equipment has to be available to keep the water under control to enable digging operations to proceed, but I have complete confidence in getting into the cavern - given the equipment if not this year then next. . . . . The prospector now desires to dispose of not more than a further twelve shares at the price of £2,000 for each share. These can of course be split, so that for example if any person desires to invest £100 he or she will obtain 1/20th of a share.*

Cruise-Wilkins continued to search for the treasure until his death in the 1980s. Now his sons have taken up the search and the dig continues, but after 40 years the sum total of their hunt is a flintlock pistol, pieces of a 17th-century wine jar and a single old coin. Presumably the shareholders are still waiting for their profits.

In the late 1940s travel writer J.A. Mockford visited Seychelles in pursuit of a perfect treasure island. He had travelled to many of the islands in the Indian Ocean: Mauritius, Madagascar and Reunion, but the place he discovered to be the essence of all his boyhood dreams of a tropical island paradise was Frégate. During his time on Mahé, he was intrigued but fairly sceptical about the tales of buried treasure:

> 'When the treasure hunters of Seychelles are mentioned, the sane and staid will tap a forefinger upon the forehead and say sadly: 'Touché'. But that there is really treasure in Seychelles I learnt from Monsieur Cadet Albert, into whose Mahé plantation I one day wandered, tired and thirsty and with only a vague notion of my whereabouts. As I drained green coconut after green coconut, I managed to launch Cadet Albert into a dissertation on the treasure trove of Seychelles. He spoke of old slaves with whom the pirates had lived, of stories handed down through the years, of parties sneaking by moonlight into the forest and along the shore with hoes for digging and a tattered chart as a guide; and when I had quenched my thirst, I asked: 'And what do you think yourself? Is there not perhaps treasure somewhere here in the Seychelles?'
> 'Yes' replied Albert with slow seriousness, 'But not pirates gold—les cocos— and he pointed to the empty husks at my feet, 'les cocos sont le veritable tresor des isles!'

Traditional Music and Dance

The **Sega** is found in Seychelles, as it is on other Indian Ocean islands, but the dance and music unique to Seychelles is the **Moutia**—a dance seen by the colonial authorities as so sexually brazen that it was banned.

After a week of hard labour on the plantations, the workers would gather under a coconut palm and dance to the sound of the **Moutia drums**. This is one of the simplest of the traditional musical instruments, made out of a goatskin stretched over a wooden hoop and heated over a fire before being played. Their lyrics reflected the daily concerns of their lives. Some of the songs express their awareness of oppression—a well known song, *Msie Bodo*, about a rich man, contains the lyrics, 'ki fere malere soufer' (who makes the poor suffer). It is the Moutia that is most closely associated with the African heritage of former slaves.

The Malagaches brought the one stringed **zez** with them from Madagascar. The zez is made from a piece of hard wood with four matches carved at one end. Tied to the other end of the stick is a large calbash, on top of which is a 'sounder', made up of a smaller calbash. A string is attached from one end of the wood to the other and music

Dance the Moutia

Flames leapt in the still night air and cast eerie shadows on the sleeping coconut palms. Over the hills yonder, a full moon rose. Drum beats, loud and sinister rose in the quiet air then were muffled by loud chants. Pearly beads of sweat on the bare chests and backs of men glistened in the firelight. Feet pounded the earth and dust rose . . . .

The dancers sit in a ring on the ground. As the drums start two men get up and walk to the centre of the ring. One of them cups his hands to his mouth and calls out 'Ehhh, He, He'. The other starts reciting a known song, or one of his own invention. His partner repeats the words, but he sings them. When the song has been completely composed, the two men, swinging their bodies, walk to the women, who are still seated. They extend their hands, at the same time making noises that resemble the gibbering of monkeys.

All the men seated in the circle, spring up and they too start calling to the women; this continues until the women respond by rising. At that stage the climax of the dance is reached. The men place themselves in front of the women, never holding each other like in waltzes. They simply swing and roll their bodies, occasionally the men extend their hands, as if to touch the women, but the latter always move back, still rolling their hips provocatively. The men all sing together and then the women repeat the words. The chant starts on a low tone, and finally rises to a higher note. The dancers stamp on the ground, sing, swing their bodies to the rhythm of the drums. From the waist upwards their bodies hardly move, only the hips and bottom roll up and down, or forward and backwards. . . .

Extract from the *Seychelles Bulletin*

(top left) *Time out for refreshment;* (top right) *Silhouette legend suggests if a man cannot weave a kapatia basket, he'll not find a wife;* (below) *A Moutia dance in full swing*

is played when the string is plucked. Four different notes can be produced on the zez and a good player, like the well known Ton pa (Jacob Marie) on Mahé, can play a wide variety of sounds.

A similar instrument is the **bonm**, which is a calbash and sounder tied at one end of a stick, which is bent like a bow. The string is attached to the calbash and played with a thin stick. Percussion is played on the **kaskavel**, a small container filled with seeds. Unlike the Moutia drum, the zez and bonm were not used for dancing, but for listening. The best players—and the best parties—usually occurred on the outlying islands.

Another instrument to come from the Malagaches is the **mouloumba**, a wind instrument made out of a bamboo knot. The musician blows through the moloumba while playing on the strings, made out of the bamboo itself.

The most well known of all the traditional music and dances of Seychelles is the **Sega**, which was originally danced only to drums. The Sega drum was a three foot high instrument, made out of a palm tree trunk and covered with goatskin. A high pitched note is sounded when the player beats the drum with his thumbs. Two drums were sometimes used, a smaller one called La Signal played with the larger Sega drum, while the dancers shook their heads, shoulders and hips to the rhythm. Nowadays the Sega performed for evening entertainment in hotels is a modernised version of the traditional dance, with fiddles, guitars and sometimes even synthesizers, but the drums and the hip swaying movements of the dancers remain.

The **makalapo** is the strangest of all the traditional instruments, made out of an empty tin can which is buried in the ground. A line is threaded between the can and a flexible stick, which is fixed to the ground a couple of feet away. Music is played by plucking the string with the stick bent, tightening or loosening the line to produce different tones.

The **Sokwe** is the strangest of all the dances. This is something more akin to a fancy dress parade than a dance and its origins are from Africa. In the past men would dress up in costumes made by binding their bodies with a wild vine, which would cover them from head to toe in leaves. They would add embellishments such as masks and hats, depending on which monster they wanted to depict. Some of the costumes were extremely suggestive or downright lewd and the men would sing and dance down the street, shouting out to all the young girls to come and look at them.

Dances originating from Europe were the preferred entertainment for 'polite society'. The general term for all the different types of country dance is **Kamtole** and this dancing is still taught in schools and encouraged by annual competitions for young people. Kamtole dances have been influenced by the French: the **Contredance** is a courtly French dance and a variation of Scottish country dancing is known as **Kotis**.

Love and Marriage

'*Out there in the Seychelles, love, like the climate, is hot*'. So wrote J.A. Mockford in his account of a visit to Seychelles in the 1940s.

Perhaps it was the lack of any church authority in Seychelles for so long after the first settlers arrived that led to a culture where marriage was seen as an option rather than necessity. These days in most countries, living together and having children outside of marriage is becoming more widespread, but in Seychelles this has always been the norm. Many couples decide not to wed, because the marriage ceremony involves holding a large party, which is prohibitively expensive. Some unmarried couples stay together for life, marrying later when they have saved enough money for the wedding feast. Some women have several children by different fathers, who themselves have children by different mothers. Family life in Seychelles is often a matriarchal affair: children are brought up in all-female households, while the men drift in and out.

In the days when the plantocracy ruled, it was frowned upon for a fair-skinned child to marry someone who was considerably darker. A fictitious story, written by English writer J.A. Mockford, tells a tragic tale of such forbidden love.

A traditional wedding in Seychelles is a large lavish affair. Wedding cars are decorated with frangipani flowers and ribbons; the bride will wear a full white gown, whether she is marrying young or has been living with her groom for many years, having had children already. If there are children, they will act as bridesmaids or page boys and the reception hall (*La Salle Verte*) will be festooned with flowers. Often arches of palm leaves and flowers (*arcs du triomphe*) are erected and the newly weds will lead their guests under the arch, accompanied by a troop of musicians with guitars, violins, banjos, triangles and a drum (called a *grosse-caisse*). They play wedding marches and other songs suitable for the occasion.

At the reception feast many toasts are made and songs sung. It is traditional for the older women of the family to sing *Romances*, sentimental ballads like *Ma fille, ma fille chérie*, with high trembling voices and tears running down their faces. After this the singing, dancing and drinking continues until just before midnight, when a song is played for everyone to join in. Then the couple kiss each gues and depart, leaving their guests to continue drinking and dancing until dawn. Traditionally, although seldom seen today, the following Sunday the couple would return to the bride's home and another big dance called *Retour des Noces* was held, thus ending the wedding feast.

Full Moon They Call Her

They called her Full Moon for the obvious reason that her face was round and yellow. Out of the East, China had come by chance to fashion her—a China engaged in such petty commerce as the little port town of Victoria, lying beneath her, had to offer. From its narrow streets she had begun to climb half an hour ago; and now the sun, sunk behind the hills into which she was now advancing, had left a reflected glory in the intricate cloud formations above Praslin island, twenty five miles out to sea, where her lover had been born.

Often, on those nights when she had lain in his arms among the palms fringing Baie St Anne, where another half hour's walk would take her, he had told her of the wonders of Praslin island; and with a sudden smile she recalled his descriptions of the coco de mer, that monstrous double coconut peculiar to Praslin island, whose jelly was said by the Indians and the Chinese to be an infallible love potion. Well, if she had fed on no other food since she had been weaned from her mother's breast, she could not (and of this she was unutterably certain) be more in love with Louis. Alas, the same could not be said of her father and mother, her numerous aunts and uncles, in a word of her grand family, for they, until the miracle of yesterday, had hated, despised and loathed him. They had spat at the mere mention of his name and then said, as if in the term were summed up all that was low and vile and outcast: 'Un chocolat!' . . . .

The pale lights of Victoria were now showing in the deep gloom beneath her, while beyond the coral reef, in the channel that twisted between the small islands scattered across the seascape, lay three schooners. One of them belonged to her father, who, during the season of the south-east monsoon, sailed it down the long beat of the archipelago, taking aboard copra from the outlying plantations. It was her father who had first vomited out the insult 'Un chocolat!' when she had told of her love for Louis; and it was her father who had now sent her a message of peace and reconciliation, telling her that she could leave her aged grandmother's house in Victoria and come home to celebrate her betrothal to Louis.

Such was the climax, the triumphant climax for her, of the long drawn out, stubborn battle in which she had refused to marry a lone Englishman who lived in a large bungalow at Baie St Anne—an old horrid Englishman, she had angrily styled him: a very rich Englishman, her father had replied with a cunning smile, an Englishman who received by each month's mailship from Bombay a remittance of many hundreds of rupees.

Well, thank le bon Dieu, she thought, as she hurried on, that all her father's nonsense was over at last, that he had seen reason, that Louis had been accepted as her prospective husband. Louis was tall and strong, a young god of the seas which he rode each day in his nimble pirogue, fishing with hand-lines and basket traps. . . .

Suddenly out of the rustling valley into which she was now descending, came the urgent thumping of drums. Her heart thumped in unison, for they were her drums, drumming in her honour the thrilling beat of the Moutia. All the plantation workers in Baie St Anne would be there gathered about the great jars of bacca, that fiery brew of sugarcane which made the black folk sing and dance in something of the mad manner their forebears had sung and danced in the jungles of Central Africa before their capture by Arab slave-dealers.

Full Moon quickened her pace. Already she could see the sweating bodies of the dancers, swaying in the leaping light of a log fire over which the drummer leaned from time to time to make taut by its heat the slackening skins of their huge tambourines. . . . she ran wildly among that mob of Moutia dancers crying: 'Louis, Louis!'. . . . It was her mother, standing with her father and other members of the assembled family on the outer fringes of the crazy crowd, who caught her by the arm and dragged her to safety. 'Where is Louis?' Full Moon asked eagerly.

'He has not come yet' replied her mother, as the family began to greet Full Moon with embraces and kisses and bantering phrases.

The family were drinking bacca as recklessly as any of the blacks, she noticed, and some, with loud laughter, were doing the detailed complicated movements of the Moutia. So was that vile, decayed Englishman, who reeled towards her uttering unintelligible words of their French patois.

Full Moon evaded him by moving swiftly through the maze of spectators . . . . she smiled her thanks at an aged negro and his aged wife, who, sitting with their backs to the fat trunk of a coconut tree, were toasting her with mugs of bacca. She wondered whether she and Louis would grow old together like that, for those two blacks were older than anybody on Mahé island, to which they had been brought as children, ninety perhaps a hundred years ago—nobody quite knew. They had been part of a cargo of 'black ivory' loaded into the racks of a slaver at Zanzibar. This aged couple, drinking and crooning together in the hubbub of their descendants, could still remember or imagine how a British ship, policing the East African coast against the forbidden traffic in human beings, had rescued them all and, not knowing where to repatriate them, had put them ashore on the Seychelles, where other slaves had been dumped before.

To grow old together . . . . But why didn't Louis come? She turned about her impatiently, to find that her father and mother had followed her.

'Come along Full Moon', cried her mother excitedly. 'We are going to have the feast now. Everything is ready.'

'Surely we must wait for Louis?' Full Moon asked.

'No, no', replied her father. 'If we wait any longer, the food will be spoilt.'

So she went with them to the family table, all set in the candle-lit dining room of their house. They gave her French wine, which made her head spin, and to sober herself she ate quickly, hungrily, the savory dish placed before her.

'You have kept all the chicken's lights for me', Full Moon said to her mother appreciatively, for in the Seychelles, where the palate sickens of insipid fowl, these tastier portions are always coveted as a special treat.

'Look,' exclaimed her father, pointing through the open door. She gazed out into the night with the others. Out there, where the sea creamed white against the barrier reef, a flambeau blazed, then faded into a glimmer and went out.

'Perhaps it is Louis', said Full Moon. 'Louis must be harpooning a turtle.'

'No,' said her father in a low voice, 'It is not Louis. Unless it is his soul passing over . . . .'

The remark bewildered her. She looked at her mother for explanation; but her mother in a trembling voice, said only: 'Drink another glass of wine, Full Moon, for your father has bad news for you.'

She drank frantically and cried out: 'Tell me, what is it?'

'You will not see Louis any more', said her father. 'He was killed by a shark this afternoon.'

She ran out of the house. Before her the bonfire of the drummers still lit up the scene . . . . she stumbled among the milling mob. Somebody seized her round the waist. With a snarl she violently freed herself, as she saw the leering face and smelt the alcoholic breath of that man of many rupees, the outcast Englishman.

Full Moon fought her way through the singing dancers, staggering into the darkness of the palm grove and clutched at a curving tree-trunk to save herself from falling. Leaning there, with madness in her brain and despair in her heart, she became aware of voices just below her. They were the voices of those freed slave-children, the aged negro and his wife. They had grown old together . . . But Louis and she would not grow old together . . . . And, O, how long and weary the days without a lover, and the nights, how weary! . . . the aged negress, sitting there beside her husband, mumbled something she could not hear; but before Full Moon collapsed, she heard the voice of the negro disputing with high-pitched, soul destroying clarity.

'No, I tell you!' cried the aged negro. 'It was not a shark, unless a shark can walk the beach with two legs. And now the Englishman will have her, for African grigris is stronger than a young girl's stubbornness. It is as I say—the chicken is for her family; but Full Moon is being feasted on her lover's lights.'

J.A. Mockford

Boatbuilding and Fishing

The people of Seychelles have evolved unique fishing methods and boats, totally adapted to their own conditions. A long canoe, called a **pirogue**, was the most popular fishing boat, easy to manoeuvre while fishing on the reefs and landing on the beaches. This was made from takamaka wood, painted black and trimmed in white, with a length varying from five to 12 metres. Since the advent of the small diesel engined boat, pirogues have declined in popularity—they capsize easily when sailed by the inexperienced. Nevertheless, some traditional fishermen still use them today.

Another traditional type of canoe is the **katyolo**, which has a narrow beam and a slightly curved shape. These are smaller boats than the pirogue, only four metres in length, again built from takamaka wood and usually painted in bright colours, in contrast to the black and white pirogue. The popularity of the katyolo has also diminished, but in days when the roads on Mahé and Praslin were non-existent or very rough going, these boats were the main transport between Victoria and outlying villages.

While many modern boats found in Seychelles are now imported from elsewhere, traditional boat-building skills have not died out. In particular, La Digue has a thriving

Fisherman with basket trap

boat-building industry and other small yards exist on Mahé and Praslin. They build the small single masted schooners used for inter-island sailing, which bear some resemblance to the fishing boats seen in Brittany or Cornwall. Larger boats are also built, including the two-masted clippers for longer journeys to the outer islands and as cargo vessels. Most boats are still built out of the most durable hardwood found on the island, takamaka.

The basket fish traps used in Seychelles are also unique to the islands. These are constructed from bamboo woven to form two flat, heart-shaped sides. These are then joined together with a long rectangular piece of woven bamboo. A cone-shaped mouth is formed, with a small opening at the narrow end, and fastened to the middle of the trap to allow fish to enter, but not

Catch of the day

easily escape. There are three trap fishing methods and the traps are given different names depending on how they are used: kazye lavol, kazye peze and kazye dormi. Fishermen who sail out for a day's fishing along the coast would take a **kazye lavol** trap with them and, at the start of the day, would lower the baited and weighted trap into the sea, attaching a buoy to act as a marker. At the end of their fishing trip, the trap would be hauled up and the contents added to their day's catch. To use the **kazye peze**, the fisherman does not need to use a boat. This trap can be taken out to the reef at low tide and anchored to the sea floor by heavy stones placed on wooden poles, skewered into the trap to keep it stable. The most common type of trap is known as a **kazye dormi**: a fisherman will have several traps, which he places around the reefs and leaves them baited, heavily weighted and marked. Each day the fisherman will sail out to check his traps, remove the fish and re-bait them. One fisherman might have up to 25 such traps, which will catch a decent amount of fish for him, while he can spend his day on the beach drinking beer and playing dominoes. No wonder this method of fishing is so popular!

Songoula: Folklore and Fable

Songoula could be a monkey or something like a monkey, perhaps a little man. No one is too sure what Songoula looks like, but he has become a part of the folklore. Songoula stories have been told to young children for many years, handed down by each generation. Some Songoula stories are obvious adaptations of European fables—'Songoula and the tortoise' replacing the tortoise and the hare story. Others have been adapted to include animals and plants that are common in Seychelles, like the tale of 'Songoula in the King's Pool'.

Songoula in the King's Pool

Once upon a time there was a King who had a large, sparkling, crystal-clear swimming pool in his palace gardens, of which he was very proud. No one apart from the King was allowed to swim in this pool. However, one night Songoula was passing the palace and saw the beautiful pool glinting in the moonlight. It looked so pretty that he decided this was the perfect place for his evening swim and dived in. The next morning the King noticed that the water was very dirty (Songoula was not noted for his cleanliness). The King questioned everyone in the palace, but no one had swum in the pool. The King set a guard to watch over the pool at night.

The following evening Songoula came again for his swim, but stopped as he saw the guard. He went home and brought back a large bottle of calou and placed it next to the guard. The guard, who was by this time getting tired and thirsty, found the bottle and soon became drunk and fell asleep. Songoula was able to have his swim. The next morning, when the King arrived for his swim, he saw that the water was dirty again. Roaring with anger, he had his guard severely punished and sent another man to watch over the pool. Songoula played the same trick on him and every other guard the King appointed (for they were all partial to a drop of calou). In desperation the King made a public announcement: whoever could keep guard over his pool would receive half of his fortune and his daughter's hand in marriage, but if they failed they would be beheaded. Several of the kingdom's best young men tried and failed. Songoula carried on swimming and the King became more and more angry.

One day the tortoise went to the palace and said to the King, in his old, slow voice: 'My Lord, I will be able to catch this evildoer.' Everyone in the palace laughed at him, because the best men in the land had failed and he was only a tortoise. But the tortoise was not deterred, for he had a plan. He coated his carapace with tar and waded into the pool, waiting and keeping very still. When the moon rose and Songoula came for his swim, he laughed and said

'Oh, the King is so kind. He has even provided me with a rock to sit on after my swim!' Songoula sat down, but when he tried to move he discovered he had been stuck with tar. The tortoise rose up from the water, saying 'At last Songoula, you wicked creature, I've got you. The King will behead you and give me half his kingdom.'

Songoula tried to hit the tortoise, to force the tortoise to let him go, but became more and more stuck. Completely captive, the tortoise triumphantly carried him to the King.

When the King and his courtiers saw that the tortoise had caught Songoula, they congratulated him. But Songoula was not ready to give up just yet. 'Tie him up and send him to the dungeon!' cried the King. But Songoula replied 'If you tie me up with the thickest rope in the land, you will not be able to keep me prisoner, for I can break free from every kind of rope!' At this the King was worried. 'Is there nothing that can keep you captive?' he asked. 'Only the thin fibre that is found on the banana plant can prevent me from running away,' was the reply. As soon as Songoula was bound with the banana rope, he snapped the rope and ran away, laughing at his own trickery. He climbed up a large banyan tree in the palace gardens. As the guards approached the banyan tree, they could see Songoula high up in the branches with his thin, brown tail hanging down. They couldn't reach his tail and each time they tried to grab it, Songoula laughed, shouting 'That's not my tail. That's a root of the banyan tree.' Songoula escaped the King's punishment and he still makes mischief everywhere he goes. He now knows that the best place for a Songoula to hide is high in the branches of a banyan tree.

A fine catch of Bourgeois fish, or Bourzwa in Kreol, otherwise known as red snapper

Food and Drink

Kreol Cuisine

The origins of the racially mixed Seychellois are revealed in their cooking. From India come many varieties of curry, some containing an explosive mix of hot chilies, others kinder and milder, often flavoured with coconut cream. From China come popular rice dishes and stir-fried vegetables, served with grilled or steamed fish, and from France the aromatic blends of garlic, ginger and herbs. All these influences, mixed with a huge selection of seafood plucked out of the Indian Ocean and a variety of tropical fruits and vegetables, make eating out in Seychelles a real culinary delight.

Food to try in one of the many Kreol restaurants should include many of the varieties of Indian Ocean fish, which are larger and meatier than the fish of the northern hemisphere. **Bourzwa** (or red snapper) is a large, round, red coloured fish, usually grilled with garlic and ginger and served whole on a buffet dinner table, from which you can take a slice of the white meat inside. It tastes something like very tender chicken and is usually eaten hot with a salad or rice and vegetables.

Tuna steaks are often served at beach barbecues and buffets. **King fish** are also delicious, served as small thick white steaks, grilled or fried in garlic butter. **Parrot fish**, so pretty swimming round the coral reefs it seems a shame to eat them, are good served deep fried in batter as fritters, with a spicy tomato Kreol sauce. **Sword fish** is served as a grilled steak and **sail fish** is smoked like salmon. **Shark** is more generally served as a 'chutney'—stir fried and seasoned with onions, herbs and bilimbi (a savoury fruit).

Other smaller fish, like the local **mackerel**, **job fish** and **rabbit fish**, are served grilled or cooked as a curry, fish soup or stew. Be careful with rabbit fish, or *kordonye* as it is called in Kreol; this is to be avoided if you have high blood pressure. One type of rabbit fish is also known locally as 'the fish that makes the women drunk'; a gland in the fish imparts a intoxicating substance to the meat—it does not taste any different, but you will feel extremely light headed after eating it! This fish affects men just as much as women, but the phrase probably originates from the hard-drinking fishermen who, of course, would not admit to becoming tipsy on a fish.

Octopus (*zourit*) is a real treat. When cooked properly it is soft and tender and can be served chopped cold in a seafood cocktail or hot in a creamy coconut curry. Either way it is a true Seychelles delicacy. The most popular shellfish are **tec tecs**, tiny white shells collected from the beaches. They are made into tec tec soup, sometimes mixed with pumpkin. They have a delicate flavour, similar to mussels. **Sea snails** are for the more adventurous—they come served with the pretty green and white shells stuffed with the chopped up meat, with herbs and lots of garlic. **Turtles** are protected under Seychelles strict environmental laws and it is now forbidden to catch them for food or any other purpose.

Millionaire's Salad is a popular choice of starter—a crisp shredded **palm heart** is the main ingredient; a slightly sweet, cool crunchy raw vegetable. It is called millionaire's salad because a whole palm tree is cut down to harvest the heart. **Bird's eggs** are another Seychelles delicacy, only available at certain times of the year. These are the small eggs of many types of seabird that nest on the islands, the most popular being tern's eggs. They are sometimes simply hardboiled or served up in a fricasseé or omelette—you will know it is a bird's egg omelette by its bright orange colour. Another typically Seychellois delicacy is **curried fruit bat**—this is occasionally on the menu of some Kreol restaurants. Fruit bat has a taste slightly similar to rabbit, but the many small bones make it awkward to eat.

Tropical fruits abound—local legend has it that if you eat **breadfruit** you will one day return to Seychelles. This can be served up either as small matchstick chips or boiled. Sometimes breadfruit is baked in the centre of a fire at a beach barbecue, then served piping hot with melted butter—it is something like potato, with a floury texture and a slightly nutty taste. Unfortunately this is not often served up as a vegetable in hotel restaurants—chefs tend to shun it, considering it too basic and common an ingredient. Another very common fruit, often seen by the roadside, is **jack fruit**, distinctive because it grows from the side of the trunk. The large long greenfruit has short spikes growing out of a tough skin. Inside the flesh is light coloured and has a rubbery, gluey texture, with several seeds running along the middle. The taste is sweet, but to some it has an off-putting odour; it is related to the infamous durian fruit, which also smells rotten. Jack fruit is hardly ever served as a fruit for tourists, so if you want to experience it for yourself, you'll have to pick your own.

Aubergines (egg plant) may be more familiar, but in Seychelles they are usually served as fritters—sliced very thinly and deep fried in batter. **Avocado pears**, **passion fruit**, **paw paws** (papayas) and many different kinds of **mango** are abundant in Seychelles. **Bananas** too can be found everywhere and there are many different varieties. The large green plantains, or St Jacques bananas, are used in savoury dishes and make the deep-fried banana chips, often served as appetizers in hotel bars. Sweet bananas come in all sizes, from the sort of size and shape common in European shops to minute cocktail-sized bananas and a small, fat, very sweet variety. Most Seychellois eat their bananas much riper than the Europeans do—so you will not find smooth yellow fruit, but much more often yellow mottled with black. The fruit inside, though, is deliciously sweet and soft.

Custard apples (or *ox hearts* as they are known as in Seychelles) are more of an acquired taste. The fruit is light green, large and heart-shaped (hence the name), with short spines on the skin. Inside the flesh is soft, pulpy and creamy white, with many brown seeds. The flesh tastes sweet and has a granular texture. Another similar fruit is the **corosol** (also known as *soursop*), which has creamy white flesh, not quite as pulpy as the ox-heart, but just as sweet. **Jamalacs** are popular with children, who can be seen climbing the jamalac trees when they are in fruit, and tortoises. These are smooth-skinned, pink, cone-shaped fruit with a texture like an apple, but with a more waxy skin.

Pineapples are grown in Seychelles, but are not always available and are surprisingly expensive: about SR20 for a good sized fruit from the market in Victoria. A traditional Kreol way to eat pineapple is to make a salad with pineapple slices, onions and black pepper. **Oranges** can be eaten this way too. Most oranges sold at the supermarkets are imported from South Africa, but some are grown locally—these are mainly green oranges and have a more bitter taste than orange oranges. Other locally grown citrus fruit are the tiny **bigerades**, miniature oranges something like kumquats—these are too sour to be eaten as they are, but can be made into juice or marmalade. Huge **grapefruit**, much larger than commercially grown varieties, are in season around April and May; these have very thick light green skins and sweet pink flesh.

Fresh **coconut** is abundant and great use is made of the flesh and milk. It is eaten raw, thinly sliced and toasted, grated or as a sticky nougat. Coconut is served on its own or as part of other dishes and desserts. Large, round, light green or yellow coconuts also provide a cooling drink of coconut water if the top of the husk is sliced off with a sharp knife or machete. These are sometimes served up at hotel bars with a cocktail inside. If you want to open one up to taste the water for yourself, be careful not to spill any of the coconut water on your clothes, as it stains.

Drinks

Besides a wide range of tropical cocktails, the best of which are served at the Sunset Beach hotel at Glacis on Mahé or the Plantation Club at Baie Lazare, there is not a great deal of choice when it comes to alcohol. Wine and spirits have to be imported, which makes them extremely expensive. There is a locally made liqueur drink, **Coco d'Amour**, which is sold in a bottle shaped like a coco de mer nut and tastes of sweet coconut cream. However, the most popular drinks in Seychelles are either beers or thirst quenching soft drinks.

Seybrew is the locally brewed beer—the brewery is on the main east coast road on Mahé, not too far away from the airport, and it is actually a pretty decent lager. The only other available lager is **Ecu**, which is a German beer brewed under licence. Chilled stout is surprisingly popular, with bottles of **Guinness** brewed at Seybrew under licence. Most bottles of beer cost around SR8 in the shops, but around SR10 from hotel bars.

There are local alcoholic brews, like **toddy** and **calou**, made from coconut sap, and **bacca**, a sweet rum-like drink made from sugar cane and pineapple. These, though, cannot be sold and are brewed for private consumption only, although you may find some restaurant Kreol dishes and cocktails laced with toddy. Some small roadside shops may sell bacca or toddy under the counter, but are unlikely to sell this to visitors.

Seypearl is the brand name for most bottles of soft drinks, costing three rupees. Keep the empty glass bottles, as there is a deposit of one rupee for each bottle returned. Tap water is drinkable, although after heavy rainfall it can sometimes appear cloudy. Locally bottled mineral water is available under the **Eau de Val Riche** label.

Grilled fish, such as these mackerel, is a popular local dish

Kreol Recipes

TEC TEC SOUP

Ingredients:

2 lbs tec tec shellfish (Clean in cold water and boiled for 30 minutes. Remove shells, strain and filter out all sand); 2 onions, sliced; 1 stock cube; 1 tablespoon of chopped thyme; 2 small carrots; 4 oz chopped pumpkin; 2 tablespoons of cooking oil; 1 and a half pints of water; seasoning.

Method:

Brown onions, thyme, tec tec and vegetables in oil, fry gently until onions are soft. Add water, stock cube and seasoning and simmer for approximately 20 minutes until vegetables are cooked. Serve hot with bread.

SHARK CHUTNEY

Ingredients:

2 lbs shark, boiled with skin removed; 2 sliced bilimbi; 1 lime; 2 teaspoons of vegetable oil; 1 teaspoon of turmeric.

Method:

Finely mash cooked shark and drain. Squeeze out bilimbi juice and add to shark. Mix onion, pepper, salt and turmeric. Warm oil and fry onion and spices for 3 minutes. Add shark and fry for a further 5 minutes. Mix in the juice of one lime before serving. Serve warm with boiled cassava.

LADOB

Ingredients:

2 green St Jacques bananas; 2 medium sized sweet potatoes; 3 grated coconuts soaked in 3 cupfuls of warm water; 8 oz sugar; pinch of grated nutmeg; 1 vanilla pod, finely chopped.

Method:

Peel and slice the bananas and the sweet potatoes and place in large, heavy-bottomed saucepan. Sprinkle on the sugar, nutmeg and the vanilla pod. Squeeze the grated coconut with your hands, or place in a blender for a minute, to express enough milk to cover the fruit. Bring to the boil slowly, stirring constantly, and simmer until the fruit is soft and the sauce is creamy. Serve hot or cold for a rich dessert.

Green Seychelles

Log books from 18th century ships that reached Seychelles record the sailors' admiration of the islands' lush vegetation and wildlife. Many of today's place names recall the animals which impressed those first visitors, such as Anse aux Poules Bleues (blue chickens), Ile Chauve Souris (bats) and Ile aux Vaches-Marines (sea-lions). The beauty of Seychelles is still very much in evidence today. The government is strongly committed to conservation and is recognised to be one of the most environmentally-conscious governments in the world.

Like many other island nations, Seychelles has a great many unique species. Isolated from the mainland for 75 million years, the islands have over 70 endemic land animals. The small numbers of most species means they are technically listed as being 'at risk', but because humans arrived a lot later than on many other islands, such as neighbouring Mauritius, fewer species have become extinct. Despite a human presence which only goes back about 200 years and consists of a fairly small community (along with visiting ships throughout the ages), people have managed to destroy much of the large hardwood forest, all of the crocodiles and two species of bird—a green parakeet and a white-eye. People have also drained many of the mangrove marshes in low-lying areas and introduced non-indigenous exotic species like cinnamon, which have quickly spread across many of the main granitic islands.

In the 19th and early 20th centuries there were dozens of distilleries producing cinnamon leaf oil for export. The distilleries were fuelled by wood, resulting in the decimation of large areas of native forest on Mahé. However, as the market for the oil declined, the distilleries closed down and the forests have been allowed to slowly recover.

The Seychelles government has set up a number of protected areas: Morne Seychellois National Park on Mahé; the Vallée de Mai on Praslin and the Veuve Reserve on La Digue. There are a number of Marine National Parks, including Port Launay, Baie Ternay and St Anne Marine Parks off the coast of Mahé and Curieuse Marine Park close to Praslin. Special reserves have also been established on the islands of Cousin, Aride, Silhouette and Aldabra. Two areas in Seychelles have been designated World Heritage Sites by UNESCO—The Vallée de Mai and Aldabra.

The Flora of Seychelles

The plant life of Seychelles varies according to altitude and can be roughly split up into four zones.

COASTAL AREAS AND LOWLANDS

These are at elevations of up to about 1,000 feet; areas most affected by man, with the greatest numbers of introduced species, fruit trees and flowering trees and shrubs.

A common species is the **coconut palm**, of which there are many different varieties, the most common of which is the tall *cocos nuciferna*, which grows in plantations or wild along the beaches. No one is sure how the coconut was introduced to Seychelles. Some think they were brought to the islands in the tenth century by Arab traders. Others believe they are endemic, but as this species of coconut palm is common throughout the tropics, it is highly improbable it is endemic to Seychelles. There is even a theory that the nuts floated over the sea from Sri Lanka or East Africa. Whatever the case, the coconut palms were certainly flourishing on all the islands when the first expedition to land in Seychelles arrived in 1609.

The coconut is a monocotlydon, a member of the Palmae family. The nut is enclosed in a thick fibrous husk and takes about five months to germinate. The tree grows quickly, producing the first fruits at six to eight years old and reaching its peak at around 60, although trees 100 years old can still produce nuts. The Seychellois have found a wide use for the coconut, which is known as the 'tree of life'.

An introduced tree which quickly spread to cover much of Mahé's slopes is **cinnamon** (*Cinnamomum zeylanicum*), or *Canelle* as it is known in Kreol. Harvested for its aromatic bark, ground to make cinnamon powder or rolled into sticks, Seychellois also use the cinnamon leaves to add flavour to stews and curries in a similar way to the European bayleaf. The cinnamon is an easy tree to identify, because the glossy green leaves each have three main veins and appear red when young. If out walking in a forest you begin to feel tired and thirsty, sucking the stem of a mature cinnamon leaf is a quick reviver.

The **casuarina** (*Casuarina equisetifolia*) or Australian Pine is a fast growing evergreen. Many casuarinas have been planted on reclaimed land and small casuarinas are also cut down annually to use as Christmas trees. There is some debate over how casuarina trees arrived in Seychelles; possibly they were planted by ancient navigators—perhaps Indonesian tribes, who are thought by some to have reached Seychelles en route to Madagascar many hundreds of years ago.

Takamakas (*Calophyllum inophyllum*) are native broadleafed trees, often found on beaches which are named after them; the wood is prized for boat building and furniture making. The huge **banyan** tree (*Ficus benghalensis*) is noticeable for the way

THE TREE OF LIFE

THE TRUNK of the mature tree produces an attractive timber, used in furniture making.

LEAFLET RIBS are made into brushes, while the main rib can be used in thatching roofs.

WHOLE LEAVES are used as thatching material. One leaf can also be cut and woven to make an instant *kapatia* basket. One story has it that the boys on Silhouette were not accepted as husbands for the girls if they could not make a *kapatia*. The leaves are also used as decorations for weddings and other special occasions.

THE TAMMY can be used as a strainer or as kindling and even made into sun hats and lampshades.

THE HUSK produces coir fibre, used in making mats and matting, ropes and even upholstery. It has been used by Seychellois to stuff their mattresses and even in earlier times as toilet paper! The husk is also used as a fuel for barbecues, especially to grill breadfruit. Whole husks, strung together are used by young children as floats, to help them learn to swim.

THE SHELL is burned to make charcoal or transformed into ornaments.

Climbing a coconut tree to collect green coconuts is only for the young and agile!

Grinding copra to make coconut oil

THE FLESH of the coconut can be dried to make copra—used in soap-making and explosives. It can be pressed to produce coconut oil, used originally as a fuel, now more commonly used as a cooking oil or an ingredient in cosmetics. The fresh white meat can be eaten or grated and soaked in water to make 'coconut cream'. The spongey flesh produced by a germinated nut can also be eaten, as it is high in protein.

THE CAKE or 'POONAC' left after the oil has been extracted can be used as an animal feed.

COCONUT WATER The natural juice inside a green coconut makes a refreshing drink; while it is enclosed within the nut it is a sterile solution, so it can be used as an emergency saline drip.

TODDY is the alcoholic brew produced from the coconut palm. The unopened flower, or spathe, is bound up to prevent it opening and the tip sliced off. The resulting juice is collected in bamboo cups. A fresh cut is made across the spathe daily and up to six gallons of toddy can be collected from just one palm.

PALMISTE or 'Millionaire's Salad' is made from the growing tip or germinal bud of the mature palm.

THE ROOT is used as *la fraichissant* by many Seychellois to cure all sorts of ailments. Some also tap the root to produce toddy.

in which the root system hangs down from its branches. There is a large specimen at Anse Étoile on Mahé, although sadly it has been ravaged in recent years by a series of fires, and now has a fence around it, to prevent further damage. Frégate island also has many impressive banyan trees.

There are many flowering trees and shrubs on the lower slopes of the islands. Many varieties of **hibiscus**, with red, orange or white flowers can be seen everywhere. Another popular flowering tree is the **flamboyant** (*Delonix regia*—a native of Madagascar) which has brilliant red flowers, as does the **poinsettia** (*Euphorbia pulcherrima*), the fully grown tree with its bright red bracts looking much more resplendent than European Christmas potted plant versions. A popular hedging plant seen around many gardens is the **bougainvillea**, which has vivid red, pink or orange bracts, as do many varieties of the smaller **croton** shrubs (*Codiaeum variegatum*). The **allamanda**, which has large shining yellow or pink bell-like flowers, is also popular.

There is not a huge variety of flower species in Seychelles—the most popular flowers are **orchids**, some of which are endemic, others introduced from the Far East. In southern Mahé there is an orchid farm, growing the flowers for export. An orchid which is seen in many a garden is the **spider orchid**, a tall slender shrub with speckled flowers that have long thin spidery petals. The prettiest is the **tropic bird orchid**—small white flowers with tapering petals, resembling its namesake.

Two types of **vanilla** grow in Seychelles. *Vanilla planfolia*, a native of Mexico, has been cultivated in Seychelles for many years for its pods. Although its value as a commercial crop has dwindled in recent years, it is still harvested and exported. These vanilla vines can be seen on Mahé, particularly at the Jardin du Roi at Anse Royale, on the slopes of Praslin and in the Union Plantation on La Digue. It has become naturalised in many places, but has not banished the endemic *Vanilla phalaenopsis*, which does not bear fragrant pods, but does have very attractive large white flowers with a peach coloured centre.

Fruit trees are also abundant in low-lying areas. The **breadfruit** (*Artocarpus altilis*, a native of Polynesia) looks like a child's drawing, with its wide trunk and branches in a large circle. **Jack fruit** trees (*Artocarpus heterophyllus*, a native of South East Asia) have large spiny fruit growing from the trunk. Several species of large **mango** trees (*Mangifera indica*, a native of India) can be seen everywhere, as can **banana** plants, **pineapples** and **passion fruit** vines.

MANGROVE MARSHES

These can be found in many low lying areas on the main inner islands. Some of these have been drained to make way for land reclamation schemes, but many of those that remain now enjoy protected status. They are home to a huge number of insect, crab and bird species.

THE INTERMEDIATE VEGETATION ZONE

This covers elevations between 1,000 and 2,000 feet and includes many of the lowland species. There is a profusion of **bamboo** (*Dendrocalamus*) introduced from South East Asia: green and giant bamboo species are especially common on Mahé. **Santol** (*Sandoricum koetjape*) is a large tree, with tiny fuzzy coated fruit containing a soft sweet pulp.

Sangdragons (*Pterocarpus indicus*) are large, graceful trees with large roots growing from the side of the trunk like flying buttresses and a sap which is blood red—from which it gains its name (dragon's blood). Sangdragons were often planted by early settlers to demarcate land boundaries and an impressive avenue of sangdragon trees can be seen at the Mission at Sans Soucis on Mahé.

Much of the intermediate zone is covered with forests of endemic trees, such as **capucin** (*Northea hornei/Northea seychellana*). The local name arises from the resemblance of the seed to the cowled head of a Capucin monk, while the scientific name honours Victorian artist and botanist Marianne North. The second part of the scientific name recognises Horne, a botanist living on Mauritius, who contributed much to the knowledge of Seychelles flora. Other endemic trees are **Bois rouge** (*Dillenia ferruginea*); **Bois blanc** (*Hernandia nymphaeifolia*); **Bois de montagne** (*Campnosperma seychellarum*) and the rarer **Bois de natte** (*Mimusops seychellarum*) — a few stunted relics appear only on Mahé.

Common introduced trees often fare better than the endemics. The fast-growing **albizzia** (*Paraserianthes falcataria*) is a dark green broad-crowned tree with horizontal branches, giving the tree a flat-topped look is a familiar sight on the mountain slopes. These trees have crowded out endemics in many of the valleys on Mahé and Praslin, growing so vigorously and demanding so much water that slower-growing trees have not fared very well beside them.

Some native palms grow in this intermediate zone, including the **palmiste** (*Deckenia nobilis*), the heart of which is harvested to make 'millionaire's salad'. Screw pines (*Pandanus/Pandanaceae*), known as **vacoas**, are distinctive for their root system, which is above the ground and forms a wigwam structure of stilts around the base of the tree. One type of vacoa, the *Pandanus seychellarum* or **vacoa marron**, has particularly long large roots, which were popular with young men. According to superstition, if a young man is not happy with Mother Nature's endowment, he can walk into the forest to find a vacoa marron and select a root branch that looks about the desirable size. The tree then has to be cut down, otherwise the part in question could keep on growing!

A number of palms called **lataniers** grow in the forests, traditionally used for thatching material. Many millions of years ago, so scientists believe, large parts of the

The Site of the Garden of Eden

The following are the reasons for the theory that the Garden of Eden is at or near Seychelles. I could even put it at Praslin, a small isle twenty miles north of Mahé.

Allow that Genesis is not allegorical, that Eden, its garden, its two trees, did exist on this earth . . . . Well, I thought there were two trees—actual trees—which had been sacramental and had ceased to be so; and in Praslin near Seychelles, and only there in the whole world, is a magnificent tree, curious beyond description, called the Prince of the Vegetable Kingdom; it is unique in its species, and on earth. The Laodicean Seychellarum, or Coco di Mir. This, I believe, was the Tree of Knowledge. I then thought if the one tree is to be found, so is the other, and this I think is the Artocarpus incisa, or breadfruit; it is a humble tree, of no great distinction, yet to an observer it is as unique in its kind and among trees as the other. This last tree is only found in the Indian Ocean. It is a life sustaining tree, and, like the other, it is full of Scriptural types.

Having thought that these were the two trees, then the question arose: where was the Garden of Eden? And first came the information that Seychelles is of granite, and all other isles out here are volcanic, granite being the more ancient formation. Then Rev D Bury mentioned casually that the verse Genesis ii, 10, could be read that the four rivers flowed into Eden, not out of it. I have been at the sources of Euphrates, Tigris etc. etc., and unless the rivers were forced to flow backwards, no spot could agree to a central basin in those lands, while a flood does not change features 10,000 ft. high. So I took the rivers Euphrates—as Eurphrates, on which is Babylon; Hiddekel—as Tigris, on which is Nineveh. They meet and flow into the Persian Gulf...

The Pison, or Nile, flowed into the Red Sea, the Gihon or Gihon Brook flowed into the Red Sea, joined, flowed down, met the Euphrates and Tigris, united near Socotra, and the soundings shown end in a deep basin, 2,600 fathoms deep, which is close to Seychelles.

Extract from an article written and illustrated with maps by General Gordon, in 1882, in the form of a letter to a missionary friend.

(right) A shapely Praslin Coco de Mer nut—dropped from the Tree of Knowledge?

tropics were dominated by latanier palm forest. Many of the ancient palm species unique to Seychelles have large spines around the base of the trunk, thought to have evolved as a protection against giant tortoises.

More recent arrivals are the smaller, variegated plants that are usually seen growing by streams and lakes, like **Dieffenbachia picta**, a native of South America. It is called *vya tangue* in Kreol, or dumb cane, because its toxic juice can cause paralysis of the tongue and throat muscles. It has been said that this was used by plantation owners to silence garrulous slaves; it had to be administered carefully, as too much of the sap can be fatal. The **icaco plum** trees (*Chrysobalanus Icaco*) have been planted along many mountainside tracks to stop erosion, but they now grow in such profusion that they are smothering endemic species and causing further problems. They are known locally as *Prune de France*—though the small red fruit tastes nothing like a plum—its white flesh is floury and bland.

The Upper Vegetation Zone

Mountain slopes and peaks above 2,000 feet, this area includes mist forest and remains the most untouched and unexplored in Seychelles. Many of the rare endemic species are to be found here, like the famous **pitcher plants** (*Nepenthes pervellei*), which can be seen on some of the mountain tops of Mahé and Silhouette. The plant has leaf tendrils shaped like pitchers, containing a sticky trap to attract and catch insects. Once they venture in they cannnot crawl back out and drown in the pitcher's liquids.

On some of the highest slopes there exists what is sometimes described as the rarest tree in the world: the **jellyfish tree** (*Medusagyne oppositifolia*) or *Bois medus*. Reaching about eight metres in height, it is so called because the stamens of the delicate white flowers resemble small jellyfish. Only about 11 plants are known to exist in the wild, hidden away in the granite clefts of the mountainside.

The Coco de Mer and The Garden of Eden

The best known of all the flora of Seychelles is the **coco de mer** (*Lodoicea maldivica*), a tall slender palm tree with straight boles up to 30 metres tall. The leaves can be up to six metres long and four metres wide, but it is the nuts that have made the tree famous. The double-cheeked nut weighs in at 22kg, making it the heaviest seed on earth, and its suggestive shape has given rise to a whole host of speculations. General Gordon thought it might be the original forbidden fruit from the Garden of Eden.

The coco de mer is an extremely slow growing tree—it takes two years to germinate, 25 years to bear fruit and seven years from fertilisation of the female flower to maturity of the fruit. Many of the giant coco de mer trees in the Vallée de Mai are reckoned to be hundreds of years old.

The coco de mer gained its name from a story that was told long before the Seychelles were discovered by Europeans. Because of its rarity and the mystery of its origin, a tale was told of strange trees growing on the seabed. References to such a tree appear in early travel literature. Antonio Pigafetta, writing an account of Magellan's circumnavigation of the world in 1519 told such a tale :

There grew a large tree in which lived birds so big and strong that they could carry away an ox or elephant. One day a small boy, survivor of a shipwreck, climbed the tree, and, unknowingly, ensconced himself under the wing of one of the giant birds which flew him back home, so that neighbouring peoples knew that the fruits which they found in the sea came from this tree.

At around the same time Portuguese chroniclers mention the coco de mer, locating it in the Maldives. Garcia de Orta, writing in 1563, claimed the coco de mer tree was submerged when the Maldives were separated from India. The nut then became known as the *coco de Maldives* and even today the scientific name for the tree, *Lodoicea maldivica*, has resulted from such early speculation.

In the 17th century the fame of the coco de mer nut grew, mainly through the writings of a Frenchman, François Pyrard de Laval. He sailed from St Malo to the East Indies in 1601, but his ship ran aground on the Maldives and for ten years he and the surviving crew were held virtual prisoners on the islands. On his eventual return to France he wrote about his travels. In his book Pyrard writes that the King of the Maldives had sent ships to look for an unknown island called Poulloys, where the coco de mer tree was believed to grow. The natives of the Maldives and southern India prized the nut highly as an aphrodisiac, he said, and anyone who found a coco de mer washed up on the beach had to surrender it to the king immediately or have his hand cut off as punishment.

In reality it is improbable that these heavy nuts would have floated anywhere— Maldivian sailors may well have journeyed to Seychelles to harvest the nuts, keeping the location a secret to enhance their value. Once the coco de mer nuts were discovered by Europeans in the 18th century, they were worth their weight in gold. The Hapsburg emperor Rudolph II offered 4,000 gold florins for just one nut. However, once the true source of the coco de mer was discovered, at the end of the 18th century, the nuts were harvested on a grand scale, which very nearly led to the extinction of the species and caused the coco de mer nut trade to crash. Today around 4,000 trees remain, mainly in the Vallée de Mai on Praslin, and they are now suitably protected.

Legends still surround these magnificent trees and the Vallée de Mai, which some people believe to be haunted. Stories are also told of the trees mating on a stormy night—the giant leaves certainly make a commotion, sounding something like corrugated iron sheeting banging together in the wind. The story continues that if anyone is foolish enough to enter the Vallée de Mai while this is happening, they will immediately die from shock.

The Fauna of Seychelles

Because the islands of Seychelles have been isolated from the mainland for so long, the wildlife remains primitive. There are few endemic mammals, but there are many reptiles and, of course, those animals not constrained by the ocean: thousands upon thousands of birds. Many animals were introduced by settlers, some of which have proven problematic, particularly goats and rats.

Goats, Tortoises and a Shipwreck

On Aldabra the presence of feral **goats**, abandoned on the atoll many years ago, has caused problems for the population of tortoises. They do not directly compete with the tortoises, but the goats ability to eat anything and everything has stripped the atoll of much of the low lying shade cover, essential for the tortoises to escape the midday heat, so intense it can literally 'cook' them inside their shells. To combat this, culling of the goats has regularly taken place, but any culling operation is a short term solution: goats are prodigious breeders and the population soon increases to a level that affects the tortoises again. In 1994 a World Bank sponsored conservation programme was implemented to completely eradicate the goats from Aldabra. The story of this project, and how it ended rather dismally in a shipwreck, is told by Raymond Rainbolt, one of the two Americans sent to cull the goats. The local press at the time referred to them as 'cowboys', though they preferred to be called 'Wildlife Technicians'.

Turtle returning to the sea having laid its eggs, Cousin

Esmerelda, the world's oldest tortoise, Bird Island

ESMERELDA

One of Bird's main attractions is the world's largest, heaviest and oldest living tortoise, who was named Esmerelda, before it was discovered that she was, in fact, a he. He weighs in at 705 pounds (320kg) and is estimated to be over 200 years old. In 1808 a ship called the *Hirondelle* went aground on the reef off the north east of Bird, which was then uninhabited. The passengers and crew came ashore, found water and collected driftwood to make a small raft so that a group could sail to Silhouette island to get help. The rest of the survivors were eventually rescued from the island. But there was one passenger that was overlooked—tortoises were kept in the ship for meat and ballast and one of these was Esmerelda, who swam to the island from the wreck. Esmerelda probably came from Alphonse, one of the outer islands of Seychelles. Having escaped amputation and certain death on board, as well as surviving the shipwreck, Esmerelda now lives a peaceful life, distracted only by the tourists who come to take photographs.

The two technicians worked successfully for several months, using what is termed 'the Judas Goat Technique': one goat is collared with a small radio transmitter and let loose. Because goats are social creatures, the 'Judas goat' soon makes his way to a herd. The men can shoot all the animals, apart from the radio-collared goat, who will then move on, leading the men to another herd. This method of culling has already been used successfully on some of the small islands of Hawaii and in New Zealand. In seven months the goat population had been reduced from some 650 animals to just over 100. The project was going well and the two men were optimistic that in just a few more weeks their task would be completed.

However, one stormy evening in April 1994, the technicians were sailing across the 70 square mile lagoon, with their workers, to the research station. They were travelling in an aluminium boat, with a small crew and several dead goats aboard. The weight of the equipment and dead goats was probably not distributed properly and, before anyone realised what was happening, a large wave rocked the boat to such an extent that it listed and started to sink. The Seychellois crew were quick to realise that the dead goats would attract sharks, which are common in the lagoon, and swam as quickly as they could towards shore. Ray Rainbolt was not a confident swimmer and he and his partner clung to any bits of floating wreckage they could find, slowly trying to head for shore, orientating themselves by the stars. Apart from sharks, the other main danger in the lagoon was the currents. Several times a day the lagoon empties its waters into the sea and, although the currents were moving into the lagoon at the time of the wreck, the men had to reach shore before the tide changed and they were swept out into the ocean.

They swam in the dark for over three hours, finally reaching the main island of Grand Terre. By chance the currents had helped the men swim towards the base camp they had left that evening. Inside the small hut they found some matches they had left behind, so they could at least build a fire. The next morning they started the long walk around the atoll to reach the research station. Two days after the sinking of their boat, they were still walking, but deciding that perhaps by now someone might be looking for them, they walked to the edge of the lagoon. Meanwhile the Seychellois crew had safely reached the research station, alerted the staff there and a rescue effort was underway. For 24 hours the two Americans were missing, presumed dead, and word had reached the American consulate on Mahé. As is often the case with 'bamboo radio' in Seychelles, a certain amount of speculation was mixed with the facts: the consulate had been notified that the men were dead and was just about to ring their parents in the United States, when word came through that they had been rescued.

Thus ended the efforts to eradicate the goats. Ray and his partner had to return home and end their project, because all the equipment was now at the bottom of the lagoon. To date, there are still a hundred or so goats left on the main island of Grand Terre, but it is hoped that a further grant from the World Bank will lead to a resumption of the project. If this happens, Ray gamely says he will give the venture another try.

REPTILES

The best known reptiles in Seychelles are the giant **tortoises** (*Geochelonia gigantea*): the most primitive reptiles surviving on earth. Scientists reckon they evolved during the Triassic period, about 180 million years ago, at a time when Seychelles was part of the supercontinent of Gondwanaland. At one time giant tortoises could be found on many of the islands in the Indian Ocean, but hunting and changing land use led to the extinction of one giant tortoise species to be found on the granitic islands (Marion's Tortoise) and reduced the wild population to the atoll of Aldabra, although many captive giant tortoises can be found on other islands in Seychelles. Until 1995 it was thought that a second species of giant tortoise (Arnold's Tortoise), which was found on the main island group, had also been exterminated by the 1840s. However two large male tortoises, discovered in a hotel garden, were shown to the Nature Protection Trust of Seychelles, along with a skeleton of a third. The shells of these animals were different to the Aldabran species, being flattened and flared over the hind legs with scalloped edges, but were characteristic of the extinct Seychelles species. A genetic study confirmed this and a conversation project on Silhouette Island is now underway with captive breeding groups, with the aim of rescuing these two giant tortoise species from the extinction that was thought to have claimed them some 150 years ago. The project is open to visitors on Silhouette.

Tortoises are well known for their longevity (some are estimated to be over 100 years old) and the older they are the bigger they get, reaching one and a half metres in length and a weight of 500 kilos, which makes their ability to swim something of a surprise. The largest and oldest tortoise is believed to be Esmerelda, on Bird Island, although George on Cousin is almost as huge.

On Aldabra a shortage of fresh water means the tortoises have developed the ability to drink through their noses, enabling them to make use of the shallowest puddle or pool they find. When a giant tortoise mates it is hardly discreet—the clash of the huge shells and the loud grunts of the male tortoise make their mating one of the loudest sounds of the reptile kingdom. After a successful mating a female tortoise will lay her eggs in soft earth, urinating frequently to turn the soil into mud, which then dries around the eggs, protecting them against possible predators. Up to 16 eggs may be laid at one time and these take three to six months to hatch.

There are four species of marine turtle in the Indian Ocean. The **green turtle** (*Chelonia mydas*) was in the past hunted extensively for turtle meat which reduced the population to negligible numbers on the main granitic islands. The hawksbill turtle

Tortoise, Cinq Cases, Aldabra

(*Eretmochelys imbricata*) was not hunted for its meat as its flesh is poisonous, but its numbers were also reduced by hunting as craftsmen sought its attractive shell. However a ban on all turtle hunting in recent years and a closer monitoring of turtle nests on some of the main nesting islands has seen a significant increase in numbers of green and hawksbill turtles. During the turtle nesting season, roughly from Christmas to mid March, turtle hatchings can often be observed on Bird, Denis, Cousine and Frégate Islands and turtles can also still be regularly seen swimming and nesting on the outer island resorts of Desroches and Alphonse.

The largest and rarest of the local turtles is the **leatherback** (*Dermochelys coriacea*), a huge turtle which has a hard leathery skin on its back, rather than a shell. Leatherbacks can reach a length of two metres and weigh 600 kilos. The **loggerhead** turtle (*Caretta caretta*) is an even rarer sight, as it does not breed in Seychelles waters, but very occasionally is seen feeding.

Until recently turtles were hunted extensively throughout the Seychelles. In Victorian times the vogue for green turtle soup in Europe led to the decimation of turtle stocks in the Indian Ocean. In more recent years measures were taken to stop the wholesale slaughter of turtles, but some hunting was still permitted and hawksbill turtle shell (usually described as tortoise-shell) was worked by local craftsmen, made into jewellery and ornaments and sold on to visitors. Under CITES law (The Convention on International Trade in Endangered Species) turtle shell products were not allowed to be imported into Europe, but they were still sold openly in Seychelles. However, in 1994 the Seychelles government bought all stocks of turtle shell from the craftsmen, in order to eradicate the trade. From January 1995 the sale of articles made from turtle shell was made illegal, while compensation and re-training in other skills were offered to the artisans. At the same time the Seychelles government introduced new regulations for the protection of the green and hawksbill turtles, whose populations in the Indian Ocean have dwindled alarmingly. Hopefully now, at least in Seychelles waters, the species will survive.

The inner islands also have three possible species of native freshwater terrapin, known locally as *torti soupap*—the plug tortoise. Two of these can be seen living in the La Veuve Nature Reserve on La Digue—the **yellow bellied** and the **star bellied terrapins** (*Pelusios castanoides* and *Pelusios subniger*). The third is the **black bellied terrapin** (*Pelusios seychellensis*), which is thought to be unique to Seychelles. Yet, as a sighting of this reptile has not occurred for many years, it could well be extinct. Even the two other Seychelles species of terrapin have suffered greatly over the last ten years due to pollution, predation and development that has drained large areas of marshland in which the terrapins live. There are now thought to be fewer than 250 of either terrapin species left in Seychelles. The Nature Protection Trust of Seychelles is now running a captive breeding programme on Silhouette island, with reintroduction of terrapins into secure reserves.

Other reptiles found in Seychelles include an endemic **chameleon** (*Chamaeleo tigris*), which can be found on Mahé, Praslin and Silhouette. It can grow to a length of ten inches and is grey or pale yellow in colour, but it turns its skin into brightly coloured yellow and black stripes when frightened. It is a beautiful creature, with the typically swivel eyes and sticky tongue of all the chameleon family. There are several species of harmless snake, which are not often encountered. The small Seychelles **house snake** (*Lamprophis geometricus*) is rumoured to suckle the milk of young mothers while they sleep, but in reality it preys on lizards and mice. The Seychelles **wolf snake** (*Lycognathopis seychellensis*) is a much larger reptile, growing up to four feet in length, but it lives only in the mountain forests, eating lizards and frogs. The **Brahminy blind snake** (*Ramphotyphlops braminus*) looks more like a worm, reaching just seven inches in length, and spends its life burrowing in the earth, eating termites and other insects.

The most common reptile in Seychelles, and the ones that live closest to human habitation, is the **gecko** (*Phelsuma*). Pink or brown geckos are often seen in houses and hotels, active at night near lights to catch insects. Vivid green day geckos are more commonly found on trees, although they do venture indoors from time to time. **Skinks** (*Mabuya*) are larger lizards, often a darker brown or mottled gold colour, slower moving and mainly living in the forest undergrowth. All these are perfectly harmless, although geckos can be a nuisance to live with—they leave long trails of their droppings down the walls and tend to die in inaccessible places, leaving behind a gruesome smell.

Crocodiles (*Crocodylus niloticus*) used to be found in large numbers in the inner islands and early sailors recount the sea around Mahé swarming with crocodiles and sharks, fighting each other and attacking the sailors as they waded ashore. Because of their aggressive nature, they were killed off quickly by the early settlers of Mahé. Today all that remains of them are a few crumbling skulls in the Seychelles Museum in Victoria.

There are at least six species of frog in Seychelles, five being endemic. One species was only discovered for the first time in 2001, so there may well be other undiscovered species hidden in the thick forests of the inner islands. The newly discovered frog was found in the forests of Silhouette and has been named the palm frog, or *Soosglossis pipilodryas* (the chirping spirit of the forest).

Other rare species include the *Soosglossus sechellensis*, unusual for the fact that the male frog carries the tadpoles on his back until they mature and hop off; and the smallest frog in the world, *Soosglossus gardineri*, which reaches barely two centimetres at maturity. This brown frog lives within the leaf litter on the mountainous slopes of Mahé and, although it is tiny, it has a loud piping call—even more remarkable since these frogs have no visible ears.

MAMMALS

Very few mammals are endemic to Seychelles, although numerous cats, dogs and farm animals were introduced by settlers. **Fruit bats** are the only truly endemic mammal—there are two species of bat or flying fox. These can be seen in large numbers, whirling about the sky at dusk. Their wing span can be a metre across and they have a small brown furry body with a fox-like snout, large brown eyes and delicate ears. Some people keep fruit bats in cages as pets. In the wild they roost in large numbers in mango trees, often hanging by just one foot with their leathery wings wrapped around them like a cocoon. A unique variety with a whitish face occurs on Aldabra.

Tenrecs are the only other wild mammal. These hedgehog-type creatures live in the forests of Mahé, after being introduced from Madagascar in the 19th century, probably for food. Tenrecs grow to about the size of a cat and they are largely nocturnal.

LAND BIRDS

Seychelles is justly famous for its bird life. At the last count 13 species and a further 17 subspecies occurred nowhere else in the world. The islands also contain a number of species considered to be particularly threatened with extinction. These include the **bare-legged scops owl** (*Otus insularis*), which for more than 50 years was believed to be extinct, until it was rediscovered in 1959. Even now a sighting of this mysterious bird is rare: it was only in 2001, during an intensive Scops Owl monitoring project in the mountain forests of Mahé, that for the first time ever a Scops Owl nest was not only discovered but was filmed by Birdlife Seychelles as the birds laid eggs and hatched a chick. Between 75 and 150 pairs of Scops Owl are thought to exist in the Morne Seychelles National Park on Mahé. They can be recognised by their distinctive call: a slow rhythmic rasping like a saw, interspersed with 'tok tok' knocking noises. It is this sound that gives the bird its Kreol name of *Scieur*.

The **Black Paradise fly-catcher** (*Terpsiphone corvina*), or *Veuve* (the widow) as it is known in Kreol, is another rare species, which now has a nature reserve named after it on La Digue. The male bird is black with a blue sheen, a blue bill and sports long black tail streamers, while the female is smaller with a brown back and wings and a blue-black head. The voice of the male is a piping whistle, which the Seychellois interpret as a sign of rain: 'pli pli pli pli'. The world population is thought to be around 150 to 200 individuals.

Another rarity is the Seychelles **Magpie Robin** (*Copsychus sechellarum*). This bird was close to extinction when numbers dwindled to a low in 1970 of just 23 birds on Frégate Island. Now there are some 110 birds on four islands. The main population is still on Frégate, but birds have also been successfully transferred to Cousin, Cousine and Aride. The bird is called a magpie robin because it resembles a robin with the white wing bars and blue-black body of a magpie, although it is actually a member of the thrush family. This bird was once widespread in all the granitic Seychelles islands, where it lived in the forests, feeding on ground-living invertebrates in the leaf litter. Once man arrived, 200 years ago, the forests were rapidly cleared and the bird population declined. The biggest threat to the birds, however, was the introduction of cats and rats to the main islands, against which the birds had no defence.

The survival of the species looked desperate, until Birdlife International intervened and a project to save the magpie robin was initiated. There is today a full time warden to care for the birds on Frégate and an extensive tree planting scheme on the island to improve the bird's habitat. Similar programmes are in place on the other islands where the magpie robins now live and it is hoped that populations on these other islands will increase significantly in the years ahead.

Another bird species recently saved from the brink of extinction is the **Seychelles brush warbler** (*Bebronis seychellensis*). This small, insect-eating brown bird is inconspicuous to the eye, but has a rich melodious song, similar to an English blackbird or an American robin. Numbers were down to 26 birds, living on Cousin island, when Birdlife International purchased the island and turned it into a nature reserve. Today the world population of this small brown bird is over 1,500.

More common bird species include the **blue pigeon** (*Alectroenas pulcherrima*), which is an attractive bird with a red cap, white front and silvery blue back and lower body. Its local name is pigeon hollandaise, named after the red, white and blue striped flag of Holland, in the days before the French flag had become the Tricolour. The **Seychelles sunbird** (*Nectarinia dussumieri*) is the most common endemic land bird, looking like a dark humming bird. It is easily recognisable by its long thin upturned beak, which it uses to suck nectar—it particularly likes passion fruit flowers. Their delicate pendulous nests are suspended from the tips of branches, often in casuarina trees.

Cattle egrets or *Madame Paton* (*Bubulcus ibis*) are the slim white herons seen waiting for fish scraps in the market at Victoria. The rarer **Seychelles kestrel** (*Falco araea*) is to be seen on the mountain slopes of Mahé. Smaller numbers of the bird can

The introduction of the non-indigenous Barn Owl, for pest control, has instead wreaked havoc with local species of small birds such as Fairy Terns

The Magpie Robin, although slowly increasing in number, is perilously close to extinction

be found on Silhouette and Praslin, where 13 birds were introduced in 1977. Local superstitions consider the birds to be bad luck: the Kreol name is *katiti*, because of its continuous call 'ti-ti-ti' when in flight. The introduced **Madagascan fody** or Cardinal (*Foudia madagascariensis*) is a common sight, noticeable for the brilliant red chest of the male during the breeding season. These small birds are very tame and will often perch on your table, seeking out scraps or raiding the sugarbowl. The cardinal is said to have been introduced to Seychelles in about 1860 and the story of how this occurred relates to an argument between two neighbouring farmers. The men were in dispute over a plot of land where one of them was growing rice. The other took revenge by sending to Mauritius for some cardinals, known to be a plague of ricefields, and he released them into his neighbour's crop. To this day, it is said, the presence of the cardinal makes growing rice in Seychelles impossible.

The cardinal's endemic cousin, the **Seychelles fody**, (*Foudia sechellarum*)—or *toc toc* as it is known in Kreol—is a larger bird with dark brown plumage and is much rarer, limited to Cousin, Cousine and Frégate. The breeding male has a yellow throat and forehead. A more common sight is the **Madagascar turtle dove** (*Streptopelia p. picturata*), a pretty grey ground dove. It is closely related to the rarer **Seychelles turtle dove** (*Streptopelia p. rostrata*), which is thought to be now almost extinct, due to inter-breeding with its more prolific cousin. The **barred ground dove** (*Geopelia striata*), a small buff-coloured dove, is one of the most common birds to be seen on the main islands of Seychelles. It is often found around houses and scavenging scraps of food from hotel gardens. These doves are not native to the islands, but appear to have been introduced to Seychelles from India via Mauritius, probably by Indian traders. Another common bird, also introduced to Seychelles by the same route, is the noisy **mynah** bird (*Acridotheres tristis*). These are large shiny black birds with a bold yellow face patch and white bars on the wing and tail. Very occasionally a mutant form of mynah is seen, in which the entire head and neck are bald, the head yellow and the neck black. Seychellois call this the king mynah or *roi martin*.

Another (less welcome) introduction is the **barn owl** (*Tyto alba affinis*), which was brought to the islands in the early 1950s to catch rats. Unfortunately the smaller rare birds offered easier prey. The owl has wreaked such havoc on bird species such as the fairy tern, that the government now offers a SR30 reward for each one killed. Apart from the mynah the noisiest birds to be seen in the granitic island forest are the **Seychelles bulbul** (*Hypsipetes crassirotris crassirostris*), which looks and sounds like a teenage delinquent, with its scruffy crest and a raucous call. This is one of the few endemic birds that does not seem to have suffered from the arrival of man. They are very curious, often flying towards a stranger in the forest to take a closer look.

The republic's national bird is the **black parrot** (*Coracopsis nigra barklyi*), which is mainly found in Praslin's Vallée de Mai and there are a few pairs on Curieuse. At one

Sacred Ibis in mangrove

time a green parakeet was also found in Seychelles; it is thought to have been similar to the Alexandrine Parakeet of Asia, but became extinct in the last century because of forest clearance and hunting. Only a few pairs of the black parrot remain, nesting in the hollow trunks of dead trees.

Sea Birds

Enormous colonies of seabirds can be found on Aride, Bird, Cousin and Desnoefs. Although Seychelles is known especially for its terns, species of noddies, boobie, frigate and tropic birds are also common.

From May to October is the best time to visit if you want to see the huge breeding colonies of **sooty terns** (*Sterna fuscata nubilosa*) on Bird Island. March and April are the best times to visit Aride, but Cousin, Frégate and other islands can be visited any time of the year and will provide good sightings of many species of sea and land birds. My favourites are the **tropic birds** (*Phaethon lepturus lepturus*), which look stunning in flight, with their long white tail feathers contrasting with the brilliant blue of the sky. Tropic birds feed much further out to sea than most of the other seabirds, elegantly diving for fish and squid. The chicks are hatched out at ground level, often in hollow trees or nooks and crannies of the rockface. They look like small round powder puffs, covered in long silky down and becoming very fat before fledging. The much rarer **red tailed tropic birds** (*Ph. r. rubricauda*) can only be seen on the outlying islands like Aldabra and, at certain times of the year, on Aride.

The beautiful Fairy Tern is found throughout the inner islands

White **fairy terns** (*Gygis alba monte*) are a common sight on many islands and on Cousin are so tame you can observe them closely as they sit on their egg, balanced precariously on the fork of a tree, as they do not build nests. On Mahé the numbers are smaller; the population has been greatly reduced by barn owls.

Other common seabirds are the **lesser noddy**, the **brown** or **common noddy**, the **red footed booby**, the **wedge-tailed shear-water**, the **bridled tern**, the **turnstone** and both the **greater** and **lesser frigate**. The male greater frigate (*Fregata minor*), the largest seabird in Seychelles, displays a spectacular red pouch in its mating display. Frigate birds never rest on the water, because their feathers would become waterlogged. Instead they hunt and feed on the wing, often scavenging scraps of food on the water's surface or chasing other seabirds in an attempt to force them to disgorge their last mouthful. Aride is the best island to see these spectacular birds.

Weighing up to five kilogrammes, giant "coconut" crabs populate Aldabra and are renowned for stealing food from unwary visitors

INSECT LIFE

There are over 3,000 insect species in Seychelles, most of which are endemic.

But don't let this large number put you off. In many ways the insect presence on the islands is far less noticeable than in Europe—flies do not occur in large numbers and, although the large wasps and bees can sting, they are like most of the wildlife in Seychelles: docile, slow moving creatures, not given to irritating humans. The **potter wasp** is a black wasp which constructs tiny mud pots in which to hatch its young, while the **mud wasp** makes a string of pots, often seen on verandahs and on rocks. The **yellow wasp** does have a painful sting, but is not aggressive unless you happen to disturb its nest, which looks like a honeycombed paper lantern.

Mosquitoes are, of course, the biggest nuisance and seem to be more ferocious on the smaller islands. The best repellent available locally is called 'Peaceful Sleep'. Cover up legs and arms, especially at dawn and dusk. Indoors, if there is no air conditioning and the shutters do not have mosquito nets, a mosquito coil is usually provided. **Cockroaches** are the other pest—they are the introduced American cockroach and you will see both crawling and flying versions at night.

Giant millipedes, up to 25cm long, look formidable but are harmless vegetarians. They mainly come out in the evening, seeking damp shade during the day, sometimes coming together to form huge communal knots around the shady sides of trees. If they are caught out in the sun they quickly die. Sometimes, after scavenging a dead millipede, a green gecko can be seen adorned with millipede segments around its neck like a large grey necklace.

Another giant is the fearsome looking **whip scorpion**, which often lives amongst rotting coconut husks on small islands. This can measure up to 30cm between the front legs, but is quite harmless. There are smaller nocturnal scorpions, which can have a nasty sting, but they are rare, occurring mainly on Frégate. Another giant occupant of Frégate is the **tenebrionid beetle**, a grey beetle with a lumpy back and thin legs, which can be seen living on the trunks of sangdragon and cashew nut trees. It is harmless, as is the large flying **rhinoceros beetle**, which occasionally makes its presence felt by flying, with a great deal of noise, to an accessible light bulb. The most interesting insects are the **stick** and **leaf insects**, but these mainly live in the forests and their disguise is so effective they can be extremely difficult to spot. One rare specimen, *Carausius scotti*, was discovered on the island of Silhouette in 1908 and later thought to have become extinct, as it was not seen again until a scientific expedition rediscovered it in 1990.

Spiders are a common sight, but the fearsome looking **palm spider**, whose giant webs are often strung across telephone poles, have no bite. The worst experience you can have with one of these is to accidentally walk into one of their extremely sticky webs. Smaller, hairier spiders do have a bite; the **wolf spider** and the **tarantula** are best avoided, but again are not often seen.

The other invertebrate with a nasty bite is the giant **centipede**. These are found in the forests and emerge from the undergrowth on damp nights. Their front legs are adapted to inflict a very painful bite and the poison they inject can cause severe swelling and an allergic reaction.

THE UNDERWATER WORLD

Nature under the waves is as spectacular as the many unique species on dry land in Seychelles. The coral reefs that form around many of the islands contain huge numbers of fish and other species and the corals themselves are well worth a closer look. Unfortunately, the El Nino weather system in the late 1990s led to widespread coral 'bleaching' as sea temperatures rose to record levels around the inner islands of Seychelles. This led to the death of many soft corals, and reduced the numbers of fish seen on the reefs that rely on the soft corals for food. Around the inner islands there are some soft corals in deeper water that have escaped serious bleaching and these will eventually re-grow back to their former glory. Hard corals were not affected and the reefs around Mahé, Praslin, La Digue and the other inner islands are still full of marine life. The reefs around the outer islands however escaped the worst of El Nino, and divers can discover the best coral gardens off Alphonse and Desroches.

Coral is a living animal. Each coral head is formed by hundreds of polyps, which are tiny animals secreting a hard external skeleton. As a result, coral should never be touched by divers or snorkellers. Apart from the fact that handling coral can kill the polyps, some coral species protect themselves against predators and kill prey by using tentacles armed with stinging cells.

Swimming amidst the life on a coral reef is like entering a huge exotic aquarium; there are hundreds of species of colourful fish that live around the main granitic islands and many are easily identified by their vivid markings. A common reef fish is the **blue-banded snapper**, which often forms large shoals. These fish display four horizontal blue bands over a yellow body. Also very common are the **gold striped fusiliers**, which have a light blue body and one golden stripe. **Angelfish** have a distinctive shape and many vivid colour variations can be seen. The **Royal Angelfish** is a particular beauty, with a golden body and tail, blue edged white stripes and a blue banded fin. Closely related to angelfish are the **butterfly fish**; they have a similar shape, but lack a gill spine.

A small, brilliantly coloured fish that is seen in shoals around the coral is the **chromis**: both blue and golden chromis are seen in Seychelles waters. Related to the chromis are the **sergeant major** and the **scissortail sergeant**, both silver and black striped fish: sometimes these fish can be particularly territorial, inflicting the trespasser with little bites, that feel like a small child is pinching you underwater. Another territorial fish is the brown **chocolate dip**, together with its cousins, the **zebra humbug** and the **two-bar humbug**.

Underwater lights help reveal the vivid red and orange hues of the coral at greater depths

Divers are bound to see school after school of fish

Despite El Nino's coral bleaching of 1998, many reefs are growing back to their former glory such as this one off Aldabra which has attracted a red grouper amongst other fish

On land the parrots are a dull black, but under the water the **parrot fish** display a rich kaleidoscope of colours. They are named because of their beak-like mouths, which are used to pick off algae growing on the coral reef. The way in which they feed, taking off tiny particles of limestone coral with each mouthful of algae, is an important contribution to the forming of the white sand beaches.

The **wrasse** is another important coral reef fish. They range in size from the tiniest specimens to the huge **humphead wrasse**, which can grow to a length of seven feet. Many of the smaller wrasse act as cleaner fish: the **bluestreak cleaner wrasse** is particularly entertaining. Each male controls a harem of six females who set up a fish cleaning station, where larger fish can actually be seen queuing up to have their irritating parasites picked off. These wrasse should not be confused with the **mimic blenny**, which is a similar colour—but when an unsuspecting large fish swims along for a clean, the mimic blenny nibbles off its fins instead.

A distinctive fish is the bright yellow **trumpetfish**, with a shape resembling the instrument. **Pipefish** are a similar shape, but they are related to the seahorse and share its peculiarities: it is the male that incubates the eggs in his pouch. Another long slender fish is the silver **needlefish**, which swims close to the surface of the water and resembles a small sword fish. They occasionally leap into the air and have been known to accidentally spear swimmers, but this is extremely rare.

A spectacular fish to see, but not get too close to, is the **lion fish**, which has pectoral fins spread out like a lion's mane. If provoked, these fish can give a nasty sting. The **scorpion fish** also has a row of poisonous spines along its dorsal fin. The fish that can cause the most harm is the **stone fish**, which lives in the rocks and so closely resembles its sand coloured environment that the unwary can tread on its highly venomous dorsal fin. The poison can paralyse its victim and hospital treatment will be needed. For this reason it is always advisable to wear flippers, or at least protective rubber shoes, when swimming on or near coral reefs and rocks.

Further out to sea from the reefs are much larger fish, like the commercially-valuable tuna and other fish that are prized as big game fishing trophies, like the **sail fish** and many species of **shark**. The most common species is the harmless **white tip** shark, but the more aggressive **tiger** shark and **hammerhead** shark are often seen on the outer islands. The largest fish of the sea is the **whale** shark and sometimes fortunate divers will be able to experience the thrill of swimming close to this giant of the deep.

Mahé

Mahé is the largest and most populated island in Seychelles. It is eight kilometres wide by 27 kilometres long and is inhabited by 70,000 people. It has the highest mountains in the archipelago, rising to 900 metres and flanked by lush dark green tropical forests, some of which have never been fully explored. The international airport is on the eastern coast of the island and a few miles further north is the marine harbour and the capital, Victoria, which has a population of 35,000, making it one of the smallest capitals in the world.

Every visitor should spend at least part of their holiday on Mahé. Besides having over 60 beautiful beaches, it has the most places to see, the best restaurants and shops and a better selection of facilities than any of the smaller islands.

Victoria

Built around the harbour, there has been a settlement at Victoria from the earliest settler days. Originally known as L'Établissement (the Establishment), it was renamed Victoria in 1841 after the Queen of England. Since then the town has grown, both upwards into the hills surrounding it and further out to sea, following land reclamation schemes. There are no distinct boundaries to the town, but in the days before cars, when people had to walk down the steep mountain slopes into Victoria, it was said that if you want to know where the town boundary lies, 'it is in the place where a girl stops to put on the shoes she was carrying on her head'.

Victoria has more of the air of a small market town than a capital city. The town's friendly character and traditional wooden shuttered shops have been preserved, despite many modern developments. The streets are always clean and tidy, there is ample car parking space and there are few high-rise office blocks—everything you would expect from Seychelles.

The small town centre makes for easy exploring. Most of the main shops and facilities can be found clustered around the colonial **clock tower**, built in 1903 to commemorate Seychelles becoming a separate crown colony, distinct from Mauritius. The clock is often assumed to be a miniature of London's Big Ben, but it is actually a replica of 'Little Ben', the clock tower which sits outside Victoria railway station. Little Ben was built nine years earlier than its Seychelles replica, to commemorate friendship between England and France. In 1903 this clock tower was on the waterfront, now it is several hundred yards away from the coast, giving a good indication of how land reclamation has changed the town.

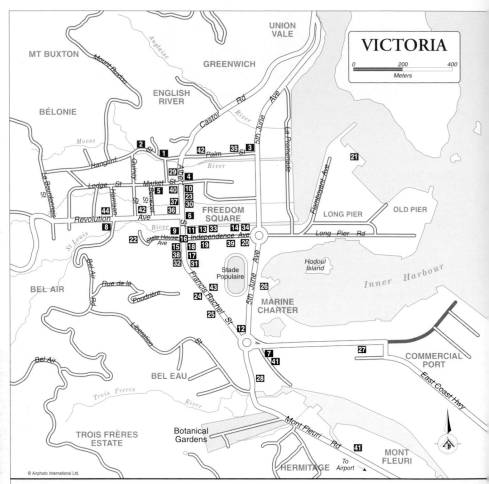

© Airphoto International Ltd.

Sites

1 Capuchin House
2 Catholic Cathedral
3 Bus Terminal
4 (&19) Barclays Bank
5 Selwyn Clarke Market
6 Camion Hall Craft Centre
7 International Conference Centre
8 Car Hire Hertz
9 Anglican Cathedral, Travel Services
   Seychelles Travel Agency,
   Banque Francaise Commercial
10 Taxis
11 Post Office
12 National Library
13 The Seychelles Natural History Museum

14 Creole Holidays Travel Agency
15 Air Seychelles Sales Office
16 Clock Tower
17 Court House
18 (&4) Barclays Bank
19 Pirates' Arms
20 Tourist Information Office
21 Ferry Departures
22 State House
23 Trinity House (Habib Bank,
     News Café, Internet Café)
24 Mosque
25 Cable & Wireless
26 Yacht Club
27 Fire Station
28 Dorothy's Florist & Garden Centre
29 Deepam's Cinema

30 SMB Supermarket
31 Petrol Station
32 Sam's Pizzeria/ Internet Café
33 7 Degrees South Travel Agents
34 Savings Bank
35 Memories Gift Shop
36 Memorabilia Gift Shop
37 Sooty Tern Gift Shop
38 Temooljees Supermarket
39 Vanilla 2000 Café
40 Sunstroke Art Gallery
41 International School
42 Mason's Travel
43 Flamboyant Night Club
44 Double Click Internet Café
45 Fiennes Esplanade Craft Kiosks
46 Kaz Zanana

On the street corner beside the clock tower is the **Court House**, outside which is a statue of Pierre Poivre, the Frenchman who, in 1772, founded the first colony in Seychelles. His name in English—'Peter Pepper'—is very apt, as he was responsible for introducing spice trees to Seychelles, including the cinnamon which now covers much of Mahé.

Banks include two branches of Barclays, the Banque Française Commerciale, Habib Bank and the Seychelles Savings Bank, all of whom will exchange foreign currency, cash travellers' cheques and give you a cash advance on your credit card. Banking hours are between 8.30 or 9.00 to 13.00 and from 14.00 or 14.30 to 16.00 or 16.30 Monday to Friday; and from 9.00 to 12.00 noon on Saturday. Bureau de Change facilities are also available in some banks in the afternoons.

The **Post Office** in Independence Avenue is open from 8.00 to 12.00 noon and 13.00 to 16.00 Monday to Friday; and from 8.00 to 12.00 noon on a Saturday. Airmail post handed in at the post office before midday will usually leave on the following day's flight. The colourful stamps issued in Seychelles can be purchased in special collectors' packs. Pictorial stamps, featuring tortoises, coco de mers, fruit and flowers of Seychelles, have become valuable collectors' items.

Naturally, sailing is quite popular in the Seychelles, Victoria Harbour, Mahé

SHOPPING IN VICTORIA

Most shops open Monday to Friday from 8.00 to 17.00, some closing for lunch between 12.00 and 13.00. On a Saturday most are only open for the morning. To explore Victoria properly takes at least a morning, but be warned, it can get very hot and humid in town and spending more than a couple of hours walking around in the heat without resting for a drink can be exhausting. Try to avoid Victoria around midday, when it is at its hottest.

VICTORIA MARKET

Named after a former governor of Seychelles, Percy Selwyn Clarke (1947–1951), the market offers a fascinating glimpse into the everyday life of Seychelles, as well as being the best place to buy fresh fruit, fish and spices. The market was renovated and expanded in 1999 and now includes an upper storey arcade of souvenir shops and a café. Rosie's Flower Shop in the market also sells a wide range of tropical flowers and can prepare wedding flowers or bouquets for overseas shipment. Saturday mornings are especially busy and the spice stalls are useful gift hunting grounds. Watch the tall egrets as they elegantly pace around the fish stalls for scraps. Smell the pungent aroma of salt fish and look out for the big catches of the day on the fresh fish stall.

There are a number of stalls selling local fruit and vegetables, all beautifully laid out, and for just a few rupees you can buy a bunch of bananas, huge avocado pears, sweet mangoes and salad vegetables, as well as the more tropical sweet potatoes, cassava, yams and chilies.

To find the market walk up Market Street, off Albert Street, past the old style wooden shops and houses and allow your nose to guide you to the market entrance, just next to the fish stalls. Morning visits are best; once the stalls begin to sell out of their produce at around lunchtime, the market tends to empty.

FOOD SHOPPING

There are three small supermarkets in Victoria, the largest of these being SMB, the Seychelles Marketing Board on Albert Street. Imported foods such as cheese, tinned and convenience foods are expensive and often in short supply: the availability of even staples like rice, lentils and flour can never be taken for granted. Visitors who are self catering in Seychelles are strongly recommended to bring some necessary food items with them.

SMB usually has the largest selection of stock, including local tea (weak but flavoursome) cartons of fruit juice and tinned tuna. Food can also be bought from the more up-market supermarket Temooljees on Francis Rachel Street, close to the clock tower, which also has an in-store café. The Continental store on Revolution Avenue will occasionally stock items that cannot be found in SMB, and has a good frozen fish and meat section. Alternatively there is a butchers and fishmongers at Les Palmes Building in Palm Street called ELS which usually has a selection of fresh fruit and vegetables in store as well.

SHOPPING FOR GIFTS

There are many **craft shops** around Victoria. The craft shops in Camion Hall contains a number of exclusive art and craft shops including local goldsmiths 'Kreol'or' who design and make fabulous gold jewellery using natural materials found on the islands such as coconut shells, green snails, tiger cowry and oyster shells. Next door but one in Camion Hall is gold and silversmith Riccardo Carbognin who creates jewellery, souvenirs and ornaments combined with precious stones or local materials, such as the Seychelles' black pearl. Also within Camion Hall is a shop selling hand made candles, other art and craft shops including clothes and textiles and a Duty Free shop.

Opposite Camion Hall is the Sooty Tern gift shop, which has been set up by three local artists to sell and display their work. The three artists are, firstly Daniel Monthy, a young Seychellois artist, who works with fibre craft to create original decorative items from coconut, bamboo, raffia and other local materials. His most popular items are tablemats, lamps and baskets. Second is 'Thoughts' Stained Glass, created by Sharon and Les Masterson, include beautifully made glass mobiles, individual glass fish, clocks, mirrors, bowls and 'Tiffany-style' lamps. Thirdly, is the work of popular British, watercolour artist Andrew Gee. His realistic paintings capture the beauty of the turquoise sea and white beaches of Seychelles.

Turning right from the Sooty Tern and then taking a first left along Revolution Avenue is another superior gift shop, Memorabilia, which is run by Catherine Mancham, the wife of the former Seychelles president James Mancham. This shop sells a wide variety of arts and crafts from Seychelles including prints from celebrated artist Michael Adams. Other gift shops well worth a visit is the 'Antik Colony' in the Pirates Arms Arcade in Independence Avenue and Sunstroke on Market Street which sells silk screen tropical clothes and textiles as well as paintings and prints of well known Seychelles' artist George Camille. There are also a number of souvenir kiosks situated along the Fiennes Esplanade, which runs alongside Francis Rachel Street. Here there are a number of stalls selling local spices, beach wraps, postcards and shells.

Apart from Rosie's Flower Shop in Victoria Market, there are a further two florists in Victoria who sell orchids and other tropical flowers, which can be ordered in advance, to be collected on the last day of your holiday to ensure they return with you in good condition. These are The Flower Box , which is behind the Pirates Arms in the street running alongside Barclays Bank in Independence Avenue, and Dorothy's the Florist which is in a restored Creole house just outside Victoria, taking the Mont Fleuri Road towards the Botanical garden. Dorothy's can be found on the left hand side approximately 500 yards from the roundabout.

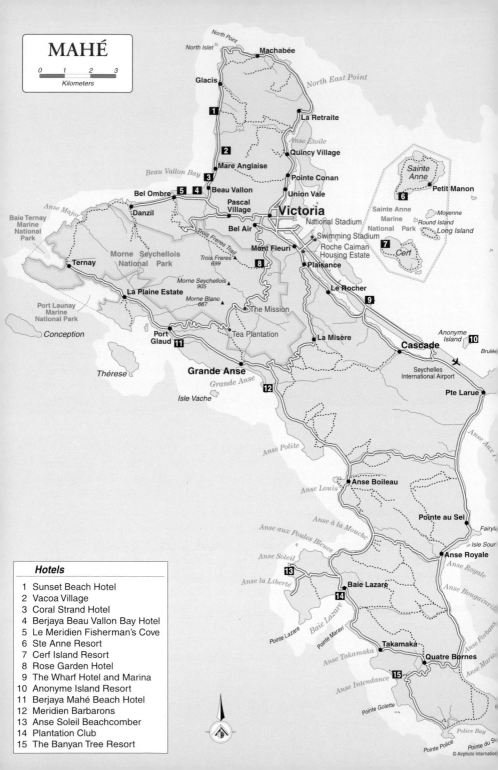

MAHÉ

Kilometers
0 1 2 3

North Point
North Islet
Machabée
Glacis
1
La Retraite
North East Point
2
Anse Étoile
Quincy Village
Mare Anglaise
Beau Vallon Bay
3
Pointe Conan
Bel Ombre **5 4** Beau Vallon
Union Vale
Anse Major
Danzil
Pascal Village
Victoria
Sainte Anne
Sainte Anne
Marine
National
Park
6
Petit Manon
Moyenne
Round Island
Long Island

Baie Ternay
Marine
National
Park
Bel Air
National Stadium
Swimming Stadium
Roche Caiman
Housing Estate
7
Cerf
Mont Fleuri
Ternay
Trois Freres Trail
Trois Freres 699
8
Plaisance
Morne Seychellois National Park
Morne Seychellois 905
Le Rocher
9
La Plaine Estate
Morne Blanc 667
The Mission
Anonyme Island **10**
Brulée
Port Launay Marine National Park
Conception
Tea Plantation
La Misère
Cascade
Seychelles International Airport
Port Glaud **11**
Grande Anse
Thérèse
Grande Anse
12
Pte Larue
Isle Vache
Anse Aux F
Anse Polite
Anse Louis
Anse Boileau
Anse à la Mouche
Pointe au Sel
Fairyla
Anse aux Poules Bleues
Isle Sour
Anse Soleil
Anse Royale
Anse Royale
13
Anse la Liberté
Baie Lazare
Anse Bougainvill
14
Baie Lazare
Pointe Lazare
Pointe Maravi
Takamaka
Anse Forbans
Anse Takamaka
Quatre Bornes
Anse Marie
15
Anse Intendance
Pointe Golette
Police Bay
Pointe Police
Pointe du Sv
© Airphoto Internationa

Hotels

1 Sunset Beach Hotel
2 Vacoa Village
3 Coral Strand Hotel
4 Berjaya Beau Vallon Bay Hotel
5 Le Meridien Fisherman's Cove
6 Ste Anne Resort
7 Cerf Island Resort
8 Rose Garden Hotel
9 The Wharf Hotel and Marina
10 Anonyme Island Resort
11 Berjaya Mahé Beach Hotel
12 Meridien Barbarons
13 Anse Soleil Beachcomber
14 Plantation Club
15 The Banyan Tree Resort

BOOKS AND NEWSPAPERS AND INTERNET CAFÉS

No foreign newspapers are on sale in Seychelles at present although British newspapers can be read in the reading room at the British High Commission in the Oliaji Trade Centre, close to the clock tower. Local newspapers and a selection of paperback books can be brought from 'Antigone' in Victoria House Arcade.

There are a number of Internet cafés in Victoria, including Kokonet in the Pirates Arms Arcade, SPACE Internet Café in Francis Rachel Street, which can be accessed by climbing the steps towards Sam's Pizzeria, and MBM Internet Café on the first floor of Trinity House arcade in Albert Street, and Double Click Internet Café on Palm Street which also serves very good coffee and snacks. All Internet cafés charge an hourly rate and most are open from 8.00 am to 8.00 pm.

TOURIST INFORMATION

The **Tourist Information Office** can be found on Independence Avenue, offering brochures on Seychelles in English, French, German and Italian. The staff will also be able to advise you on boat charter or travel to other islands. **Tour Operators** in Victoria who can offer arranged day trips are: TSS (Travel Services Seychelles), on Albert Street close to the Anglican Cathedral; Masons Tour operators on Revolution Avenue plus Creole Holidays and 7 Degrees South, which are both in Kingsgate House along Independence Avenue. Premier Holidays are also along Albert Street. All the main

Fisherman sort the day's catch on the quay for the fish market

airlines also have offices in Victoria, where you may need to confirm your return flights. **Air Mauritius** is in Kingsgate House Arcade on Independence Avenue. The **Air Seychelles** sales office is in Victoria house on Francis Rachel Street.

SIGHTSEEING IN VICTORIA

Apart from shopping, Victoria has other attractions. The **Roman Catholic Cathedral** is the remains of an impressive French colonial style building on the north side of town, perched on the hillside of Oliver Maradan Street. It is called the Cathedral of the Immaculate Conception and has a bell tower with the famous clock that, chimes twice on the hour. The interior of the cathedral has a modern, airy feel and the Saturday evening and Sunday morning masses are well attended to the degree that latecomers usually have to stand outside in the cathedral gardens.

To the west of the cathedral is **Capucin House**, the Catholic bishop's residence. This is not open to the public, but is worth a glance from the outside—it is an impressive three storey house, with balconies supported by grand stone pillars.

The **Anglican Cathedral** is a new building, completed in 2004. The older, smaller stone and corrugated roofed cathedral, which had stood in the same spot since 1859, was demolished apart from the bell tower. This was then incorporated into the new more spacious design that also features modern stained glass windows and a copper roof. Services are held here every Sunday morning. Other religious buildings in Victoria include a Hindu temple in Quincy Street and a small mosque with a golden dome, which can be found up a tiny alleyway off Frances Rachel Street.

The **Seychelles Natural History Museum** on Independence Avenue is a useful diversion on a rainy day. This small museum contains hidden treasures: there is a collection of shells and dried insects, including some of the biggest beetles in the world—thankfully rare! You can also see skulls of the now-extinct Seychelles crocodiles (killed off by early settlers) and some sad-looking stuffed giant tortoises and turtles. The **National Museum of History** is an informative display of the history and settlement of Seychelles and can be found within the impressively modern National Library, on Frances Rachel Street.

Within the museum are permanent exhibitions on slavery and British rule, as well as temporary exhibitions, on themes such as shipwrecks and Seychelles in the Victorian age. Open five days a week except Wednesdays and Sundays, the National Museum of History also houses some of Seychelles' most prized monuments, such as the Stone of Possession placed on the islands in November 1756 by Captain Nicholas Morphey as a formal act of possession, and the world's smallest statuette of Queen Victoria, which was erected outside Victoria's court house buildings in 1841. The museum offers guided tours for an admission fee of SR10.

State House is at the top of State House Avenue. Formerly Government House, this two storey Edwardian-style mansion was the former home of the British governors, but now houses the offices of the President of Seychelles, whose office is situated in a modern extension to the old house. State House is often used to host state parties and ceremonies. The house was built in 1913, when Sir W E Davidson was governor. His wife played a major role in its design, but apparently forgot to include a staircase in the plans: fortunately this oversight was noticed before the house was actually completed. It is, however, a fine example of colonial architecture: a report written in the 1950s states that "few of the British colonies possess such a splendid residence of the King's representative".

The gardens surrounding the house are just as impressive as its architecture. Thirteen gardeners are employed to tend to the large collection of exotic flowers and trees, planted by successive governors and collected from the then huge expanse of the British Empire. Shaded arbours, water gardens and sweeping lawns make these the most beautiful gardens to be found in Seychelles. At one time the grounds covered some 13 acres of land, occupying what is now State House Avenue and including the area behind the house, right up the hill behind Victoria to the area of St Louis. The entrance to the house must have been very grand, with an avenue of 40 huge sangdragon trees. Sadly, only one ancient giant remains, the rest having been cut down after their branches began to fall onto the road with fatal consequences.

Besides the garden and a glimpse inside the house, there are some interesting historical sites: the imposing tomb of Seychelles' most famous governor, Queau de Quinssy, and nearby a monument to the well-liked British Governor, Sir John Thorpe, who drowned while swimming at Grand Anse in 1961. The remains of part of the original settlement can also be seen—crumbling stone barracks, or possibly storerooms, and the surgeon's quarters are still just about standing. These date back to 1778, when Lieutenant Romainville arrived on Mahé with a small military detachment and a number of slaves to set up an official headquarters. In those days the State House was very close to the sea and the original buildings a humble affair—simple stone structures housing the Commandant's quarters, Surgeon's quarters, a store, a small hospital and barracks for the soldiers. The Commandant's quarters could be described as the very first government house, but the building measures just 30 feet by 12 feet, with only one storey. There is also an old cemetery, which was dug by the original settlers: its existance was marked on a map dated 1794. It was in use until 1862, when the lower half was obliterated by 'La Grande Avalasse'. Seychelles' most famous corsair, Jean François Hodoul is buried here.

Sadly, because it is still used as the offices of the Seychelles President, State House and its gardens are no longer open for guided tours except by special arrangement.

The Best Beaches on Mahé

PORT LAUNAY

For many years this splendid beach was closed to the public as it formed part of the campus belonging to the National Youth Service. Now, however it is easily accessed and there are plans to develop a 5 star resort on this beach in the future. Port Launay is a wide perfect bay in National Marine Park protected waters. The beach itself is long and wide, with plenty of shady spots under the overhanging takamaka trees. The sea is good for swimming, with a gradual drop and calm waters particularly during the Southeastern trade winds (April—September). Snorkeling here is excellent. During weekdays the beach is generally empty, however at weekends and in particular on Sundays this is a popular venue for picnics and can become busy. The beach can be found by following the signs from Port Glaud. If the beach is too busy, there are a number of other smaller pretty beaches and coves on the road between Port Launay and Baie Ternay (where the road ends), which are often deserted.

INTENDANCE

Hailed by many travel writers as one of the best beaches in the Indian Ocean, Intendance is half a mile of powdery white sand and huge rolling waves. There is no reef here and occasionally you can see dolphins jumping beyond the breakers. The long beach is framed by mountains and behind it are mangrove marshes, coconut palms (including the island's only double-headed coconut palm) and takamaka trees. The Banyan Tree Resort is situated on the edge of the beach and the hotel chalets can be seen spreading up from the beach into the hillside overlooking the bay.

Turtles often nest on this beach, and the Banyan Tree Resort has introduced a turtle conservation policy to ensure that the presence of the hotel does not interfere with the turtles' breeding habits.

During the southeast monsoon, between May and October, the waves are fearsome. You will need to get beyond the white horses to the deeper, calmer water beyond to swim properly; not recommended unless you are a very capable swimmer, as there can be a strong undertow. However, you can enjoy the waves without getting out of your depth. Bikinis are not recommended—they can be washed off and swept away by the strength of the water.

In the northwest monsoon—October through to April—the sea is a lot calmer; although the waves are still large they will not throw you about as much, so normal swimming is possible. At this time of the year you can also snorkel by the rocks to the side; there is not a great deal to see, as there is no coral here, but you can occasionally glimpse quite large fish.

The only drawback to this beautiful beach are the flies at certain times of year. Living in the mangroves behind the beach, these large flies have a bite that feels like being jabbed with a needle. However, they are slow moving and can be swatted easily—but if there is more than one or two bothering you, it is often better to move somewhere else.

To get to Intendance take the small turning at Quatre Bournes, in southwest Mahé, following the road down to the right, drive past the entrance to the Banyan Tree Resort and continue along the road until it widens to become a small parking area behind the beach. Do not park (or sit for that matter) underneath a coconut palm though: falling nuts can cause a lot of damage.

POLICE BAY

To the south of Intendance is another spectacular beach, with rolling waves and soft white sands. Take the road to Intendance from Quatre Bornes and, instead of turning right to Intendance, carry straight on— the road will bear left, taking you straight down to the southernmost tip of the island. The road terminates at a security barrier— visitors are not allowed past this, as the area is used for military training.

The beach to the right of the road from the security barrier is Police Bay, fringed with coconut palms and vines. Unfortunately it is not suitable for swimming, as the strong currents make it dangerous, but it is very photogenic and perfect for a long walk across the sand.

BEAU VALLON

The most popular beach on Mahé, it can get busy at weekends. It is a good place for watersports and a number of places along the beach hire out windsurfers and small catamarans. You can also paraglide from Beau Vallon; harnessed to a parachute, a motor boat carries you off from the beach into the air, where for ten minutes it circles the bay, giving a wonderful bird's eye view of the two mile long beach and surrounding mountains. Landing is surprisingly gentle—the boat gradually slows down, either allowing the glider to slip gently into the sea or float down onto the beach. Paragliding can also be done in pairs.

Coral Strand Hotel has a diving centre, which provides regular lessons and diving excursions. Other centres, at both the Coral Strand and the Beau Vallon Bay Hotel, offer water skiing and a 'water sausage' ride—this is an inflatable tube you sit astride while it is towed behind a speed boat. When the boat makes a sudden turn, the sausage tips its passengers into the sea. If all this action is too much effort, Beau Vallon is still about the best place for a leisurely swim. The clear warm waters have a gentle drop, making swimming a real pleasure. It is also very safe for children—no big waves, soft sand underfoot and no strong currents.

Anse Lazio on Praslin remains one of the world's most beautiful and unspoiled beaches

(top) *Port Launay, Mahé;* (bottom) *Police Bay, Mahé*

ANSE ROYALE

During the northwest monsoon, between October and the end of April, this is a wonderful beach for swimming and snorkelling. However, in the southeast monsoon the winds churn up the water, making it cooler and cloudy, and high tides and seaweed combine to make the beach less desirable.

At its best this beach is heavenly. The water is clear and warm and the long stretch of sand is divided into several little coves by huge granite boulders, so it is possible to have a small beach all to yourself. The tall takamakas and palms at the edge of the beach also make for good shady areas for sitting in when the sun gets too much. It is probably the best place for snorkelling on Mahé, especially for beginners.

Anse Royale is on the southeastern coast of Mahé. The beach is just beside the main coastal road; there is no car park, so drivers will need to park by the side of the road. There are also no nearby restaurants or bars; the nearest places are in the village of Anse Royale, to the south of the beach, so do take supplies with you.

ANSE SOLEIL

If you want total seclusion and don't mind a bumpy ride to get it, this is the beach for you. Anse Soleil is a beautiful small bay with clear waters, good for swimming and snorkelling, and a wide stretch of sandy beach. A wide variety of fish, big and small, inhabit the rocky waters.

Anse Soleil may well be off the beaten track but it is an increasingly popular beach, with a small hotel and self catering apartments along its shore as well as a local Kreol café, which serves very good curry lunches and is always full at weekends. The only drawback is the bumpy road to the beach and the lack of parking space close to the beach itself.

At weekends it is best to follow the road to Anse Soleil from Baie Lazare and stop before the small right hand fork that takes you on to the beach itself. There is a space for parking cars here and a footpath to the left leading towards the pretty bay of Anse La Liberté. After parking the car the beach is a short walk to the right, past the Anse Soleil Beachcomber Hotel and down the steps to the side of the Anse Soleil Café.

ANSE À LA MOUCHE

Situated on the southeastern side of Mahé, Anse à la Mouche is a large secluded bay, with very calm, clear waters. At high tide it is possible to swim here, although the water in the bay will never get more than chest-deep for an adult, and at low tide you will only be able to paddle! The shallow waters, however, make it a good swimming spot for children.

The water by the rocks to the side of the main bay is excellent for snorkelling, but it is very deep here, so is only for confident swimmers. There are many smaller fish that feed off the corals around the rocks, but there are also some much bigger fish around, as there is no barrier reef here. At certain times of the year bio-luminescence can be seen in the bay—micro-organisms which give off light as fish move through the water. A night snorkle to see this phenomenon is magical—the sea is lit up by myriads of tiny lights whenever a fish swims past you.

Outside Victoria: Sightseeing on Mahé

There are many things to see and places to visit, besides Victoria and the beaches, most of which have no admission charge. Probably the best way of exploring Mahé is to hire a car for a day. However, most of the places listed are also on the main bus routes and tour operators like Masons Travel, Creole Holidays and TSS offer day coach tours of Mahé, taking in most of the main sightseeing spots.

**ROUTE ONE: FROM THE BOTANICAL GARDENS
UP THE SANS SOUCI ROAD TO PORT LAUNAY.**

THE BOTANICAL GARDENS

The gardens are just outside Victoria, on the south side of town. Coming out of town, down Francis Rachel Street to the fish tail roundabout, take the third exit to 'Mont Fleuri'. The Botanical Gardens are just a few metres down the Mont Fleuri road, past the large Pentecostal Assembly Church, on the right hand side of the road. There is a small car park for visitors on your right. The Botanical Gardens also have a small thatched restaurant, *Le Sapin*, which serves simple snack lunches for a reasonably price.

For a few rupees you can buy a guide to the plants and flowers in the gardens from the information booth next to the car park. The gardens were laid out in 1901, by Frenchman Rivaltz Dupont, so many of the trees are now fully grown. The main pathway cuts through the middle of the gardens—there are many striking tropical plants, not only those native to Seychelles but also specimens from around the world. There is also a tortoise pen, where giant tortoises laze and wallow in the shady mud. Unfortunately the tortoises here have to be caged, because the gardens are so close to the main road and town. Beautiful aquamarine orchids frame the wooden archway at the back of the orchid garden in August.

THE SANS SOUCIS ROAD

Coming out of the Botanical Gardens, turn left past the Pentecostal Church and take the next road on the left, called Liberation Avenue. Climbing up the road, stop at the lay-by on the right to view the town and harbour of Victoria. If you continue you will arrive at the area known as Bel Air; turn left at the T-junction, which leads on to the Sans Soucis road proper—this winding mountain road crosses the centre of Mahé. It

Cinnamom Zeylanicum by Rosemary Wise

is a particularly steep climb with several hairpin bends and frighteningly steep drops. About half-way up the mountain is an impressive driveway, marked 1776, the former residence of the US Ambassador and the house in which the exiled Archbishop Markarios of Cyprus resided during his time in Seychelles. Just around the next bend on the right is a shop known as the island's "health haven on the hill". **Lily Moon** sells healthy herbal tonics, homeopathic remedies, rejuvenating facial lotions and revitalising body potions. Many of the items make interesting and attractive souvenir gifts that are unique to Seychelles. Around a couple more bends from Lily Moon, on the right, is a sign showing the beginning of the **Trois Frères Mountain Trail**. If you don't have energy or time for the whole walk, drive up the unmade road to the car park to see the panoramic view of the coast and islands below.

Driving along the Sans Soucis road takes you past another sign for a mountain trail walk, Copolia, and the Indian Ambassador's residence. At the very top of the road is L'Exil which used to be the residence of long-serving Seychelles President France Albert René. It has been reported that during the coup d'etat, which swept him into power in 1976, René was directing the military action taking place in Victoria by walkie-talkie as he sat on his lawn with his binoculars trained on the streets below. This property would have certainly given him a good vantage-point. It is now occupied by one of René's ex-wives. Although you will not be able to see the house as you drive past, you will notice the two ornamental cannon at the front of the driveway and the old guardhouse by the side of the road. Beyond L'Exil the road begins to wind downhill. A few bends later you will see the sign to the mission.

THE MISSION

Once run as a school for the children of liberated slaves, the Mission is now a few crumbling ruins. Venn's Town, as it was known in colonial times, was established in 1875 by the Anglican Church Missionary Society. Although slavery was abolished by law in the British colonies in 1834, Arabs and others were still buying slaves from Africa and Zanzibar and transporting them across the Indian Ocean.

Many of the slaves released by the British were children, who had either been orphaned or separated from their parents when they were captured. On arrival in Seychelles the government was responsible for them and, as they were keen for them to have a Protestant education, financed the mission. Built high on the mountainside, this was the cheapest land the missionary society could buy. There were no roads up to the school in those days; people and goods had to be transported by horse up the long, steep climb.

On average the school housed about 100 children at a time, 7–10 years old. They were educated in English (a disadvantage when the rest of the population in Seychelles only spoke Kreol or French) and were taught woodwork, arts and crafts. The school eventually stopped taking children in 1879 and in 1892 was closed down and abandoned. The ruins consist of one room, probably occupied by the warden, and a larger room which was the children's dormitory. Many people believe the site is haunted—there is certainly an eerie atmosphere about the place!

Exploring the atmospheric ruins of the Mission, Mahé, which was once a home for liberated slave children, run by the Anglican church

Beyond the ruins there is a footpath surrounded by giant sangdragon trees. The trees were planted here in 1875. In the forest around the pathway you may be able to see many of the endemic birds of Seychelles—a pair of rare Seychelles kestrels nest nearby; if you are lucky, you may catch a glimpse.

At the end of the pathway is a wooden viewing lodge, built for the Queen's visit to Seychelles in 1974, where she sat sipping tea and admiring the view. Standing in the lodge you can look out over the lush tree canopy, stretching out towards the ocean. This is best seen on a fine clear day—the view can be totally obliterated by mist and rain.

THE TEA PLANTATION

A little further down the Sans Soucis road from the mission, towards Port Glaud, is the Tea Plantation and Tavern. There are walks which take you around the plantation land, which lines the mountain slopes. During weekdays it is possible to visit the small tea factory, to see how Seychelles tea is made and blended. Afterwards take a visit to the thatched tea tavern to taste vanilla and other flavoured teas. The tavern also sells dried *citronelle*, or lemon grass, which can be used to make a refreshing infusion. If you want to try citronelle for yourself, you can easily pick it from the side of the road nearby. Look out for bushy clumps of tall bright green grass; if you crush the blades in your hand it will impart its distinctive lemony scent. Simply take three or four stems, put them in a cup or teapot and pour over boiling water.

Coming out of the tea tavern, carry on down the road, which will take you to the west side of the island at Port Glaud. A little further down from the tea tavern, along a few more hair-raising bends, is a stunning view, looking out over Port Glaud towards the islands of Thérèse and Conception.

PORT GLAUD AND PORT LAUNAY

The Sans Soucis road ends at the intersection with the coastal road at Port Glaud (pronounced *Por-Glow*). Turn right and past the Port Glaud church there is a short walk to the Port Glaud waterfall. Follow the river behind the church for about a quarter of a mile—the walk is not hard and should only take 15 to 20 minutes. The waterfall is not huge, but it is attractive and the trees and rocks that surround it a cool and peaceful beauty spot. Take a dip in the icy cold river water—if you dare. However do not try to climb the rocks around the waterfall—they are very slippery and there have been accidents here in the past.

Continuing along the main road to the right leads to **Port Launay**. This is one of the best beaches on the island and its wide expanse of white sands and clear calm waters makes a beautiful spot for sunbathing, swimming, snorkelling and beach picnics. Further along the road there are a number of other smaller pretty coves fringed with granite boulders and coconut palms. The road ends at **Baie Ternay**, a beach that is, unfortunately, closed to the public.

ROUTE TWO: GRANDE ANSE TO ANSE ROYALE, SOUTH MAHÉ

GRANDE ANSE

Grand Anse, on the southwestern coast of Mahé, has a large bay. Although not suitable for swimming, because of the strong undertow (a former British governor drowned here), it is a spectacular beach to walk down, with high surf and a long sandy shoreline. There is also a lot of farmland around the bay, which is part of the government's agricultural research station. The rocky outcrop visible from this shoreline is known as **Isle Vache**.

Taking the road from Grand Anse to the south, you will pass the left hand turning to La Misere, which is a mountain pass across the centre of Mahé which leads back towards Victoria. Carrying along the coastal road is the **BBC Relay Station**, with its large radio masts broadcasting the World Service to Eastern Africa. Just past this and before you reach the Le Meridien Barbarons Hotel, there are two small nature walks which are clearly signposted from the road.

On the left hand side of the road is a signpost and small car park leading to the **Vacoa Trail**. This is a walk, taking approximately 40 minutes, alongside a small river. There are a number of vacoa trees along the route, along with other plants and trees of interest. The notice board in the small car park at the start of the trail is an informative guide on the path and points of interest along the way.

Just across the road from the Vacoa Trail is the **Mangrove Board Walk**. This leads across the mangrove marshland to a viewing platform which is particularly good for bird watchers, as there are a good number of birds including plovers and herons that live in the mangroves. This is a short walk, of around 15 minutes, and is particularly good for taking small children, even with a pushchair. My children enjoy looking out for the many crabs, fish and mudskippers along the way.

Carrying along the coastal road from Barbarons, the land is still very much agricultural in this part of Mahé. On the left you will pass a large Orchid Nursery, not open to the public, and about a kilometre further on from here, past a small shop and the Chateau D'Eau guest house there is a nursery and building site which will be home to a new tourist attraction in the future. The Barbarons Botanical Gardens are presently being planted and a museum, gallery and cafeteria are being built. The project is being administered by the Seychelles government. The gardens however are not likely to be fully open until 2010. They will predominantly display much of Seychelles' rare endemic plants within some 20 acres of grounds.

Taking the coastal road again, the next large bay is Anse Boileau, a pretty small fishing village with one or two small guesthouses by the beach which has calm, shallow waters.

Continuing south, the palm trees by the side of the road give way to steep granite rocks and boulders, some of which seem precariously balanced on top of one another. It is amazing to think they have stayed like this for thousands, if not millions, of years. One of these rocks has been named **Pig Rock**—jutting out into the road from the seaward side, its shape is very similar to a pig's head, snout and all.

ANSE À LA MOUCHE

Just past Pig Rock is Anse à la Mouche. It is a wide, sheltered bay; the absence of a reef means you occasionally find small sharks basking in its shallow waters. An eccentric, retired English

(top) *Cascade Church, Mahé* ; (above) *Victoria Inter Island Quay, Mahé*

missionary called Winifred Gas spent the last 20 years of her life living in a small bungalow here, taking her early morning swim every day in the shallow waters of the bay. One morning she saw a group of children on the beach waving energetically to her as she swam. She gaily waved back and continued her 100 strokes. It was not until she came out of the water that they told her several sharks were swimming in circles around her. She was not in the least put off, saying she was all skin and bone and so a shark would not look twice at her.

There is a small roadside café just past the Blue Lagoon Bungalows—the *Anchor Café*, run by an American who came to Seychelles to work at the satellite tracking station at La Misère. When his term of duty ended, he decided to stay on, marrying a Seychelloise and opening his café, which serves US fare such as hamburgers and pizzas as well as fast food Kreol style.

TOM BOWERS

The road to Les Cannelles, to the left of Anse a là Mouche, leads to Santa Maria and the gallery and studio of sculptor **Tom Bowers**. His exquisite sculptures are mainly lean, sensual figures of Seychellois people, cast in bronze resin. His figures are usually naked, he explains, because "their bodies are so beautiful they look better without their clothes". Tom Bowers sculptures can be seen in some of the public buildings in Seychelles and there is also a display of some of his smaller pieces for sale at the

Watercolour painting by Christine Harter

Banyan Tree Gallery at Intendance. Tom is a former advertising photographer who abandoned his camera for his love of Seychelles and sculpting. He does undertake special commissions, but all other works are in editions of ten only and are exclusive to Seychelles.

After taking this little detour, return to the coastal road, carrying on south, to meet another well known English artist—Michael Adams.

MICHAEL ADAMS

Michael Adams is the best known artist in Seychelles; he has lived there since 1972, painting mainly jungle landscapes in vivid colours with a wealth of detail. His studio is part of his house at **Anse aux Poules Bleues** (Bay of the Blue Chickens). A sign by the right-hand side of the road reveals the driveway up to his quaint, pastel blue wooden house. Inside is a display of his prints and paintings, which have sold all over the world. There is also a book of press cuttings and exhibition reviews. Originals are an expensive investment, but his prints (both colour and black and white) are more affordable and capture the vivid beauty of the Seychelles forests. Michael Adams is often home and his burly, bearded figure is instantly recognisable.

ANSE SOLEIL AND BAIE LAZARE

Beyond Anse aux Poules Bleues the road cuts across a peninsula to Baie Lazare, a small village where there are a few shops a petrol station and a roadside cafe. Just before the petrol station and opposite Harvey's roadside cafe there is a turn to the right which leads to **Anse Soleil**, a beautiful beach which was a well-kept secret on Mahé for many years. The area is now more accessible following the development of two small hotels nearby, although to get to the beach you have to park the car where the road ends and then walk up a small track to the left, past the Anse Soleil Resort, to an area on the left where there are several small houses. In between these houses are some steps down to the beach.

Once there, you will discover that Anse Soleil is a wide sandy beach with calm seas, suitable for swimming and snorkelling and plenty of welcoming shade along its edges. There is also a small café just beside the steps that lead to the beach between the houses. This café, which is really just a couple of tables on a verandah overlooking the beach, and I don't think even has a proper name, is open for lunch only and serves great prawn curries.

Back on the main coastal road, just past the village of **Baie Lazare**, is the **Plantation Club Resort**. This large hotel complex has a swimming pool open to non-residents but it does get crowded on a Sunday afternoon. There is a restaurant by the pool which serves a variety of light lunches. Opposite the main entrance to the Plantation Club there is the **Val Mer Art Gallery**, which showcases the work of local artists, in particular abstract painter Gerard Devoud.

Following the main road south from here, the last beach on the west coast road is **Anse Takamaka**, named after the takamaka trees that surround it. It is a beautiful beach, but strong currents make swimming difficult. There is also an excellent Kreol restaurant alongside the beach that can be reached by following the roadside sign down a narrow sandy path. **Le Reduit** is the epitome of a relaxed beach eatery, serving curries and seafood in a ramshackle house overlooking stunning Anse Takamaka.

Leaving Anse Takamaka the road then curves to the left, turning inland towards the eastern side of the island.

INTENDANCE

Coming to a crossroads at **Quatre Bournes**, you may wish to take the small concrete road to the right, signposted **Intendance**. A few kilometers down this road is another right hand turn, which is also signposted for the hotel resort the Banyan Tree. Take this road, driving past the main Banyan Tree entrance on the left, and there is parking space at the end of the road for the beach.

Intendance is one of Mahé's very best beaches and the water here is an amazing vivid blue, with waves that can knock you over if you stand in their way. The trick to swimming here is to dive straight into the middle of a wave just as it is about to break. Dolphins can occasionally be seen jumping beyond the surf. But be warned—the powder-like white sand churned up by the sea will get everywhere.

ANSE FORBANS AND ANSE ROYALE

From Intendance, take the minor road back to the main costal road at Quatre Bournes and then turn left towards the east coast and **Anse Forbans**. From Quatre Bournes the road winds along the eastern coast, less scenic than the western side of the island, there are nevertheless some pretty beaches and coconut plantations along the way. The first major beach you will come across on this road is Anse Forbans, and there is a small hotel here, **The Allamanda**. This is a good place to spend a Sunday afternoon, with a Kreol buffet lunch, plenty of Seybrew and a sleep in the shade of sandy Anse Forbans.

The next village is **Anse Royale**, site of the Seychelles Polytechnic campus. Apart from the polytechnic, Anse Royale has some shops, a petrol station, and a pizzeria, *Kaz Kreol*.

JARDIN DU ROI

Before entering the village of Anse Royale, there is a road on the left, just opposite the Anse Royale Anglican church which is signposted **Les Canelles**. There is also a blue sign advertising the Jardin Du Roi here too. At the next crossroads turn left into Sweet-Escott Road, then first left, following the road to the right up the hill. This leads to the Jardin du Roi, newly-created spice gardens, a restaurant and small museum set in nearly 100 acres of land; a visit here could easily make a day trip.

(top left) *On the road, Mahé*; (top right) *Bridge at Anse Royale*; (bottom) *Anse Royale Beach*

The original Jardin du Roi (King's Garden) was a spice farm planted by the first French settlers. Early farming efforts proved disappointing—the spice plants did not flourish as was hoped, although this seems due more to the ineptitude of those looking after the gardens than the choice of location. In 1779 the spice garden was burnt, to prevent it from falling into enemy hands. The ship turned out to be French, but it was too late and only the cinnamon trees had withstood the flames. They later flourished and spread right across the island. The new Jardin du Roi is a grander recreation of the original or, to be more accurate, what the gardens could have been.

The car park is on the left hand side of the driveway and next to this are several old farmhouses. One of these has been transformed into a crêperie, serving pancakes stuffed with the fruits and spices grown on the estate. Close by women roll cinnamon quills, which can be bought in the shop, along with other locally made goods—dried vanilla pods, nutmeg and citronelle, jars of chutneys and hot, spicy sauces.

There is also a reptilarium and several enclosures housing giant tortoises and turtles, together with an aviary of exotic birds, mainly imported from Australia. Further along the hillside there is an outside drying area, where the ripe vanilla pods, peppers and cloves are laid out to bake in the sun. There is also an old sugar cane press, where visitors can try their hand at pressing the cane through a type of old-fashioned wooden mangle, to extract the sweet sap.

The grounds of this estate continue right up the hillside. Marked pathways lead to the top of the mountain, where there are panoramic views of the coastline at Baie Lazare. The Jardin du Roi is open during daylight hours, Monday to Saturday.

ANSE ROYALE BEACH FAIRYLAND
The beach at Anse Royale is a few kilometres north of the village. Just off the coast is **Isle Souris**, where you can safely swim to get the best views of the fish living around the coral reef. The point of land including the beach area is known as **Fairyland**.

Driving north from Anse Royale will take you towards the airport at **Anse aux Pins**, where the sea gradually gets shallower. Between Anse Royale and the airport, though, are two places well worth visiting for those interested in the history and culture of Seychelles.

LA MARINE AND CRAFT VILLAGE
Driving north from Anse Royale, you will come across La Marine, a centre that makes and sells intricate wooden models of large sailing ships. It is a tradition that was founded in Mauritius, but was introduced to Seychelles some years ago. The models are beautifully handmade, with great attention to detail. They are very expensive, but a look around the workshops to see how they are made is fascinating. The designs for the ships come from the French Naval Museum in Paris and each model is made to scale. A team of 15 craftsmen and women make about ten models a month.

A few kilometers further down the road from La Marine is the **Val du Pres Craft Village**, complete with Kreol restaurant and restored plantation house. In the village there are two imposing wooden plantation houses: one is **The Vye Marmit Restaurant**, serving the traditional 'real cuisine' of the Seychellois. The grilled snapper on banana leaves is recommended, and do try the traditional island dessert of 'Ladob'—a rich mixture of soft breadfruit and bananas in a syrupy coconut milk and vanilla sauce. The other large wooden house in the village is a restoration of how a plantation house would have looked like a 100 or so years ago. Entrance to the house is free. You can go into all the rooms, which have been furnished as they would have been by the French plantation owners—dark mahogany furniture, lacy bed linen, mosquito nets and old photographs revealing stern matronly faces. There are five main rooms—two bedrooms, a sitting room, bathroom and nursery, all with a wonderful atmosphere of faded grandeur.

To the front of the plantation house are a number of craft stalls, each one housing different types of local craftsmen and their workshops—carpentry, shells, artwork and wickerwork are all on display and everything is for sale.

Continuing north along the eastern coastal road, the next landmark is another large and newly-restored plantation house, the **Lenstiti Kreol**. This is the institute responsible for the encouragement and advancement of Seychellois culture, particularly the Kreol language. The Lenstiti Kreol also organises Kreol festivals on a regular basis, joining up with other French-based Creole speaking nations from the Indian Ocean and the Caribbean.

Further on, passing the International Airport, take the main east coast highway, the only dual carriageway in Seychelles, towards Victoria. To the right of the road is a light industrial area, which then makes way for views of the ocean and small, reclaimed islands, awaiting development. The Wharf Hotel and Marina is on the right hand side, while a little further on, past the rusting wreck of the **Isle de Farquar** ship, now stranded in a man-made lagoon, and opposite the large Roche Caiman housing estate, is another marina, where yachts, catamarans and big game fishing boats can be hired. At the roundabout, drive straight on towards Victoria, or turn right towards the **sports stadium** and national swimming pool.

For a longer, more meandering route towards Victoria, ignore the East Coast Highway and take the old coastal road, which runs through a small industrial estate; the Seybrew brewery is located here and often smells strongly of hops. The next major turning on the left is signposted La Misère, one of the main mountain roads. Half-way up is a viewing post offering sights of the eastern coast of Mahé from Victoria, across the newly reclaimed land, to the airport and the islands scattered just outside the harbour. A wooden guide to the scene points out the names of the islands—Cerf, Round, Moyenne, Sainte Anne and Long Island.

Seashells by Rosemary Wise

Returning down the hill, the coast road winds its way into the village of **Mont Fleuri**, the road then takes you into the southern suburbs of Victoria, past the hospital, the Botanical Gardens and into the capital itself.

ROUTE THREE: NORTHERN MAHÉ—BEL OMBRE, BEAU VALLON AND NORTH EAST POINT
From Victoria take the St Louis Road towards Beau Vallon. The road will wind its way uphill past the **Chinese Embassy**, its resplendent white marble tiles in stark contrast to the humbler corrugated iron houses that surround it.

BEL OMBRE
From Le Niol the main road to Beau Vallon winds downhill. Past the petrol station the road forks right to Beau Vallon and left to Bel Ombre. Take the left hand fork, past the entrance to the Berjaya Beau Vallon Bay Hotel and the more upmarket Le Méridien Fisherman's Cove Hotel. Bel Ombre is a small village, with houses scattered over the hillside above the coast. The beach here is usually empty and a good retreat from the busier main beach. There are also some exclusive gourmet restaurants, including *Le Corsair* and *La Scala*.

Just past Le Corsair restaurant, on the rocks going down to the sea, is a reputed pirate treasure site. The area has been fenced off and workmen are usually busy draining and digging, still searching for that elusive fortune. Visitors are not allowed inside the site, but standing by the edge of the road you will be able to see the work being carried out below, which is most active at low tide. The road peters out at Danzil and from here there is a footpath to the secluded beach at **Anse Major**.

BEAU VALLON
This is the most popular and by far the busiest beach in Seychelles. A stunning wide sheltered bay overlooking the islands of Silhouette and North and fringed by hotels, this is the place for sunbathing, water-sports, dive centres, bars and restaurants. During the day the Baobab pizzeria and El Mare restaurants both offer Italian food; the Bird Cage bar is open for drinks and snacks and the Sun Resort has excellent take-away pizzas and ice creams that can be taken onto the beach. The Coral Strand and the Berjaya Beau Vallon Bay hotels also have beachside bistros and bars. This beach also offers a good viewpoint to see the setting sun.

GLACIS AND NORTH EAST POINT
The main road north from Beau Vallon is a lovely scenic drive, taking in most of the northern coast of Mahé. Past the Northolme Hotel and Vacoa Village you arrive at Glacis, with fine beaches between a rocky coastline. The Sunset Beach Hotel has a

superb beach, which is now, unfortunately, only accessible to residents at the hotel. Past several more small guest houses, you will arrive at a long stretch of beach at the northern tip of the island. Anse Nord D'Est, or North East Point, is a good beach to walk along, but collecting shells is prohibited.

Just past the beach is a small studio and shop selling locally made perfumes. *Kreolfleurage* sells perfumes containing tropical flowers and spices. There are three different perfumes packaged in wooden cased bottles. The most popular scent is called *Bwa Nwar* and is made of 42 different essences, including patchouli, vanilla, cinnamon and passionfruit flower.

ANSE ÉTOILE TO VICTORIA

The north coastal road winds round the coast to Anse Étoile, which is perhaps the least attractive part of Mahé's coastline. Seaweed washed up here makes this stretch of road decidedly pungent. To the left out towards the ocean is land recently reclaimed from the sea. This new land will perhaps one day be used for a new highway and housing projects but at the moment sits empty, apart from casuarina trees which have been planted to strengthen the soil, awaiting future development.

The coastal road continues south, past **La Bastille**, an old building which houses part of the Seychelles National Archives. Most of the archives are now kept at The National Library in Victoria. It is possible to view the old documents, including letters written during colonial days, but the archives are not really geared to the tourist. Researchers are able to use the library, for a small fee, and the staff there are very enthusiastic, knowledgeable and helpful.

The road then runs past the **Seychelles Broadcasting Corporation** radio studios, back into Victoria, becoming the 5th of June Avenue. The roundabout is called the *Twa Zwazo* (Three Birds). The sculpture is meant to represent the three cultures of Seychelles: Africa, Asia and Europe. The road to the left leads down to the old port, which now acts as the terminal for Inter Island Ferries and is also the mooring place for Sunsail yacht charters. The Cat Cocos catamaran service to Praslin also leaves from here. Further along the 5th of June Avenue the road will take you behind a sports stadium, where there is another sculpture—*Zomn Lib* (Free Man)—a metalworked monument to a man freeing himself from the chains of slavery.

On the left hand side of the road is the **Yacht Club and Marine Charter**—the yacht club is only open to members, but from the marine charter you can hire yachts, take excursions to other islands or go on big game fishing trips. At the next fishtail roundabout, the new industrial port is to the left, down Latanier Street, while to the right is the Mont Fleuri road, which takes you to the Botanical Gardens and the hospital. Straight on is the new East Coast Highway—the shortest route back towards the airport and the southeastern side of the island.

Island Hopping

Not all tropical islands are the same and an island hopping holiday to Seychelles can be particularly rewarding. In Seychelles there are three main types of island: the granitic, heavily-forested mountain scenery of the main inner islands (such as Mahé, Praslin and La Digue); the flat coralline islands and atolls (the Amirantes); and the faraway limestone islands, which have a bizarre, almost moonscape quality (the Aldabra-Astove group).

Travelling to most of the islands is fairly simple; either by ferry, plane or helicopter. Some of the smaller islands can be explored in a day or an afternoon, while others merit a longer stay. (See hotels section for further information on accommodation.)

The Inner Islands

Thirty-two of the islands are made up of different types of granite; brown on Mahé, pink on Praslin and La Digue. The rocks of Silhouette have a unique syenite formation (granite without quartz). To the north of the central granite group are two coralline islands, Denis and Bird.

Cocos Island provides an idyllic setting for watersports

A pirogue, serving as a water taxi, is poled through Anse Source d'Argent, La Digue

Geologically, the existence of the granite islands has been explained by the theory of Continental Drift. In the Primary Era, 150 million years ago, it is thought that South America, Africa India and Australia were a single supercontinent, known as Gondwanaland. By 100 million years ago all the continental masses of Gondwanaland, including Madagascar, had separated and geologists estimate that the inner islands of Seychelles were formed as Madagascar and India broke loose from one another.

ARIDE

Bought in 1973 by chocolate baron Christopher Cadbury for the Royal Society for Nature Conservation, this is the most northerly of the granitic islands, lying about 30 miles north of Mahé and 10 miles north of Praslin. Aride (pronounced *Ah-reed*) is only one mile long by a quarter of a mile wide, but its scented forests rise over 150 metres above the ocean.

Aride was discovered in 1756 by Captain Nicolas Morphey and was originally called Ile Moras, after the French Marine Minister. The island was colonised around 1850, when the forests were felled to make way for coconut plantations and citrus trees, while the seabird eggs were harvested for human consumption. Despite the loss of much of the native forest on the island, the fact that a jetty was never built meant the wildlife on the island was not irreparably damaged by the introduction of rats and cats.

RESCUED FROM NEAR EXTINCTION:
THE RARE BIRDS OF SEYCHELLES

The many islands of Seychelles are a fragile home for many of the world's rarest bird and plant species. Their survival is threatened by human activities, past and present, and some bird species were on the very brink of extinction just a few years ago. Thanks to the imaginative and ground breaking work of conservation organisations many of Seychelles rare birds are well on the way to recovery.

It is thought that the first early seafarers who stopped off in Seychelles, left coconuts behind so that coconut trees would grow on the many small isolated islands of the archipelago and so provide future sustenance for sailors. While coconut palms swaying on the edges of the white beaches typify for many the image of Seychelles, the resulting coconut plantations grown on the majority of the islands resulted in long lasting damage to the fragile island ecosystems. The monoculture of palms led to the decline or destruction of many endemic trees and shrubs that provided essential habitat for many unique bird species. Once human settlers arrived on the island they not only chopped down even more native trees, but also introduced animal species that preyed on the eggs and chicks of rare birds, such as rats and cats. Over 60% of the islands in the Seychelles archipelago have extensive coconut plantations and only six small islands are cat and rat free. This situation led to endemic birds like the Seychelles Warbler declining to less than 30 individuals in 1968 and the Seychelles Magpie Robin, which had a world population of just 23 birds only found on Frégate Island.

Birdlife International purchased Cousin Island in 1968 as a nature reserve, specifically aimed at helping the endangered Seychelles Brush Warbler. The island was transformed from a coconut plantation to a lowland forest teeming with seabirds, reptiles and rare land birds. The number of Warblers grew from less than 30 to now over 1,500 birds, spread out over three neighbouring islands. The Seychelles Warbler, a small brown bird, which compensates for its rather plain appearance by having a beautiful song, is now considered to be out of immediate danger of extinction but is still considered to be 'vulnerable'. Further populations need to be established before this species will be totally out of danger.

In 1998 Birdlife Seychelles was formed, and took over much of the work that Birdlife International was involved in, including the day to day running of the Cousin reserve. Birdlife Seychelles also has projects on other islands to improve the habitats of three of the four critically endangered birds of Seychelles: The Scops Owl, the Paradise Flycatcher and the Magpie Robin whose population has now increased to 110 birds on four islands. The success of these projects has resulted not only in the restoration of these endangered bird populations but also other biodiversity.

Other organisations, including the Seychelles Ministry of Environment, are involved in bird conservation: the Seychelles White Eye is a critically endangered species of bird whose main world population of just 300 birds is on the small island of Conception. In 2001, a successful transfer of 31 birds from Conception to Frégate Island was completed, and after six months there was evidence that the transferred birds were thriving in their new island home, and four chicks were sighted in February 2002. The five star resort on Frégate is working alongside conservation organisations to restore endemic plants and a more natural habitat on the island which not only helps White Eyes and the beautiful Magpie Robin, but other rare species too.

The Nature Protection Trust of Seychelles, while more famous for its tortoise and terrapin conservation work, is also involved in bird conservation and research. It manages a Bird Sanctuary at Roche Caiman on Mahé and is involved in the conservation of the magnificent Seychelles Kestrel.

Thanks to all these organisations, the birds of Seychelles can look forward to a better future in the 21st century. And not just the birds: it is true to say that birds are a very visible indicator of the general well being of an eco-system—so when the birds are happy and thriving it usually means that other animals, plants and invertebrates are happy and thriving too!

Contacts: Birdlife Seychelles, PO Box 1310, Mahé, Seychelles.
Email: birdlife@seychelles.net Tel (248) 225097

The Nature Protection Trust of Seychelles
Ron Gerlach, Silhouette. Tel 323711, Email: npts@seychelles.net
Website: www.members.aol.com/jstgerlach/

The Seychelles White Eye Rehabilitation Project
Dr Gerard Rocamora and Elvina Henriette, Conservation Section,
Ministry of Environment, Seychelles.
Email contact for information or donations: whiteye@seychelles.net

The Greater Frigate, such as this fine specimen on Aride, is the largest seabird in Seychelles

Now Aride is a Nature Reserve under Seychelles law; the birds, animals and plants are all protected, including the turtles that come ashore to lay their eggs, as are the fish, shells and coral of the reef.

Aride houses the greatest collection of sea birds in the region. As the boat sails towards the island, the noise and sight of hundreds of thousands of nesting birds is overwhelming. The best time to visit the island is between May and October, when over a million birds are nesting. It is celebrated for the world's largest colony of lesser noddies; nearly a quarter of a million nest in the island forest. The most important sea bird, however, is the rare roseate tern: Aride has the last major breeding colony in the Indian Ocean.

The most impressive bird on the island is the greater frigate, which has a wingspan of over six feet. They breed on Aldabra and come to Aride after their season is over, roosting in the tallest palms and casuarinas. Another bird to look out for is the red-tailed tropic; it is much rarer than its white-tailed cousin and can only be found on Aride and Aldabra. Other sea birds that also nest here are brown noddies, sooty terns, bridled terns and fairy terns.

The island is also famous for its Wright's gardenia, or *Bois Citron* as it is known locally; a bush with masses of white blossom and lemon scented leaves, which grows nowhere else in the world. The second species unique to the island is a type of peponium, an inedible cucumber. Aride is also said to have six times more insects than the rest of Seychelles and possibly the world's densest population of lizards.

The island is open to day visitors all year round, but during July and August some excursions are cancelled because of rough seas. Tour operators may tell you that they will have to telephone the island first, to check that landing is possible. Aride can be reached by a 40 minute sail from Praslin. Be prepared for a wet landing (keep your cameras and other valuables in a waterproof bag): there is no jetty and boats are not allowed access, because of the danger of introducing rats onto the island.

From November to April a guide will take a tour up into the mountainous interior, where there is a viewpoint facing north, to see some 2,000 frigate birds and the occasional red-tailed tropic bird. The rest of the year there are huge numbers of nesting birds on the hillsides, so the tour is restricted to a coastal walk, but the spectacle of all the birds together is very impressive. Usual visiting days are Wednesday, Thursday and Sunday, although it may be open on other days for party bookings. Bookings can be made through all the main tour operators on Mahé and Praslin and most of the larger hotels on Praslin arrange day trips. Each visitor to the island pays a landing fee that goes directly towards conservation.

BIRD

Thirty minutes by air from Mahé, this island is, as its name suggests, an ornithologist's dream come true—but there's much more to it than bird life. More visitors stay here for the laid-back ambience and beauty of the island than to see the birds. The attraction of the island is not what it has got, but what it hasn't. Staying on Bird there are no decisions to make or activities to plan. The island lodge has deliberately avoided building tennis courts or investing in water-skis and power boats. It is simply somewhere for people to do absolutely and gloriously nothing, apart from enjoy the sun and the sea and the fine food of the hotel.

The minimum stay on Bird is one night, but most people tend to stay for two nights. It has been known for some world-weary types to stay a full two weeks.

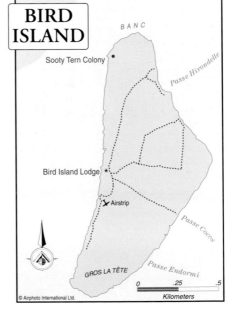

map © Airphoto International Ltd.

Even if you are no bird watcher, the spectacle of so many nesting birds at the height of the breeding season is well worth seeing. Several million sooty terns nest on the northeastern corner of the island every year from May to October. In early April, when the birds begin to arrive, a dense cloud of sooty terns can be seen hovering above. They do not land immediately, but fly over for two to three weeks before they land and nest. Mid-July is the time to see the largest number of sooty terns nesting—a colony of some 3,000,000 birds. It is possible for visitors to approach their nests to within 20 feet or so—but go any closer and you will risk being mobbed! There are some hides on the island to allow for bird watching and photography.

If you miss the main nesting period for sooty terns on Bird, there are always large numbers of resident birds, including noddies, fairy terns, ground doves, tropic birds and egrets. Migratory birds also come and go at different times. The main season for spotting rarities is November and December; these include turnstones, crab plovers, crested terns and bridled terns, but the list of birds seen is endless, as many more obscure species arrive on the island after being blown off course. Another time of the year worth visiting Bird is in October, when there is the chance to see turtles coming ashore to lay their eggs—at least five or six turtles come ashore each day during the breeding season.

Bird Island is located at the end of the Seychelles Bank, about 70 miles from Mahé, where the sea suddenly drops to over a 1,000 fathoms, so it also offers fantastic big game fishing. Swimming is superb, with an average water temperature of between 26-28 degrees centigrade (78-82 degrees F). Bird is a low-lying island and is much drier than Mahé or Praslin, so it has more reliably sunny weather. It is really not much more than a giant sand dune, its shape altering with changes in sea currents. Since 1988 over 75 metres has been lost from the main beach, while the sand spit at the north of the island has become longer. In effect this means the island is becoming longer and narrower. How long this trend will continue, no one knows, but perhaps once the shape of the island is back in tune with the ocean currents, it will return to its former stability.

A stay on Bird Island can be booked through travel agents or through the Bird Island office in Victoria, Mahé. The hotel and the flights are often fully booked, but sometimes a last minute reservation can be had for less than the full price.

CERF

A small island just off Victoria Bay on Mahé, which can be reached by small boat in 10-15 minutes, Cerf (pronounced *Serf*) is a popular weekend picnic spot. There is a small restaurant, which offers Kreol buffets, and the shallow seas and coral reefs around the island are part of the Sainte Anne National Marine Park. It is safe to snorkle off the beach, without getting out of your depth, to see the vivid colours of the fish and corals.

Cerf ('The Stag') was named after the frigate commanded by Corneille Nicolas Morphey, who took possession of Seychelles in the name of the King of France in 1756. Today several families live on the island, including the author Wilbur Smith, who has one of his homes on Cerf and often chooses it as his location to work from when he is writing one of his best-selling novels. There are several guest houses and chalets on Cerf as well as a small five star resort, all close to the island's sandy beaches. Day trips to Cerf can also be arranged from Mahé.

On the southern side of the island is a small islet, which can be reached by walking across the beach at low tide or wading at high tide. This islet was used as a quarantine base for slaves arriving in Seychelles from Africa some 200 years ago.

COUSIN ISLAND

Cousin (pronounced *Coo-zan*) is owned by British-based conservation organisation Birdlife International (formerly the International Council for Bird Preservation). It was purchased by them in 1968, when the only brush warblers that existed in the world (less than 30) survived on Cousin and were being threatened with extinction. Now over 1,500 brush warblers are thriving on three islands, including Cousin. Cousin is also a nature reserve for many other rare bird and animal species, including Seychelles ground doves, weaver birds, toc tocs, Wright's skinks, giant millipedes and the obligatory giant tortoises.

For a small landing fee visitors are shown around the island by one of the rangers, who live and work there and can explain its natural wonders in English, French or Italian. The tour lasts just over an hour and will take you around the island and up to the cliffs to watch the beautiful tropic birds circling high above. The birds on the island are tame and wonderful photographs can be taken of fairy terns and tropic birds sitting on their nests or with young chicks; they barely blink an eye as you point your lens at them. A trip to Cousin will last for half a day and the best time to see the island is when all the birds are nesting in April and May. Only 20 visitors to the island are allowed at any one time and flashlight photography is not allowed. All visitors have to be accompanied by a guide at all times. Swimming is not permitted.

Boat trips to Cousin can be arranged through tour operators or through the Maison de Palmes hotel on Praslin, either as a half- day or as a full-day trip, combining a trip to Curieuse and a buffet lunch. The sailing time is around only 15 minutes, but at certain times of the year the beach landing—by dinghy—can be very rough. Take your camera equipment in a waterproof bag and strap it around you carefully, in case a wave overtakes the dinghy on landing and you have to wade onto the island.

Cousin Island is open to the public every week from Tuesday to Friday from 9.00 to 16.00 hrs. The island is closed at weekends and public holidays. Landing of visitors takes place between 9.00–10.00 hrs and 14.00–14.30 hrs only. Because of the sensitive nature of Cousin's wildlife, visitors are urged to remember the following guidelines:

The two best ways to get around Seychelles: helicopter and boat off Cousin Island

(top) *Cousine Island;* (bottom) *Dining terrace at Cousine Island Lodge*

- Respect wildlife: do not touch, feed or harass any of the animals.
- Visitors most be accompanied by a guide at all times.
- Please leave all shells, corals, seeds, feathers and all other natural materials where you find them.
- Please do not use a flash when taking pictures as it disturbs the animals.
- Please do not smoke: the risk of fire is too great.
- Don't forget to bring plenty of mosquito repellent—you will need it!

There is no overnight accommodation on the island apart from small groups of scientists who have made prior arrangements with the island manager. Rough weather can prevent landings at times.

COUSINE ISLAND

Cousine is a privately owned island lying 6km off the west coast of Praslin, close to Cousin Island. Cousine, like Cousin, is a nature reserve but additionally has a five star small hotel on the island, which finances conservation projects.

Cousine covers an area of 26 hectares, with a long stretch of sandy beach that overlook Cousin and Praslin. There is a flat area of land close to the beach, which is now the location for the Cousine Island Lodge, while the rest of the coastline remains wild and rocky. For many years the plateau area of the island was used primarily as farmland, including rearing of pigs and chickens. In 1992 the island was privately purchased and set aside as a nature reserve, primarily for the protection of nesting sea turtles, but also to maintain populations of endemic land birds and provide protection for nesting sea birds. Giant tortoises who had been living in poor captive conditions on Praslin were also bought and 'emancipated' on Cousine.

Conservation workers have extensively restored the island to its natural state: removing foreign and invasive plants and animals, including a rat and cat eradication programme. All the chickens remaining on the island from it's farming days were also shot—all apart from one, who was shot in the initial chicken cull and with much blood and feathers fled into the bushes, so was presumed dead. A week or so later she re-emerged from the bush only to be shot again: there was more blood and feathers and she disappeared again only to re-emerge several days later, very much alive. Nicknamed 'Lucky', she now remains on the island to live out the rest of her hen years in peace. There are a small number of fruit trees and herb garden for the hotel kitchen on the plateau, but besides that, the rest of the island is being restored to its natural state by a programme of planting endemic trees and plants.

Efforts have been made to ensure Cousine's survival as a nature reserve and to allow visitors to become an integral part of this unique tropical island. For the first 8 years, the Cousine nature reserve was supported through private funding. Since the opening of the hotel, in April 2000, the conservation programme has been maintained through the formation of the Cousine Island Conservation Trust. All profits from the hotel are allocated through the Trust to conservation projects, including the monitoring of the rare Seychelles Magpie Robin, which is now successfully breeding on the island.

Cousine, like many of the small islands in Seychelles, was also believed to be a pirate base in days gone by and there are some who still believe there is treasure hidden in some underground location on its rocky north coast. If there is a hidden treasure trove, it hasn't been found yet!

CURIEUSE

Curieuse (pronounced *Cure-i-ers*) is one of the larger small islands, just a mile or so from Praslin, with a summit reaching over 170 metres and spectacular granite rock formations. The island was named in 1768, after the schooner of French explorer Nicolas Marion Dufresne, who also named Praslin and La Digue.

In 1771 sailors set the island ablaze, intending to make it easier to harvest the coco de mer nuts. The fire virtually destroyed the island's forests, including many coco de mer trees, and evidence of the blaze can still be seen. Sixty years later the island was used as a leper colony, on and off, until 1965. The ruins of the old leprosarium and other buildings can still be seen. The old doctors house has recently been renovated and turned into a very attractive and informative museum which tells much of the poignant story of the leper colony and history of the island.

Since the leper colony was closed, the island has become a breeding centre for giant tortoises and turtles and a huge turtle pond was created by building a stone barrage in Laraie Bay. A footpath winds around the old leprosarium and turtle pond, running across the island, through mangrove swamps, to **Fond Blanc**, where the few inhabitants of Curieuse live. The turtle pond was never a huge success—being so close to the mangroves, the water was not clean enough for the turtles to thrive. On the other side of the pond there is a farm for raising giant tortoises. Visitors are able to walk around the pens which house the young tortoises, from the tiny hatchlings to the giants they will become by the time they are five years old.

Day trips to the island can be arranged through tour operators on Praslin, which will also take you to the Curieuse Marine National Park, which offers good snorkelling and scuba diving among the corals.

DENIS

Denis Island is a coralline island some 95 kilometres north of Mahé and three degrees south of the Equator. The island is at the edge of the Seychelles Bank which plunges to depths of 2000 metres into the dark abyss of the Indian Ocean.

The island was discovered by and named after Frenchman Denis de Trobriand in 1773. Somewhere on the island is buried a bottle containing the Act of Possession, claiming the island in the name of the King of France. This historical treasure still awaits discovery today. In 1814 King Louis XVIII turned Denis, together with the rest of Seychelles, over to the British Crown through the Treaty of Paris.

Denis is a crescent shaped island with a land area of 375 acres. It is some 1300 metres at its longest point and 1750 metres at its widest point, taking between one and a half to two and a half hours to walk around the island. Much of the island is surrounded by coral reefs, creating a natural lagoon and brilliant white sandy beaches. The waters around the island are renowned for their fishing, and several record-breaking dogtooth tuna and bonito have been caught here. The biggest yellowfin tuna caught in these waters weighed in at a hefty 83 kilos. Fly-fishing for bone fish is also excellent here, and fishermen can cast their rods from the sand flats around the island as well as from a boat. The seas here are teeming with life, and guests taking boat trips from the island can often see schools of dolphins and the occasional whale. Hawksbill and green turtles also come up onto the beaches of Denis to lay their eggs.

Between 1929 and 1941 over 16,000 tons of guano were exported from Denis and extensive coconut plantations were established. A lighthouse was built here in 1910 as a joint venture—the French built the lighthouse and the British supplied the light. In recent years the lighthouse has been renovated, and visitors are now able to climb the steep cast iron steps right to the very top. Denis Island also has the only ecumenical chapel in Seychelles. This tiny church only has around three services a year, when priests are flown over for Christmas and for other church festival occasions. For the rest of the year the main inhabitants of the chapel are the bright green geckos.

Close to the chapel is an old cemetery used in the times when maritime communication was rare. Unfortunately there are no known records of the first burial to take place on Denis and most of the graves are so ancient that the names of those buried have sadly long weathered away. The most recent graves date back to the 1940s and 1950s.

Denis is a privately-owned island with all its 100 inhabitants employed by Denis Island Lodge, which is owned by Seychelles tour operators Mason's Travel and managed by the Indian hotel group, Taj Resorts.

FÉLICITÉ

Félicité, the French word for bliss (pronounced *Fell-i-si-tay*), is a small island about a mile from La Digue. It can be rented as a private hideaway for anything from two to eight visitors at a time, the ultimate 'honeymoon island' for the very rich—the cost of staying here is akin to that of the Paris Ritz, with staff ready to cater to every whim. One famous visitor to Félicité did not have to pay for the pleasure—the exiled Abdullah Khan, Sultan of the Malay state of Perak. He was responsible for the death of the British consul in Perak and was exiled here between 1875 and 1879, when he was transferred to Mahé until 1895.

Grande Soeur south beach, just north of Félicité

Félicité is only about 680 acres in size. Small, rocky and covered with coconut palms, its highest peak is just under 750 feet. There are two colonial-style houses, one of which dates back to the last century and is thought to have been the residence of the exiled Sultan. Air conditioning, ceiling fans and attached bathrooms are more modern luxuries.

Swimming is good at the beach at La Penice, which is close to the Lodge. The beach overlooks **Ile aux Cocos**, which provides the best snorkelling in the area. There is also a small tennis court on the island, for which racquets are provided. Deep sea fishing, boat trips to other islands and windsurfing are all available. The interior of the island is also intriguing to explore, with its lush vegetation and the remnants of a shy herd of French cattle that have returned to the wild.

FRÉGATE

Frégate is a privately owned island with an exclusive resort, Frégate Island Private. The island is just two square kilometres in area and has spectacular beaches, including the award winning Anse Victorin, which has consistently been voted by the press as 'The World's Best Beach': it is truly magnificent, with dazzlingly white sand, clear turquoise seas and beautiful granite rock formations dotted around and along the beach. Frégate is worth visiting for this beach alone, but the island has much more to offer as well.

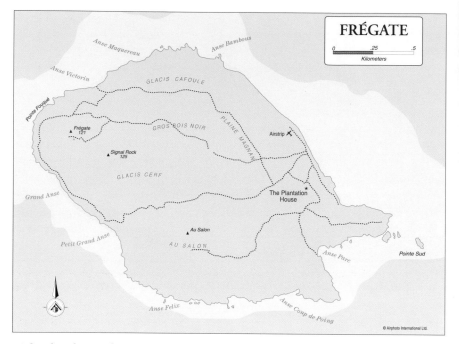

Other beaches such as Anse Parc and Grand Anse may not be such beauty stars, but they are wonderful for beachcombing, walking, viewing turtles hatching at night or sunbathing during the day. For children, the beach close to the harbour is the safest and most accessible for swimming. Snorkelling is excellent around the rocks at Anse Victorin as well as the coastline that runs close to the airstrip.

The hilly interior of the island has not only a small farm and plantation which grows produce for the hotel but also plenty of tropical forests in which live many rare and endemic species found nowhere else on earth, such as the giant tenebroid beetle, and Frégate's most famous inhabitant, the Seychelles Magpie Robin, a beautiful and very tame black and white bird which was rescued from near extinction by the efforts of conservation organisation Birdlife International. A resident Birdlife warden lives on the island to care for the birds and the resort's Eco Manager, Steve Hill also assists in the conservation effort to remove the old coconut plantation and replace it with the endemic trees and shrubs necessary for the bird's habitat. When the resort was being built here an unfortunate side effect was the re-introduction of rats to the island. To counter this, a major rat eradication programme was put into place, which meant the capture of most of the island's land birds and giant tortoises to a safe area while helicopters dropped poison around the island to kill the rats. This was a hugely successful project: the birds were so well looked after that they actually bred while in captivity and the rats were totally destroyed. Frégate is once again a rat free island and preventative measures are in place to ensure that rats do not return. A large fence around the harbour is one of the measures, as is the rule that no yachts or other sailing vessels are allowed to moor close to the island.

The island peak, Mt Signal, can be easily reached by foot and the resort here occasionally hosts champagne trips to view the sunset from the top of the island. There are no cars but guests at the resort are able to drive petrol driven buggies or ride mountain bikes to explore the island. Pirate treasure is rumoured to have been buried on this island, once a pirate stronghold—so far it has not been found, but there are a couple of ancient crumbling graves, said to hold the remains of ancient corsairs.

Frégate is not open for day visitors. The only way to explore this island is to stay at its one very exclusive resort.

LA DIGUE

La Digue (pronounced *La Deeg*), of all the islands, definitely should not be missed. There are very few cars and no paved roads, so it offers a charming glimpse of what life in Seychelles was like before the intrusions of the modern world. The only means of transport cost just a few rupees. Bicycles, can be hired at a daily rate, or an ox cart is driven for you by a young island lad, who will also point out the main sights. However, an ox cart can only travel on the main, flatter roads and tracks—a typical tour will take you through the **Union Plantation** to Anse Source d'Argent. To see more of the island cycling or walking is best.

If you are going under your own steam, rather than on an organised tour, take a ferry to La Digue from Baie Sainte Anne on Praslin in the morning. The sail takes about 30 minutes and you can look out for dolphins in the choppy waters between the two islands.

On arrival take a right turn down the main track, towards La Digue Island Lodge hotel and the south of the island. This is what could loosely be termed the town centre of La Digue, with about 2,000 inhabitants; there is a post office, a few quaint-looking shops, police station and jail and two banks: Seychelles Savings Bank and Barclays. The islanders are known in Seychelles as Digueois and are considered rustics by the people on Mahé. Talk to the Digueois and you will find them very open and friendly—amazingly many of them rarely leave the island and consider life on Mahé to be living in the fast lane!

Passing La Digue Island Lodge Hotel and the pretty Roman Catholic Church of Notre Dame de l'Assomption, a small track leads into the Union Plantation Reserve. For a small entry fee you can walk or cycle around coconut palms and vanilla plants, to see what a plantation would have looked like in the past. A sleepy-looking ox yoked

LA DIGUE

0   .5   1
Kilometers

Anse Patates

Anse Sévère

Anse Gaulettes

Pointe Cap Barbi

Anse Grosse Roche

Ferry to Praslin

LA PASSE

CAP BAYARD

La Digue Cross

● Police

Hospital

Anse Banane

Post Office

NID d'AIGLES

La Digue
Island Lodge ★

● **La Réunion**

Anse La Réunion

Anse Fourmis

Veuve Nature
Reserve

La Digue
333

Anse Caiman

ROCHE BOIS

LA RETRAITE

FOND PIMENT

Union Plantation
Reserve

Anse Cocos

Anse Union

Pointe Ma F...

Pointe Source d'Argent

▲ Citadelle
150

Pointe Turcy

Anse Source d'Argent

Pettite Anse

Pointe Bélize

Grand Anse

Anse Pierrot

Anse Songe

Pointe Canon

Grand Anse

Grand l'Anse

Anse Bonnet Carré

Grand Cap

Anse Marron

Pointe Camille

Pointe Jacques

Anse Source d'Argent, La Digue

Many of the old wooden houses on La Digue retain a well-worn tropical charm

to a wheel crushes coconut husks as he slowly circles, producing coconut oil from the mill in the centre. There is also an old cemetery in the reserve, a relic of early French settlers, many of whom died young in the harsh conditions they experienced. The official residence of the President of Seychelles, a thatched plantation house, is also in the reserve and there is a large tortoise pen at the back of the house.

Taking you through the Union Plantation Reserve, the track will lead you towards **Anse Source d'Argent**. As the track turns into soft sand, abandon your bicycles and walk the remaining few yards. Reputed to be the most photographed beach in the world, you will often see scantily clad models posing on the sand. The reason for this is the remarkable granite rocks that have tumbled out of the mountainside onto the sands; huge boulders balanced haphazardly on top of one another, so smooth they look like polystyrene replicas. There is one rock in the middle of the first cove that you can climb into—the middle has been weathered out into a slight dip, which makes it an excellent place for a comfortable and very private sunbathe. The further you walk the more you will see—Anse Source d'Argent consists of many small coves, separated by rocks and caves.

A 20 minute cycle ride from the jetty takes you to **Grand Anse**, on the other side of the island. It is a bit of an effort to get there: take the road into the centre of the island, just past the Island Lodge, carry on past the small shop with a cage full of fruit bats, and through the **Veuve Nature Reserve**, where the rare Seychelles Black Paradise fly catcher bird lives (the Kreol name for it is *Veuve*). The track gradually climbs up the hill. Past a small shop on the left, there is a track on the right, sloping steeply down towards the coast. There are no signposts here, so taking a map of the main tracks on La Digue with you is useful.

The long ride is rewarded by the sight of Grand and **Petite Anse**. A very different coastline can be found on the southeast of La Digue. Here the beaches are much wider, with fewer rocks and big waves. They look beautiful, but unfortunately swimming is not always safe. Look out for the warning sign at the edge of the beach: if it forbids swimming, do not ignore it. While the waves may not look too rough, the undertow can sweep you out to sea very quickly.

Grand Anse is, predictably, the larger of the two beaches, which lie side by side, separated by rocks. Petite Anse is still pretty big and can be reached by taking the footpath across the rocks at the northern end of Grand Anse. This beach is often empty, so if you're lucky you can have this huge beach all to yourselves.

There is a small footpath on to **Anse Cocos**, **Anse Caiman** and back to the road that leads on to **Anse Patates**, the best beach for swimming in this area of La Digue. This is only to be recommended on foot, as the footpath is too rocky for bicycles.

(previous pages) *Yacht mooring at Grande Soeur (Big Sister Island), northeast of La Digue*
(previous pages inset) *Diving off Desroches Island*

A snorkeller explores Anse Source d'Argent, La Digue

While La Digue is a popular day tour, to see the best that the island can offer and appreciate the romantic atmosphere, a two or three day stay is recommended. La Digue Island Lodge is the biggest and most expensive hotel, but there are several smaller, more reasonably-priced guesthouses scattered across the island.

LONG ISLAND
One of the islands situated just outside Victoria harbour on Mahé, this island is off-limits to the general public. It houses the jail, where there are about 100 men and just five women prisoners. Tour guides will tell you that this is either because women do not turn to crime or, if they do, they are too clever to get caught! The prisoners spend their time farming the land on the island, making the prison virtually self-sufficient in fruit and vegetables. When there is a festival on Mahé, the prisoners are also sent over to erect the marquees.

MOYENNE
A day trip including a visit to Moyenne plus a trip in a semi submersible boat to the Ste Anne National Marine Park is offered exclusively by Masons Travel. Moyenne is the best of the several small 'inner islands', that are scattered just outside Victoria harbour on Mahé. After a look at the marine life on the reef, the boat sails on to Moyenne, where visitors are often greeted by the owner of the island, Brendan Grimshaw. He will give an entertaining potted history of the island, including some spine-chilling tales of pirate ghosts and buried treasure. Afterwards visitors are left to their own devices to explore the island.

A walk around the clearly laid out island path takes around 30 minutes. The remains of early settlers' houses, pirate graves and a small thatched chapel can be seen. An excellent Kreol buffet lunch is provided, followed by another trip to the reef, where you can leave the boat for a short snorkel. The marine life here is so rich, it is like swimming in an aquarium and the colours of the fish and corals are much more vivid when seen close up.

NORTH ISLAND (ILE DU NORD)
North Island, or Ile du Nord, lies seven kilometres north of Silhouette and, on a clear day, can be seen on the horizon from Mahé's northwestern coast.

As far back as 1609 an expedition, led by English Captain Alexander Sharpeigh, encountered North Island. Their charts were inadequate and they thought it was part of the Amirantes. The log entry says, 'these islands seemed to be an earthly paradise . . . . except the allagartes. You cannot discerne that ever any people had been there before us'. The English sailors did not stay long though—they were unable to find water on the island, so they took some giant tortoises aboard to eat and sailed on towards Praslin.

North Island lies 32km north west of Mahé and 5 km north of its nearest neighbour, Silhouette. The island covers some 210 hectares of land and is about 2.5km long and 1 km wide. Three large granite outcrops dominate the island and drop straight into the sea. Between these lies the island plateau, which was extensively farmed in the past.

There are three main beaches, Grand Anse on the western side of the island, which is protected by coral reefs, to the south of the beach is the small cove of Bonnet Carre, where the island's only Barrington Trees drop their delicate pink flowers into the sand. At Anse d'East on the eastern side of the island is the North Island Resort, built around this large wide bay. There is also a further small beach, Petite Anse on the south eastern coast.

During the 19th century North Island was mined for guano and remains of this is still evident at Petite Anse, where there is the remains of a small jetty and a small dome of ancient guano at one corner of the beach. Early in the 20th century copra replaced guano as Seychelles' main export and coconut plantations were established on the plateau. When eventually the copra market collapsed, North Island was sold on in the 1970s to be used as a farm, producing many fruits and vegetables that were sent to Mahé.

Today North Island is home to one of Seychelles' most exclusive resorts. The North Island resort offers 5 star luxury and remote island privacy in individual thatched chalet style rooms. The island is also a film star: the 2004 Thunderbirds movie was partly filmed here after the producers had searched the globe for the location of the International Rescue headquarters, 'Tracy Island', North Island was chosen for its strikingly similar look to the tropical island hide-away featured in the original animated television programme of the 1960s.

PRASLIN

Praslin (pronounced *Prah-lan*) is the second largest island in Seychelles and can be reached from Mahé in two and a half hours by ferry or 15 minutes by plane. The island is home to the second largest population after Mahé, about 5,000 people, who make their living mainly from farming, fishing or tourism.

Praslin was first named Ile de Palmes by the man credited with discovering Seychelles, Lazare Picault, in 1744. It was renamed Praslin by Marion Dufresne, after Gabriel de Choiseul, the Duke of Praslin. In his log Dufresne comments on the lush vegetation of the island and the huge crocodiles, which he said were six metres long. The crocodiles are long gone, killed off quickly by frightened settlers, but the rainforests remain.

The **Vallée de Mai** is the main reason to see Praslin—a primeval rainforest, designated a World Heritage Site. For the admission fee of SR25 you can either arrange for a guided tour or take a brochure and follow the well-marked path, seeing the many exotic plants and perhaps catching a glimpse of the rare black parrot that lives here.

(left) *North Island stood in for 'Tracy Island' in the 2004 movie* Thunderbirds

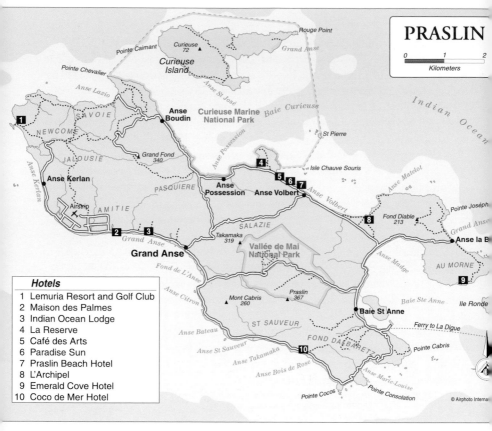

PRASLIN

0   1   2
Kilometers

Rouge Point

Pointe Caimant

Curieuse
72

Curieuse
Island

Grand Anse

Pointe Chevalier

Anse Lazio

Anse St José

SAVOIE

NEWCOME

Anse
Boudin

Curieuse Marine
National Park

Baie Curieuse

Indian Ocean

St Pierre

JALOUSIE

Grand Fond
340

Anse Possession

Isle Chauve Souris

Anse Kerlan

Anse Kerlan

Airstrip

AMITIE

PASQUIERE

Anse
Possession

Anse Volbert

4

5 6 7

Anse Volbert

Anse Matelot

Pointe Joseph

Grand Anse

Anse la B

Fond Diable
213

8

SALAZIE

Takamaka
319

Vallée de Mai
National Park

Anse Mudge

AU MORNE

9

2 3

Grand Anse

Grand Anse

Fond de L'Anse

Anse Citron

Mont Cabris
260

Praslin
367

Baie Ste Anne

Ile Ronde

Baie St Anne

Ferry to La Digue

ST SAUVEUR

Anse Bateau

Pointe Cabris

Anse St Sauveur

FOND D'A BARETZ

10

Anse Takamaka

Anse Bois de Rose

Anse Marie-Louise

Pointe Consolation

Pointe Cocos

© Airphoto Internat

Hotels
1 Lemuria Resort and Golf Club
2 Maison des Palmes
3 Indian Ocean Lodge
4 La Reserve
5 Café des Arts
6 Paradise Sun
7 Praslin Beach Hotel
8 L'Archipel
9 Emerald Cove Hotel
10 Coco de Mer Hotel

All the plants are larger than life and you will see many giant specimens of the small house plants you get at home. There is also a spectacular waterfall, which can be seen from the main island road that passes through the park. The Vallée de Mai is steamy, exotic and full of atmosphere

It is forbidden to take anything out of the Vallée de Mai, most especially the coco de mer nuts, but they can be bought from the Agricultural Department Offices, further down the road at Fond D'Offay, costing SR400 each. They are sold in their natural state and are very heavy. For a few more rupees an empty nut, either in its rough state or polished up, can be purchased from many small craft shops on Praslin and Mahé. A licence is needed to export the nuts and should be obtained from the vendor.

There are a number of superb beaches on Praslin. The largest is the **Côte d'Or** (the Gold Coast) on the north side of the island. The main beach is also known as Anse Volbert. Most of the hotels and restaurants on Praslin are situated beside these sands. Watersports are available here too, although not as much as Beau Vallon on Mahé. The main facilities include sailing, windsurfing, snorkelling and diving. The Praslin Beach

Horsing around on Anse Lazio, Praslin

Enjoying the view of Praslin's Anse Volbert from the shade of a verandah

Hotel has a good diving and watersports centre. The sea is fairly shallow, so at low tide a long wade is necessary to find waters deep enough to swim in. But they are very calm, safe and suitable for children and nervous swimmers. The best snorkelling can be found around the northern edge of the bay or around the small island of **Chauve Souris**. The Praslin Beach Hotel also offers snorkelling trips by boat to the islet of **St Pierre**, where there is a treasure trove of brightly coloured corals, fish and the occasional turtle.

Going west, further along the coast, past a number of pretty coves and bays like **Anse Possession, Anse Takamaka** and **Anse Boudin**, there is the wonderful **Anse Lazio**. This superb beach has been voted the best in the world—it has everything a tropical beach should have: safe, calm waters for swimming, a wide expanse of soft white sand and a bay fringed with spectacular granite rocks and coconut palms. It is never busy, although rarely empty. It is a bit of a trek to get to the bay, but its reputation means visitors will always make the effort to spend a day or afternoon here.

The road to Anse Lazio is not for the faint-hearted; it is very steep and full of potholes. From Côte d'Or the journey will take about 20 minutes by bike, 30 minutes if you walk or an extremely bumpy ten minute car ride. Once beyond the main hotels it turns into a dirt track—keep going, first uphill then steeply downhill past the bays of Anse Possession and Anse Boudin. At Anse Boudin the track turns inland and uphill—carry on, taking the fork to the right which leads straight down the hill to Anse Lazio.

Because of its remote location, bring plenty of drinks and food if you are intending to spend the day here. Alternatively the small restaurant by the side of the beach, *Le Bon Bon Plume*, offers a good lunchtime menu. There are no watersport facilities here, but the rocks around the bay are good for snorkelling, as are the two secluded coves to the far end of the bay.

Turning back towards Côte d'Or, take the track from Anse Boudin, which leads inland for a good view from the summit of Grand Fond, where the radio tower is, across the ocean towards Curieuse. Further east, past Côte d'Or, the beach peters out and an avenue of casuarina trees will take you to Baie St Anne, where the schooners leave for La Digue. On the right is the main mountain road which cuts across the island, taking you towards the Vallée de Mai and to the beaches and the airport on the western side of Praslin.

On the west coast most of the hotels are clustered around **Grand Anse**, not too far away from the airport. Grand Anse is a quieter bay than the Côte d'Or, but not as pretty and, at certain times of the year, rather pungent-smelling seaweed is washed up. There are a number of small hotels and guest houses scattered along the bay, a few shops and banks, a fish market, police station and the Cable and Wireless office. There is also the much-photographed Seychelles Independence Monument, which features a large coco de mer nut.

To the south of Grand Anse are the pretty bays of **Anse Consolation** and **Anse Marie Louise**, although the water is sometimes too shallow to allow anything but a quick dip. The coast northwest of Grand Anse is full of small coves. Close to the airport on the coast at Amitie is also the Seychelles Pearl Farm which produces black pearls. (Black Pearl Ltd, Tel 233150). It is open to the public and the Italian owners can explain how the pearls are cultured and harvested. There is also a gift shop where visitors can buy black pearls individually or set in hand made jewellery.

Anse Kerlan and Petite Anse Kerlan have granite rocks very different from the beaches on the other side of the island. Here the granite is rough and weathered. The sea, too, is a different colour—at Côte d'Or it is a light turquoise, here it is a brilliant green. The sea is rougher and in December and January, when the northwest winds are strong, the waves can be too fierce and the currents too strong for swimming. However, on calm days these bays are great for snorkelling and swimming, though you should always watch out for strong currents.

Further on down the road from **Amitie** there is the small beach of **Anse Bateau** and further along the coast, the beaches of **Grand Anse Kerlan** and **Petit Anse Kerlan**. These beaches, the rocky peninsula between them, known as **Pointe Saint Marie**, along with the gorgeous beach **Anse Georgette** now form part of the **Lemuria Resort**.

To explore Praslin fully you will need to spend at least a couple of days on the island. Indeed many visitors to Seychelles choose to exclusively stay on Praslin at one of the island's many excellent hotels. Praslin is also a useful base for exploring other islands nearby, like La Digue, Cousin and Curieuse. Day trips to Praslin from Mahé including a trip to the Vallee de Mai can however be arranged through all the tour operators.

ROUND

Round is another of the small islands that lie just outside Victoria harbour on Mahé. A walk right around this tiny island can be accomplished in less than half an hour, but it is a good spot for picnics and there is an excellent restaurant here, providing an exhaustive Kreol buffet dinner. The open air restaurant is centred around an old leprosarium, from the days when the island served the settlers as a leper hospital.

Boat trips to Round island can be arranged through the main tour operators on Mahé. Most arranged trips to Round also include Cerf Island and a trip on a glass-bottomed boat over the Sainte Anne National Marine Park.

SAINTE ANNE ISLAND

This is the largest island in the Marine National Park off Mahé, with a peak reaching 800 feet. Discovered on Saint Anne's Day, it was the first place the early French settlers lived, before colonising nearby Mahé. In its recent history the island has been used as a place of refuge for escaped prisoners and as a whaling base during the early 20th century. Up until 1992 it was used to house the National Youth Service, where young people aged between 15 and 17 would spend some time living on the island as part of their state education. From 1999 to 2001 it was used as the base camp for the British based Shoals of Capricorn environmental programme (now adopted by the Government of Seychelles and housed at Port Launay on Mahé). Ste Anne is now home to the brand new **Beachcomber resort.**

Ste Anne has some beautiful sandy beaches, such as **Anse Cimitiere** and **Anse Manon** which overlook the **Ste Anne National Marine Park** where there is fantastic snorkelling and a wild and hilly interior with many nature trails and walks.

SILHOUETTE

This is the third largest granitic island in Seychelles and reputed to have the least disturbed original forests. Its highest peak is the 2,400 foot (751 metre) Mont Plasir, covered with the rare Seychelles Sandalwood and a significant amount of Bois de Natte, the finest of all Seychelles timber, which has been severely plundered on Mahé. The mistforest remains largely unexplored and provides a habitat for the endemic Soosglossus frogs and pitcher plants. New biological discoveries are still being made here.

Silhouette has no roads, only pathways and tracks. About 200 people live on the island, mainly farmers and fishermen. An old sugar cane mill and a large wooden plantation house can still be seen in the main settlement of **La Passe**. It is also reputed to have been the home of the French corsair Jean Hodoul. Rumours still circulate that his treasure is somewhere on the island and there is an old stone wall, of the type believed to have been built by pirates, which can still be seen today.

Island history suggests there may be some truth to the theory that the earliest discoverers of Seychelles were Arab tradesmen, sailing the Indian Ocean centuries before the first Europeans. On the eastern coast is a bay called **Anse Lascars** (*Lascar* being the Kreol word for Arabs), where there are some ancient tombs, believed to be the final resting places of 30 Arab sailors whose dhow was wrecked on the island.

Silhouette lies some 12 miles north of Mahé and can be clearly seen on the horizon, looking out from Beau Vallon Beach on Mahé. Day trips by helicopter can be arranged through tour operators on Mahé and accommodation is provided by the only hotel: the Silhouette Island Lodge at La Passe.

The real treasure of Silhouette Island is its surrounding lagoon

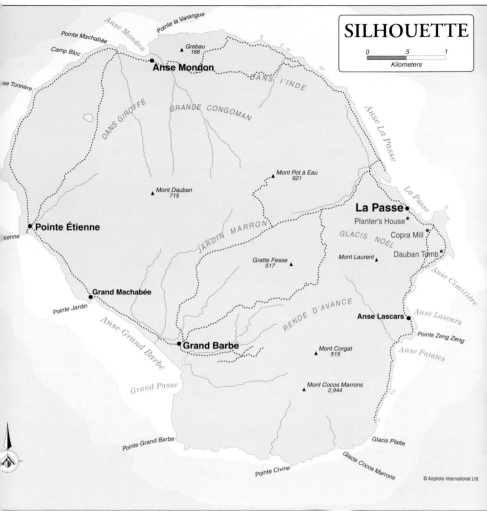

SILHOUETTE

0   .5   1
Kilometers

Pointe Machabée
Camp Bloc
se Tonnère
Anse Mondon
Pointe la Varangue
▲ Grebau
166
Anse Mondon
DANS L'INDE
DANS GIROFFE
GRANDE CONGOMAN
Anse La Passe
Mont Pot à Eau
621
La Passe
▲ Mont Dauban
715
La Passe
Planter's House
Copra Mill
Pointe Étienne
tienne
JARDIN MARRON
GLACIS NOEL
Gratte Fesse
517
Mont Laurent ▲
Dauban Tomb
Anse Cimitière
Grand Machabée
Pointe Jardin
Anse Grand Barbe
RENDE D'AVANCE
Anse Lascars
Anse Lascars
Pointe Zeng Zeng
Grand Barbe
Mont Corgat
515
Anse Patates
Grand Passe
Mont Cocos Marrons
2,944
Pointe Grand Barbe
Glacis Platte
Glacis Cocos Marrons
Pointe Civine
© Airphoto International Ltd.

THÉRESE

Isle Thérèse (pronounced *terr-raise*) lies off Mahé's southwestern coast and is popular for watersports. Also on the island is **Petite L'Escalier**—rock formations resembling a giant's staircase. Watersports available include scuba diving, water skiing, sailing, windsurfing and deep sea fishing. The island restaurant serves Kreol lunches and the twenty minute boat trip across can be arranged through the Berjaya Mahé Beach Resort at Port Glaud.

The Outer Islands

The outer islands of Seychelles consist of four groups, the Amirantes, Farquar, Coetivy and Aldabra. There are landing strips and resorts at some islands, while others can only be reached by boat. For many years, the outer islands were used as coconut plantations until the decline in copra prices made them largely uneconomic for much of the second half of the 20th century. Now tourism is beginning to bring new life back to these far flung atolls: their very remoteness has meant that their beaches and marine life are absolutely pristine: beautiful desert islands, awaiting discovery.

THE AMIRANTES

The Amirantes (pronounced *Ammi-rants*) are the closest to Mahé of all the outer island groups, consisting of 28 islands and islets, lying between 193 and 322 kilometres from the Seychelles capital. The first humans to step onto these islands were probably Arab traders in the ninth century. But the islands were named by the Portuguese after explorer Vasco da Gama discovered them in 1501. Maps from the 16th century referred to them as 'Illhas do Almirante'—the Admiral islands. Five are now inhabited: Desroches, Alphonse, Daros, Marie-Louise and Poivre and three of them have airstrips.

AFRICAN BANKS

African banks used to consist of two islands—North and South, but in recent years South Island has slowly slipped under the waves, with just a large sandbank remaining. What was North Island is now the main African Banks island. This is home to thousands of birds from May to October each year, with the largest breeding site of sooty terns in the Amirantes as well as a breeding ground for Roseate Tern, Black-naped Tern and Crested Tern. It is also an important turtle nesting site. Visitors here are rare and confined to serious bird watchers and conservationists who visit by boat from Desroches.

ALPHONSE

The Alphonse group is some 450 kilometres south of Mahé, 7 degrees South of the Equator and has three islands extending some 16 kilometres from North to South around a magnificent lagoon: Alphonse, St Francois and Bijoutier.

The biggest island of Alphonse is a triangular shaped island with sides just over a kilometre long. It was named after Chevalier Alphonse de Pontevez, the commander of the French frigate 'Le Lys', who discovered the island on the 28th January 1730. The name St Francois was given in honour of Saint Francois de Salles and Bijoutier was given its name because the island's pure beauty reminded the early explorers of a gem.

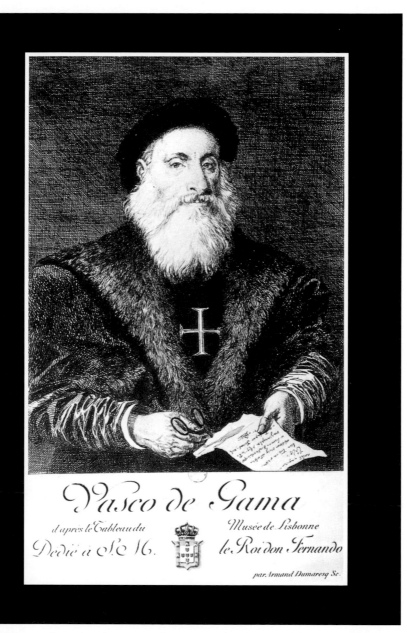

Portuguese explorer Vasco da Gama's Indian Ocean endeavours in 1501 found the Amirantes

For many years the islands were left undisturbed, although it has been speculated that pirates and early navigators may have left troublesome prisoners or crew on the island, which acted as a very effective prison: its very remoteness from any other inhabited land and lack of hardwood trees meant no escape. But there were coconut palms and fresh water on the island, so it was not necessarily an immediate death sentence either.

During the Second World War some survivors from the Australian ship 'Tulagi' found refuge on the islands after the ship was torpedoed by a Japanese submarine. It was the Alphonse island administrator who managed to help them eventually return home.

Alphonse was a large coconut plantation, in the colonial days when copra was king. Some cotton production was also harvested here. Usually the island Administrator ruled some 70 plantation workers who toiled in the hot sun, in the days when visiting schooners with supplies and news of the outside world visited every three months or so. A visit to the old island cemetery reveals a few tantalising facts about some of the people who lived–and died–on Alphonse, including a three month old baby and a number of unmarked graves which are suspected to be a mass burial during a smallpox epidemic. There are grander graves here too, including a pirate grave of one Marcelle Dupont, who died on Alphonse on the 16 January 1908 at the age of 35. Mr Dupont was, apart from engaging in a bit of pirating, one of the 'big men' of the island, lording

Bijoutier Island, gem of the Alphonse group

A coconut plantation, Alphonse

it over the lowly plantation workers and supposedly riding around the island on a white horse. How he met his untimely end, no one quite knows (or isn't telling)...

These days Alphonse is home to a luxurious hotel resort, with the best diving in Seychelles and the best salt water fly fishing in the world. Visitors fly to this remote atoll from all over the world to experience its amazing marine life. The huge lagoon teems with life and even non-divers can enjoy the experience of snorkelling or even just walking along its shores to see huge manta rays, basking baby sharks, turtles and spectacular corals and shells. The fly fishing off St Francois is second to none, and the small island is also home to numerous seabirds, in particular the Crab Plover.

D'ARROS AND ST JOSEPH ATOLL

This atoll was named after Baron D'arros, who was the Marine Commander in Mauritius, or Isle de France as it was then, from 1770–71. D'arros is privately owned by an Iranian prince and was home to Seychelles writer Glynn Burridge for many years. His book, 'Voices' is a collection of short stories, some fiction and some based on his own experiences, which have been gathered by him from the many 'tall tales' told by the outer islanders in traditional story telling during the long tropical nights spent on this atoll.

'VOICES' BY GLYNN BURRIDGE
'THE LAMENT OF ANGELINE'

...the man whom we shall call Matthew Boniface the fisherman, settled himself to begin his story...

"I came to this island when I was just ten years old. My mother had met a man who had set up camp on one of the islands in the Amirantes and we moved down to live with him. There must have been fifty or so people at that time living on and off the island, and here I am talking about some eighty or so years ago.

The settlement was a loose collection of huts built around a makeshift chapel, a warehouse and a calorifer too, for the coconut industry". Boniface paused thoughtfully, trying to recall details of a distant past. "Fishing was plentiful and everyone pitched in and grew basic crops around their homes to supply the community with food. The schooner visited once or perhaps twice a year and brought new additions to the work force and supplies for the island. The round trip could take many weeks and if things went wrong, even months. It would depart with sometimes fifteen tons of coprah which would be sold on Mahe. These were the main activities of the island back then, along with some mining of 'guano'. Believe me it was a desolate place to be, year in year out. People grew sick and died for want of medicine, relying on plants that only some people knew how to use. Poor bastards, many good men went down there I remember, and women and kiddies too. Some died in agony with their friends looking on, wondering if they would be next. They were planted in the cemetery."

"How long had your mother known this man?" The visitor interrupted.

"A month or so." Boniface shrugged. "Maybe more, anyway transport on the island was a giant pirogue that could carry twenty men under oar. She was a mighty vessel but damned dangerous in the heavy swells, then there were two or three smaller vessels as well. For animals there were chickens, ducks, pigs and two oxen for the heavy work of moving timber and coprah around the plantation. As amusement people would make their own brews and tapped the 'toddy', and from time to time there would be a 'moutia'—a real moutia that is, not one of those electronic affairs of today. It would be by torchlight and the dust that would be kicked up would stay in the air 'till morning. During that dance grievances would be aired, marriages formed and broken and many a dark crime committed such as rape ... and even murder. All too often these offences went unpunished, particularly if the 'sandiq' or watchman was involved, or friends of his. Gangs would form and break and then reform again—just like the debris you find collected on the seashore. That was our existence. We lived from day to day, remote from the cares of the outside world and too far from that world to care about us, even if it had a mind to."

"Remote from the cares of the outside world," a Desroches beach collects debris

D'arros is also home to vast numbers of seabirds and also has a good population of the rare land bird, the Seychelles Fody, which was introduced on the island by Birdlife International from the Cousin nature reserve. Close to D'arros is St Joseph Atoll which is made up of 13 small islets. Here can be found myriads of frigatebirds and, unusually, pelicans.

DESROCHES

The most accessible of all the outer islands, Desroches (pronounced *De-rosh*) is a long narrow sandy cay, named after Monsieur Desroches, who was governor of Mauritius from 1767 to 1772. It can be reached from Mahé by plane in 40 minutes. Its position on the edge of a circular, submerged reef makes it the ideal place for watersport, diving and fishing enthusiasts. There is also an exclusive holiday resort on the island, Desroches Island Lodge, with a dive centre, water sports and deep sea fishing facilities.

POIVRE

This atoll lies due south of D'Arros, some 200km southwest from Mahé and consists of three islands: Poivre, South Island and Florentin. This is the largest atoll in the Amirantes and was for many years a privately owned coconut and cotton plantation. Florentin is home to large numbers of grey herons, and is named after them, florentin being the kreol word for the grey heron.

Poivre, named after Pierre Poivre, is famous for the legend of Louis XVII; a French settler on the island, Pierre Poiret, claimed he was the son of the ill-fated French King Louis XVI and queen Marie Antionette, escaping the guillotine for exile in Seychelles. Poiret worket at the cotton ginning factory on Poivre between 1804 and 1822, after which he became a respected cotton planter on Mahé. It is said that on his deathbed he confessed that he was indeed the legitimate heir to the French throne and this was a popular legend in Seychelles for many years until in the 1990s DNA samples were taken from Poiret's descendents, who still live in Seychelles, to conduct genetic tests of his claim: sadly these did not match and this story remains just another of Seychelles' many tall tales.

This remote atoll is now managed by the Seychelles government, but is rarely visited and the birds and turtles there are left alone. Fishing trips to around Poivre are often organised from Desroches, as the big game fishing here is excellent.

REMIRE

Also in the Amirantes group, this atoll is managed by the Island Development Corporation and is generally out of bounds to the general public, as it is a very private retreat for the former President of Seychelles, Albert René and his family.

THE FARQUAR GROUP

The Farquar Group of islands lie some 692 to 805 kilometres from Mahé and were discovered and named by Portuguese explorer Juan Nova in 1504, but later renamed after the governor of Mauritius, Sir Robert Farquar. The islands that make up this group are the Farquar atoll, St Pierre and Providence. These islands have been earmarked for tourism development in the future but in the meantime they are only accessible by sea.

PROVIDENCE ATOLL

This is a long thin atoll with two small islands at each tip: Providence to the north and Bancs du Providence to the south. In-between there is a massive very shallow lagoon which is home to hundreds of grey herons.

ST PIERRE

This rather desolate island is a strange looking raised coral platform, which rises to only about 10 metres above the sea level. There is no beach here, just a tiny strip of sand at one corner of the island only visible at low tide. This island was once mined for guano, but is now abandoned and uninhabited.

Fishermen, using a traditional pirogue, hunt for rays in the calm ocean shallows

THE FARQUAR ATOLL

Ten islands make up the Farquar Atoll. The main island is called North and there is here a tiny settlement producing a small amount of copra. In the lagoon lie three much smaller islands, the Manahas, and to the south of the lagoon is the larger South Island which is an important nesting site for Red-footed Boobies. The most southerly island in this group is also the most southerly island in the Seychelles archipelago, Goelettes. This is a bare, almost treeless windswept isle, but again important to nesting seabirds, in particular Sooty Terns.

THE ALDABRA GROUP

The Aldabra (pronounced *Al-dabb-rah*) group of islands can be divided into two halves—in the east are Astove and Cosmoledo and to the west Assumption and Aldabra Atoll. Over 700 miles from Mahé, this group of islands are closer to the African coast and Madagascar and are the most remote of all Seychelles' islands. Even though they are remote, they can be visited, by small cruisers or yachts and often by diving groups, who can charter the Indian Ocean Explorer between November to April and explore the waters around Cosmoledo and Astove with expert David Rowatt.

ALDABRA ATOLL

The atoll is a huge, eroded coral sponge, 35 by 15 kilometres, at the centre of which lies one of the largest lagoons in the world. At high tide the lagoon is three metres deep and twice a day it is home to a huge influx of marine life—manta rays, hammerhead sharks, barracuda, whip tailed sting rays and turtles.

Eighty thousand years ago there was a volcano where Aldabra now stands—the tip of it can still be seen. Now the coral atoll covers 50 square miles and encompasses a unique ecosystem. It is the sanctuary of the flightless white-throated rail (a bird distantly related to the Dodo) and the last remaining natural habitat for wild giant tortoises in the Indian Ocean. Many green and hawksbill turtles come ashore to lay their eggs on the sands of Aldabra and a whole host of sea and migratory birds, like flamingos and herons, roost here.

The Arabs are credited with landing first on Aldabra in the tenth century. They called the atoll *Al Khadra*; the Portuguese changed it to *Al Hadara* and in time it ended up as Aldabra. French settlers tried to make a living here in 1899, but the remoteness of the islands and the difficult conditions meant it was never developed extensively or for very long. The island has no fresh water source and months often pass without a drop of rain falling. Tales are told of shipwrecked sailors who resorted to drinking tortoise urine in order to survive. The only reminder of early settlers is a coconut plantation on Grande Terre island and a large herd of goats.

Sailors landed on the atoll throughout the 19th century to raid the islands of their many giant tortoises, as a source of food for the sailors. In 1842 two ships alone are reported to have taken more than 1,200 of the creatures. By the turn of the century the tortoises were almost extinct and the crew of one ship had to hunt for three days to find just one.

Aldabra has been designated a World Heritage Site and is administered by the Seychelles Island Foundation, based on Mahé. A disaster for the island was narrowly averted in the 1960s, when Britain entered into negotiations with the United States to turn Aldabra into a military air base. Such a move would have condemned the unique wildlife on the atolls. After the plans were made public, there was an international outcry by ecologists. Their lobbying led to the military plans being abandoned and the area and its wildlife receiving full protection.

COSMOLEDO ATOLL, ASTOVE AND ASSOMPTION

There are 13 islands in **Cosmoledo** Atoll, which are totally uninhabited. The islands are harvested for birds' eggs, eaten as a national delicacy: 100,000 sooty tern eggs were taken in 1990. The taking of the eggs is strictly monitored. Due to a decline in bird numbers in 1991, for example, hardly any eggs were harvested that year.

Astove, 35 kilometres south of Cosmoledo, has an intriguing history. In the 18th century a Portuguese slaver was shipwrecked on the island. Only the slaves survived the wreck and they managed to exist very happily on Astove for over 40 years, resisting any attempts to rescue them. Astove is still home to a few families, who make their living mainly from the production of coconut fibre brooms.

Assomption is 140 kilometres to the northwest of Astove and is the second largest of the outer islands. It is seven kilometres long and two and a half wide. An airstrip has been recently built on the north of the island, with the intention of using it as a base for tourists heading for Aldabra. A small hotel is also under construction.

The Aldabra group is now open, not just to the biologists and scientists who work there, but also a strictly limited number of visitors each year. All inquiries about Aldabra, from scientists and from the general public should be made to: The Executive Officer, Seychelles Islands Foundation, c/o The Ministry of Tourism, PO Box 92, Mahé, Seychelles. Tel: 225333.

Practical Information

Getting There

The biggest single expense of a holiday to Seychelles is the flight. Prices are kept high for the ten hour flight from Europe, which has the effect of both limiting the number of tourists and restricting them to the 'champagne class'. Seychelles is not generally not listed in the cheap flights section. At the time of writing, three airlines offer flights into Seychelles: **Air Seychelles**, **Qatar Airlines** and **Emirates**. There are regular scheduled flights from UK, France, Dubai, Singapore, Mauritius and South Africa.

Island Hopping in Seychelles

Island hopping packages in Seychelles are sold by most of the main travel agents. Transfers to islands are mainly done by either Helicopter Seychelles or Air Seychelles. There is also a ferry and a catamaran service between Mahé and Praslin/La Digue. Helicopter Seychelles Website: www.helicopterseychelles.com.

When To Go—Weather Guide

Stepping off the plane onto the runway at the Seychelles International Airport on Mahé, the first thing to hit you is the heat and humidity. It is like stepping into a sauna and the airport can be about the hottest place on the island at midday.

The temperatures in Seychelles are a fairly constant 29 degrees Centigrade or 84 degrees Fahrenheit throughout the year. The islands are outside the cyclone belt, so high winds and severe thunderstorms are rare. Seychelles is just four degrees south of the equator, so there are no distinct seasons, but there are two monsoons. Monsoons are the trade winds not rain, but they do affect the rainfall pattern.

If you are travelling off-season, try to avoid the rainiest months of January and February. However, Seychelles is in the tropics, so it can rain buckets, even in the so-called drier months of July and August. The good news is that the rainfall, whilst heavy, is usually short-lived. And even if it does rain all day, it is still very warm and

(left) *Anse Source d'Argent, La Digue*

doesn't stop you from swimming. When it is really raining heavily, try washing your hair in it: the rainwater makes a very good conditioner! A table follows, showing monthly rainfall and temperature averages for Mahé, the island which receives the most rain. Other smaller islands, like Frégate or Bird, receive considerably less rain.

AVERAGE CLIMATIC TABLE FOR MAHÉ

Also worth noting are the humidity levels throughout the year. If you are averse to high humidity, then avoid the northwest monsoon between October and April/May and visit during the slightly breezier and drier southeast monsoon, from June through to September. If you are visiting Seychelles for a diving or sailing holiday, then the sea is much clearer and calmer during the northwest monsoon.

The monsoon will also affect the weather and sea around different parts of Mahé at different times. During the southeast monsoon, for example, the sea is very rough on the southeast side of the island. And even on an island as small as Mahé, which is just 17 miles long by nine miles wide, it can be raining hard on one side of the island and beautifully sunny on the other side, just a 20 minute or so drive away. If it is raining on your side, try ringing a hotel on the other side of the island and ask the receptionist what the weather is like there. Of course you then take the risk that the weather could have changed by the time you get there!

Month	Daily High	Nightly Low	Daily Hours of Sun	Humidity	No. of Days with Rain
JAN	30C	24C	5	82%	12
FEB	30C	25C	6	80%	15
MAR	30C	25C	7	79%	15
APR	31C	25C	8	80%	14
MAY	30C	25C	8	79%	14
JUN	30C	25C	8	79%	12
JUL	28C	24C	7	80%	12
AUG	28C	24C	7	79%	11
SEP	29C	24C	8	79%	12
OCT	29C	24C	7	80%	13
NOV	30C	24C	7	80%	17
DEC	30C	24C	5	82%	19

Most cloud bursts are short lived, such as this rainshower passing Cote d'Or, Praslin

Travel Preparations

VISA REQUIREMENTS
You must have a valid passport to enter Seychelles, plus onward or return tickets, valid travel documents, accommodation and sufficient funds for your stay. There are no visa requirements for Seychelles. The tourist visa will allow a stay of up to a four week holiday visit and it can be renewed for up to three months, free of charge. A disembarkation card will be handed out shortly before landing in Seychelles, which you need to fill in, stating where you are staying and for how long.

VACCINATIONS AND HEALTH
If you visit your doctor and say you are going to Seychelles, you will get a variety of jabs from tetanus boosters to cholera and typhoid vaccinations. Truth is though, there are no vaccination requirements for Seychelles and, for a typical two or three week stay on the islands, they are not needed. Seychelles is an extremely clean country. There are no serious tropical diseases, the water is clean and very drinkable and tummy upsets

rare. Although there are mosquitoes, they do not carry malaria. If, however, you are combining a holiday to Seychelles with a safari trip to Africa, then do consult your doctor. Yellow fever vaccinations are compulsory when arriving from Africa and malaria precautions advisable.

Victoria has a general hospital at Mont Fleuri, next to the Botanical Gardens, and there are clinics elsewhere on Mahé, Praslin and La Digue. Private clinics on Mahé include Dr Haresh Jivan, behind Jivan's Arcade at Mont Fleuri, just south of Victoria, a few kilometres further on down the road from Victoria hospital (Tel 324008) and Dr Chetty in Market Street Victoria (Tel 321911). Both private and state medical clinics will charge consultation and prescription fees. Some pharmaceutical products can be purchased from chemists, but these are often in short supply, so it is advisable to bring any necessary and basic medicines with you for the duration of your stay. The main chemist in Victoria is Behram's Pharmacy in Victoria House Arcade (Tel 225 559).

For serious emergencies dial 999 for fire, police or ambulance. Medical evacuations from the outer island resorts can be arranged with Helicopter Seychelles. It is advisable to take medical insurance cover for your stay.

TIME DIFFERENCE
Seychelles is four hours ahead of GMT and nine hours ahead of EST, three hours ahead of BST and eight hours ahead of EST in daylight savings months.

WHAT TO TAKE
Pack lightweight and loose cotton clothes, plenty of T-shirts and shorts, beach shoes and sturdy trainers for walking. You will need at least one change of swimwear, long trousers to cover up in the evenings (some hotels do not allow shorts in their evening dining rooms). Sundresses and sarong beach wraps are useful for women. While the dress code is casual throughout Seychelles (evening gowns and dinner suits are not worn) it is not advisable to walk around Victoria in beach wear. A local policeman may well pull you aside and tell you to cover up!

Take plenty of film for your camera, since buying new film is expensive. The same goes for suntan lotion. Also recommended are antihistamine cream and tablets for mosquito bites.

Pack a large umbrella for sudden downpours, but not an anorak or plastic mac—it is simply too hot. Beach towel, mask, snorkel and flippers if you have them; if not it will not matter much, unless you are going to self cater, as most hotels and guest houses will have snorkelling equipment.

Also bring a hairdryer and electric razor, if you usually use these at home. The electricity supply and sockets are the same in Seychelles as in Britain (240 volts, 50Hz, 3-pin plugs).

For security reasons always make sure that the baggage going into the hold is securely locked. Air Seychelles will allow only one piece of hand luggage and it cannot be bigger than the overhead luggage bins. The luggage allowance for all the airlines is around 20 kilos per person, but if you are intending to do a lot of island hopping it is better to travel on the lighter side, as baggage allowance for the smaller inter-island planes is only 10 kilos per person.

Arriving

As the aircraft approaches Mahé it provides a good view of the island, with its steep dark green slopes, white beaches and the dappled colours of the coral reefs under the ocean. From the air it looks practically uninhabited; only as the descent to the airstrip begins can houses be seen, dotted about under palm trees. Building regulations in Seychelles mean that no construction can be higher than the tallest palm tree.

The International Airport runway is on reclaimed land on the eastern coast. The landing strip is almost 3,000 metres long. Built by the British with American money during the 1970s, at the height of the cold war, it was agreed that it would be constructed to be large enough to be used as a military strip if ever needed (it never has been).

Before the doors of the aircraft are opened, a disinfectant is sprayed into the cabin, as required by Seychelles law. If you wear contact lenses, keep your eyes shut while the hostess walks up the gangway with the aerosol can. Even arriving in the early morning or late evening, the heat will still come as something of a shock. There is a short walk to the terminal building across the runway, a queue through passport control and then a wait of around twenty minutes for your baggage. The airport is not air conditioned and has a tin roof, so it can become furnace-like in the sun. Light clothing for arrival is recommended.

CUSTOMS

Customs laws in Seychelles permit the following importations for passengers of 18 and over: 200 cigarettes or their equivalent, 1 litre of spirits and 1 litre of wine, 125cc. of perfume and 25cl. of toilet water, plus other duty free items with a total value not exceeding SR400. Non-prescription drugs, firearms (including spear-fishing guns) are totally prohibited, as are all forms of pornographic material. Animals, food and agricultural produce are strictly controlled and subject to licensing. As alcohol is very expensive in Seychelles it may be worth buying drinks from the Duty Free Shop at your home airport.

Of the handful of airlines servicing the islands, Air Seychelles is the only carrier to offer direct flights

ARRIVALS HALL

If you are on a package holiday, your rep will be waiting for you in the Arrivals hall. For those going it alone, a taxi can be hired to take you to your hotel or cars and mini-mokes can be hired from the airport. A small Bureau de Change stand is in the airport hall; car hire firms will accept most credit cards and travellers' cheques.

The airport is on the east side of Mahé, on the main north–south coastal road. So if your hotel is in southern Mahé, you will turn left; for northern Mahé, Victoria and Beau Vallon, turn right. Most car hire companies provide a simple road map. Before setting off from the airport, glance upwards at the sheer granite cliff on the other side of the road; this is what Mahé is made of and why the airport had to be built on reclaimed land.

Getting Around

You may think that on such small islands walking would be the best mode of transport. It is for tiny islands like Frégate or Bird, which are small enough not to need roads, but on the larger islands of Mahé and Praslin some form of transport is necessary. The heat and humidity makes it intolerable to walk anywhere for very long and most of the roads are steep mountain passes.

TAXIS

A row of taxis awaits you at the airport; prices are calculated by meter. Taxi cabs are easy to find at the major hotels on Mahé and Praslin, at the airports and at a central stand near the clock tower in Victoria. Smaller hotels can contact cabs for guests.

CAR HIRE

Even though it is expensive, it is worth hiring a car for at least one day of a visit to Mahé or Praslin. The most widely available hire vehicle is the mini-moke, which provides a fun, bumpy, breezy ride, though not very practical in the rain. A jeep is useful if you want to explore some of the smaller dirt roads, like the potholed path to Anse Intendence or the treacherous road to Anse Soleil.

There are several car hire operators based at the airport, including well known international companies like *Hertz* and *Avis*, which can be booked in advance, as well as local firms like *Kobe* and *Tropicars*. It is possible to save money by ringing around the car hire operators for a quote. Most car hire is expensive—at least SR350 per day for a jeep or mini-moke (there are no mopeds or motor cycles for hire)—and air-conditioned cars are more expensive still. The prices include compulsory third party insurance. There are no extra charges for mileage. To hire a car the driver must have a full current driving licence and be over 21. A deposit is usually required. Speed limits are 24 mph in the town and generally 40 mph outside, although on the dual carriageway the limit is 70 mph.

Mahé and Praslin have good tarmac roads, apart from the occasional beach road. Driving is on the left and signposting is good. There are few roads on Mahé and even fewer on Praslin, so it is difficult to lose your way. A driving tour of the whole island of Mahé will take less than a day. Make sure there is plenty of petrol, as steep mountain roads make cars very thirsty. Speed limits are 25 mph in the town and 40 mph outside. The hairpin bends with sharp drops on many of the roads mean you will rarely be out of second or third gear and require careful driving.

THE BUS SERVICE

The bus services on Mahé and Praslin are reasonably reliable, but not often used by tourists, partly because the timetables are not usually posted at the bus stops. Ask the hotel receptionist, or simply note the time when a queue starts to form at the nearest bus stop, to get a general idea.

On the main roads crossing the islands there is usually a bus once every half an hour. The bus service is cheap and the only time buses get crowded is early in the morning, with people travelling in to work or school, and at around 4.00 pm as offices close. The main bus depot is in Palm Street in Victoria and to get from one side of the island to the other, you will need to change buses here. The terminals for the various areas around Mahé are clearly marked. There is a flat fare for every single journey of SR3. The bus service operates from dawn to dusk only. All the main hotels are on bus routes. Just tell the driver where you want to get off.

CYCLE HIRE

Not widely available or really recommended for much of Mahé's sometimes steep and increasingly busy roads, although in South Mahé and around the flatter coastal roads cycling is an alternative form of transport and mountain bikes can be hired from some of the larger hotel resorts. Cyclists should watch out for the hazards of wet, slippery mountain roads (there are very few barriers between the road and sharp drops below) and also for the large TATA public buses, which hurtle around the bends at breakneck speed...

Newlyweds take to the trails of La Digue

Ox Cart

This is only available on La Digue and a novel way of getting both a reasonably priced ride and a guided tour of the island in one. The ox carts are usually available from the jetty or by the La Digue Island Lodge Hotel and can take you to your hotel or the beach, or give you a tour through the Union Plantation and across to the beach at Source d'Argent.

Inter-Island Flights

For island hopping holidays the quickest and easiest mode of transport is either by light plane on the Air Seychelles inter island service, or by helicopter, flying Helicopter Seychelles. The Inter Island Terminal is part of the main airport on Mahé and situated about 100 yards north of the International terminal. There are scheduled and charter services between Mahé and Praslin, Desroches, Bird, Frégate, Denis and Alphonse islands using prop aircraft: an assortment of six and nine seater Twin Otters. La Digue, Silhouette, Cousine, North, and Frégate are reached by helicopter transfer. There are several daily flights from Mahé to Praslin. Check in is 30 minutes prior to departure.

The Inter-Island Ferry and Catamaran Services

The ferry is the cheapest option for travel between Mahé, Praslin and La Digue. The schooner leaves from the old port at Victoria from Tuesday to Saturday and the cost from Mahé to Praslin is around SR35 each way. The ferry can be crowded, so it is best to arrive about 30 minutes before sailing time. A new catamaran service, the Cat Cocos, is significantly faster but more expensive, from SR140 each way. Tickets are available at the inter-island ferry quay and check-in is 15 minutes prior to departure.

There is also a ferry service from Praslin to La Digue, at the Baie Ste Anne Jetty. Tickets can be reserved in advance and the crossing takes 30 minutes.

Typical Journey Times from Mahé to Main Island Destinations

	PLANE	HELICOPTER	FERRY	CAT
PRASLIN	15 mins	20 mins	2hrs 30 mins	55 mins
LA DIGUE		25 mins	30 mins from Praslin	
COUSINE		15 mins		
BIRD	40 mins			
FRÉGATE	20 mins	35 mins		
DENIS	35 mins			
DESROCHES	1 hour			
ALPHONSE	1 hour 5 minutes			

Money Matters

The local currency is the Seychelles Rupee (SR), made up of 100 cents. Notes come in denominations of SR10, 25, 50 and 100, coins from SR5 downwards.

The exchange rate has been as high as ten rupees to the pound sterling, but is more usually between seven and a half and eight. You'll get a better rate (in rupees) for your currency in Seychelles, so it is advisable to buy them there, rather than ordering them in advance.

There are a number of Bureau de Change facilities dotted about the islands. Most large hotels have one and there are a number of banks, including Barclays, in Victoria. Bank opening times are from 8.30 or 9.00 to 13.00 or 13.30 and from 14.00 or 14.30 to 16.00 or 16.30 Monday to Friday; from 9.00 to 12.00 on Saturday mornings. Some Bureau de Change counters are open after banking hours at the airport and in hotels. Banks do offer better rates though. Travellers' cheques can be changed at banks or hotels and can be used for car hire and hotel bills.

Most shops, hotels and restaurants will accept credit or debit cards. Visa, MasterCard and Access are accepted almost everywhere; Diners and American Express in fewer places. Due to economic problems within Seychelles, which have led to a shortage of foreign exchange, many visitors find themselves being approached by Seychellois and asked if they would like to change money for a much higher rate than that at the bank. Please note that such transactions are illegal and those caught dealing on the black market will be subject to prosecution. Due to economic pressures, all hotels are now charging visitors in dollars rather than Seychelles Rupees for room rates and also for the cost of all food and beverages. Some hotel gift shops and the airport Duty Free Shop will not accept payment in Seychelles Rupees and entrance fees to all of Seychelles National Parks including the Botanical gardens in Victoria and the National Marine Parks is now in US Dollars.

Business and Communication

Seychelles is a growing business centre, with good communications with the rest of the world. An off shore business centre, the Seychelles International Trade Zone, is being developed on reclaimed land just south of the capital Victoria with facilities for international company registration. Possible investment opportunities lie in the huge tourism market as well as in fisheries and marine farming. All enquiries should be directed to the Investment Desk at the Ministry of Finance, PO Box 313, Victoria (Tel 248 382016, Fax: 248 224936, Email: ideasio@seychelles.net). The British High Commission's website also has some advice for those seeking to do business in Seychelles: www.bhcvictoria.sc

THE INTERNATIONAL CONFERENCE CENTRE

The International Conference Centre of Seychelles provides a main auditorium for 600 people. It has been fitted out with the latest simultaneous interpretation facilities and audio-visual aids and also offers two main committee rooms for 200 and 150 delegates, plus a range of other smaller rooms. This can be booked through the Seychelles Tourist Offices or directly through the Ministry of Tourism in Seychelles. Tel: 611100.

Media and Telecommunications

Local and international telecommunication links are handled by Cable and Wireless and Airtel. Both companies sell mobile phone cards and phone cards to use in public telephones on Mahé, Praslin and La Digue. Cable and Wireless operates a 'ship to shore' service, (ISDN) lines and both companies offer roaming services for mobile phones although at present there is no GSM service. Direct international dialling is available on fixed line and mobile telephones, but mobile call rates are more expensive. Most hotels have internet and email facilities. There are also several internet cafés on Mahé and Praslin.

The only daily newspaper is *The Nation*, which reflects government views and was for many years the only locally published newspaper available. The governing SPPF party also publishes a weekly paper *The People*. The opposition SNP party has its own weekly paper, *Régar* that is on sale every Thursday afternoon. There is also a weekly Saturday newspaper, *Isola Bella*. Foreign newspapers can sometimes be available from larger hotels and resorts but are not stocked in local shops. There are occasional foreign magazines on sale, mainly South African publications, available sporadically in and around Victoria.

Radio and television broadcasts are run by the Seychelles Broadcasting Corporation, SBC. There are two terrestrial channels, SBC (which broadcasts locally produced programmes in Kreol and some English language programmes including morning and lunchtime broadcasts from CNN and BBC World news), and TV5, the French channel. Larger hotels offer additional satellite television channels.

SBC has a radio service on Medium Wave that broadcasts mainly in Kreol. Paradise FM is a 24-hour music station that broadcasts on 93.6 and 92.6FM. The BBC World Service is relayed on FM, on 106FM and the French international shortwave service, RFI, is relayed on 103FM.

Living and Working in Seychelles

There are some visitors to Seychelles who fall sufficiently in love with the islands that they don't want to leave at the end of their vacation. If you are thinking about living and working in Seychelles, this section offers a few guidelines—and cautions.

Firstly, those wishing to work in Seychelles have to obtain a Gainful Occupation Permit, or GOP which is granted by the Government of Seychelles and costs in the region of SR20,000 per year. You cannot undertake any work without one. However if you obtain a job, your employer is likely to obtain and pay for a GOP on your behalf. A GOP is only issued to a foreign worker if the government of Seychelles is satisfied that there is no suitable local person who can fill the vacancy. The Government of Seychelles is the country's biggest employer and recruits a number of expatriates as doctors and health workers; teachers, customs officials and other professionals. The two main private schools in Seychelles, the International School and the Independent School also recruit some expatriate teaching staff. Foreign companies operating in Seychelles employ expatriates as senior management staff only, including Cable and Wireless, Barclays Bank, Seychelles Breweries (a subsidiary of Guinness) and Indian Ocean Tuna (Heinz). Many hotels also employ expatriate staff in senior positions. Some pilots working for Air Seychelles or Helicopter Seychelles are also expatriates. Most job opportunities in Seychelles require English speakers, preferably with French as a second language, although this is not always essential. The tourism industry however will

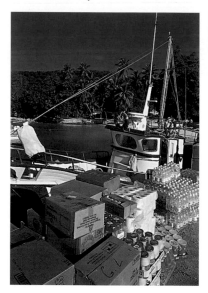

Off loading cargo at La Digue Harbour

require workers with at least three European languages. Expatriates working for the Government of Seychelles are generally paid in Seychelles Rupees, and changing this into hard currency to be sent overseas can be problematic if not downright impossible at times.

Enquiries about job vacancies can be made directly to individual companies, or to the Ministry of Education, Box 48, Victoria. Tel (248) 283283, the Ministry of Health, Box 52, Victoria Tel (248) 388000. The British High Commission's website www.bhcvictoria.sc also has some useful advice on living and working in Seychelles.

Building a roof from latanier leaves

Grinding copra the traditional way is still done on La Digue

Houses are readily available to rent and details are usually advertised in the classified ads section of the daily newspaper 'The Nation'. Monthly rents start from around SR5000 for a basic bungalow to SR7,500 and above for a larger house with swimming pool. Some houses are rented out with a maid and/or gardener. Houses to rent along Mahé's more popular north-western coast are usually more difficult and more expensive to obtain.

There are three private schools on Mahé, all close to the capital Victoria. The International School takes pupils from 3 years of age to 18 and follows the British National Curriculum. This is an excellent school but it does have long entrance waiting lists. The Independent School is aimed more at Seychellois pupils, but education is in English and pupils can be taken from 3 to 16 at present although there are plans to open a sixth form. There is also a smaller French School, which offers primary and secondary education in French and follows the French education system.

The International School, Mont Fleuri, Mahé:
Tel (248) 610444. Fax: (248) 322641.
Website: www.internationalschool.sc
The Independent School, Union Vale, Victoria, Mahé. Tel (248) 322337
Ecole Francais, Riverside, Victoria, Mahé. Tel (248) 224585

There is also an excellent Montessori Pre School on the hillside above Victoria on Mahé, which takes children from 18 months old to up to 6 years old. Teaching is primarily in English, but there are teachers who specialise in French and Kreol teaching too. This is The Children's House, Bel Air, Mahé. Tel: (248) 550677

The level of primary health care in Seychelles is generally good, both at the state run hospitals and clinics and at the private medical clinics. Expatriates have to pay a small fee at both. However some drugs are not always readily available in Seychelles and patients in need of specialist care are usually sent abroad.

Security in Seychelles is better than most other African or Indian Ocean countries: there is a certain amount of petty crime, mainly opportunistic thefts and house burglaries, but little in the way of violent crime and virtually no car crime. As long as there are adequate prevention measures in place: burglar bars on windows, mortice locks on doors, there is very little to worry about. As a mother of three I find Seychelles is a wonderfully safe and generally healthy place to bring up small children.

The cost of living in Seychelles is extremely high. Most foodstuffs and everyday essentials are expensive: approximately twice the price of similar items in the UK, even for items produced in Seychelles (you can buy cheaper fresh pineapples in Europe than you can here). The cost of purchasing a car is also pretty steep: for example an imported small saloon car will cost in the region of SR130,000 or the equivalent in foreign exchange and second hand cars are also pricey: for instance a ten year old second hand saloon in good condition would cost around SR80,000. The good news is that depreciation value of cars is not great, so those working on a two or three year contract may well end up getting most or even all of their money back when they sell the car on.

A word of caution: living in 'paradise' has its drawbacks. Living on a remote island

in the middle of the Indian Ocean can cause some to develop claustrophobic 'cabin fever' type symptoms, that causes them to leave Seychelles after the initial honeymoon period is over. Other drawbacks include frequent shortages of imported food and other necessities and leads to some food queues (or scrums) when items not seen in the shops for some time

A pause from work in the midday sun

Shops may run out of stock from time to time. Victoria, Mahé

suddenly reappear, such as breakfast cereals, toothpaste, tinned vegetables and chocolate. Seychelles is not the place to live if you live to shop! But for those that do not mind the hardships of going without a few western luxuries and a wide range of food; who can cope with water restrictions at certain times of the year and the occasional power cut; who enjoy the climate and can be patient with a certain amount of laid back tropical lassitude when it comes to the workplace, then this paradise could be for you.

(right) *The views from the mountain tops of Mahé are well worth the climb*

Where to Stay

There are a range of small hotels and guesthouses on the main inner islands of Mahé, Praslin and La Digue and full details of all accommodation on offer can be viewed at the Seychelles Tourism Marketing Authority's website :www.aspureasitgets.com or at the Seychelles supersite www.sey.net

Family Holidays

Seychelles is generally a couples market when it comes to tourism, but there are some resorts which allow and make provisions for children. In the luxury bracket, Lemuria and Plantation Club are both aimed at families as well as couples with supervised children's activities and programmes and babysitting services. Other smaller hotels and guest houses do welcome children but there may be a lack of child-friendly facilities. Not all the beaches and islands are suitable for children either: as a general rule, Beau Vallon on Mahé is a safe destination for children, as is the Cote d'Or coast on Praslin.

Luxury Hotels on Mahé

The following resorts are five star or equivalent on the main and outer islands that are recommended to offer guests sublime tropical holidays and showcase the best of what Seychelles has to offer.

LE MERIDIEN FISHERMAN'S COVE HOTEL
Bel Ombre, Mahé. Tel: (248) 247247. Website: www.lemeridien.com
Following a $12 million refurbishment, taking almost a year to complete, the Fisherman's Cove re-opened in 2004 as a more luxurious five star resort. A new thatched reception area contains a waterfall, which tumbles down through the hotel's main public spaces, which have been built into the rocky slopes at the edge of the beach, until it reaches a 70-metre infinity pool that seems to stretch out into the ocean.

The guestrooms have been re-styled, some with an open bathroom, or with showers in the middle of the room, while others have a wooden deck accessible through the shower area. All rooms have a view of the sea and are set out in colourful tropical gardens situated on the northwestern side of Beau Vallon Bay.

A decked boardwalk extends from the rooms to a new restaurant and bar, Le Bourgeois. This then extends out to a rocky promontory, where a new traditional thatched sunset pavilion offers a place to sit and watch the sun go down. Le Bourgeois is a casual restaurant, offering a menu of freshly-caught grilled fish, while the hotel's second restaurant is the more formal Le Cardinal, offering a gourmet a la carte menu.

A new spa, located in a 'zen' corner of the grounds, includes two massage rooms, a plunge pool and an exercise room.

While the beach directly in front of the hotel is not the prettiest stretch of Beau Vallon, and swimming is much better further along the beach towards the middle of the bay, this newly designed hotel offers comfort and luxury and yet, unlike the other luxury resorts in Seychelles, is close to Mahé's main beach resort with its restaurants, bars and sports facilities.

THE BANYAN TREE, Intendance, Seychelles
Tel: (248) 383500. Fax: (248) 383600. Website: www.banyantree.com.
This flagship hotel offers oriental style luxury and beauty spa treatments, and recently won the Condé Nast Traveller award for the best hotel spa in the Africa, Indian Ocean and Middle East region. There are 36 luxury villas each with private swimming pool and sundeck, within a stones throw of one of Mahé's most spectacular beaches, Intendance, on the south-western corner of the island. The hotel is around a 30 minute transfer, by private jeep, from the International airport and around a 45 minute drive from Victoria.

The villas are built with sensuous pampering in mind: aromatherapy oils can be lit in the room; there is a spacious bathroom with every five star amenity and a huge television and DVD player hidden away in a mahogany cabinet. There is also a CD player in each bedroom with a selection of soothing 'new age' music.

Buggies take guests to either hillside or beach front villas, which have been built on a strip of land between beach and lagoon. There is also a Presidential Villa recommended for families or small groups travelling together: here there are two bedrooms with separate entrances and a spacious living and dining area, two swimming pools and a Jacuzzi. However Banyan Tree is not aimed at family groups: Intendance beach is spectacular but with huge crashing waves it is not suitable for small children. The hotel itself is aimed at couples wishing to holiday in style and be pampered by the beauty treatments on offer.

The Banyan Tree Spa has a wide range of massage, body and beauty treatments carried out by Thai masseuses and beauty therapists. There is a Health Club and Gym and a health conscious juice bar. For the not so figure conscious there is also a Verandah Bar offering cocktails and snacks all day and The Jardin d'Epice Restaurant has All-Day Dining in a verandah setting overlooking Intendance Bay. The Saffron Restaurant serves evening a la carte Thai cuisine and has a private dining room for small private functions, which has been named 'The Peter Sellers Room', in recognition of the fact that the British actor Peter Sellers once owned the property that the hotel now occupies.

This is a hotel for those that enjoy Thai style luxury and food combined with solitude and the tropical setting of Intendance Bay.

THE PLANTATION CLUB
PO Box 437, Victoria. Tel 361361. Fax 361333. Website: www.plantationclub.com
Situated on the secluded south western side of Mahé, the Plantation Club is a large hotel built on a 180 acre coconut plantation between imposing granite cliffs and sandy beach. Transfer from the airport takes around 30 minutes by car, or less than ten minutes by helicopter.

The resort has 200 large rooms and suites all within two storey apartments well spread out within large grassy gardens. The suites have ample living space and even the double rooms are on a split level with a separate living area. There are three restaurants, with a selection of themed buffet evenings and a la carte dining, a cocktail bar, casino, water sports facilities, floodlit tennis courts, Jacuzzi, gym, sauna, masseur, hairdresser, art gallery and one of the biggest and best swimming pools on the island.

Tropical gardens lie between the rooms and the beach and a lagoon slips past the cocktail bar in the main hotel building. There are a number of organised activities for guests each day and evening meals include dinner dances, live music and international food evenings. The hotel is also one of the main sponsors and hosts of an International Festival of Classical Music, held in Seychelles every two to three years. The Plantation Club is particularly recommended for families with a range of facilities and activities aimed at children including an outdoor play area and children's swimming pool.

Well-appointed chalets have all the trappings of a five star resort at Le Meridien Fisherman's Cove, which was renovated and refurbished in 2004

The dining area at Le Meridien Fisherman's Cove;
(below) The pool at Le Meridien Fisherman's Cove appears to stretch out into the sea and become part of the ocean itself

The Banyan Tree, at Intendance on south-west Mahé offers award-winning beach-front accommodation, with all the health spa facilities that this hotel chain is best-known for

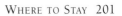

Stunning scenery of the Curieuse Marine Park, looking over the top of Curieuse island, over the turtle pool in the bay and towards its larger island neighbour, Praslin; (inset) Sharp granite rocks are a feature on Curieuse island

Luxury Hotels on Praslin

LEMURIA RESORT OF PRASLIN, Anse Kerlan, Praslin.
Tel (248) 281281. Fax: (248) 281 001
Email: resa@lemuriaresort.com. Website: www.lemuriaresort.com
Lemuria is the newest, largest and most exclusive resort on Praslin. Entering the hotel through imposing and rather daunting security gates, the resort occupies over 100 hectares of land and includes an 18 hole championship golf course and three beautiful beaches.

The resort is just five minutes away from Praslin's airport and limousine transfer can be arranged by the hotel. Alternatively the resort has a helipad for helicopter transfer from Mahé's International Airport.

The main building of the hotel hugs the hillside and overlooks the two coves of Grand Anse Kerlan and Petit Anse Kerlan. Across the ocean lie the nature reserve islands of Cousin and Cousine and on the horizon is the main island of Mahé. The main lobby overlooks the large swimming pool which has been built around the natural granite rock formations and spills down into three levels leading to the sandy beach of Petit Anse Kerlan. Around the pool is an informal eating area open for lunch and occasionally for a romantic candlelit dinner. The main bar is to the right of the lobby area and has a relaxed atmosphere with sunken bar and easy chairs instead of bar stools. The décor is that of wood and stone with African style prints and accessories.

The resort has three restaurants, the main dining area, The Legend, a Beach Restaurant, open for lunch only, and an Italian eatery, The Sea Horse, which is adjacent to the golf course and overlooks the 11th hole. There are also four bars, including a beach bar set on the rocky peninsula between the two beaches of Anse Kerlan and in the perfect location to sip and sundowner and watch a tropical sunset.

Lemuria has 88 suites, spread out within a stone's throw of the beach. Each suite has air-conditioning, spacious living area, bedroom and bathroom, TV, VCD, CD and internet facilities. The senior suites have additional living area and sofa beds for children as well as a Jacuzzi and wide sundeck.

This is a resort for the whole family: surprisingly for a top notch 5 star resort, Lemuria has many facilities for children and welcomes families. There is a Turtle Club for children aged between 4 and 12 which supervises and organises activities for children throughout the day as well as a babysitting service in the evening. There is an extensive Health and Beauty Spa featuring a range of massage techniques, beauty treatments, hair salon, sauna and Jacuzzi. Nearby is a fully equipped and air conditioned gym open from 7am to 9pm.

The sports facilities at Lemuria are the most extensive in Seychelles. The truly spectacular golf course has been landscaped around the hills in this corner of Praslin with views to take your breath away. A golf pro is on hand to provide lessons and it is hoped that major tournaments will be played here in the future. Non-residents of the hotel can play here for a daily green fee and clubs can be hired. There are also two tennis courts with a tennis pro who can teach adults and children. Plus all the water sports activities one would expect in Seychelles: a PADI 5-star dive centre, sailing, kayaks, windsurfing, pedalos and so on.

One would expect, from the description, that Lemuria is an all-inclusive resort. But it isn't. All guests come on a Bed and Breakfast basis, and not all of the facilities on offer are free to hotel guests. So come prepared—your wallet could be seriously hit! The advantage of this, however, is that guests here do not feel obliged to eat at the resort's restaurants and can enjoy exploring the rest of Praslin and visiting other eating places whenever they wish.

Lemuria is large and grand, seriously swanky, with some 400 staff on hand to

Health Spa at the Lemuria Resort on Praslin

look after their privileged guests. This is a resort for families and couples who can make use of and enjoy the many facilities this resort has to offer.

HOTEL L'ARCHIPEL, Anse Gouvernement
PO Box 586, Praslin. Tel: 232040/232242. Fax: 232072. Email: archipel@seychelles.net. Website: www.larchipel.com
This small and exclusive Seychelles owned hotel is set in a tropical gardens on the hillside overlooking the secluded sandy beach of Anse Gouvernement.

The 30 rooms vary from deluxe to suites, all overlooking the sea and are spacious and elegantly decorated. A colonial style building houses the reception, bar and main restaurant. Lunch and dinner is served à la carte, with a gourmet dinner served in the main restaurant. The fresh seafood here is highly recommended.

The hotel has massage and gym facilities and offers snorkelling, windsurfing canoeing and boat trips to the nearby St.Pierre Island all free of charge to guests. Deep-sea fishing and diving excursions can be arranged upon request.

(clockwise from top left) *Lemuria's golf course has been voted one of the most beautiful in the world; the hotel's pool cascades into three levels; wind-swept towering palms complete the tropical-island paradise ambience; the thatched chalets at the resort face towards the sandy cove of Anse Kerlan*

(left, from top down) *North Island Resort's inclusion of natural tones and elements creates an harmonious interior decor; while away a relaxing evening with tic-tac-toe; warm interior lighting complements twilight's magnificent palette of hues;* (below) *Seychelles sunsets set passions ablaze*

Small Island Resorts

Accommodation away from Mahé and Praslin is more basic. Small hotels or island lodges have that 'back to nature' feel about them, often made of wood with palm thatched roofs. The emphasis is on simplicity rather than luxury. But staying at these lodges is far from 'roughing it'. The cuisine is excellent and the atmosphere totally different from any large hotel: sleeping in a small thatched chalet and listening to the waves lap on the beach, just a few yards from your door, gives you a wonderful experience of the Tropics.

ALPHONSE ISLAND RESORT
PO Box 1273, Victoria, Seychelles. Tel: (248) 229 030. Head Office: (248) 323220.
Fax: (248) 229034. Head Office: (248) 322026. Email: alphonse@seychelles.net.
Website: www.alphonse-resort.com
Alphonse Island Resort combines tropical five star luxury on one of the most remote and spectacular coralline atolls in the Seychelles archipelago. The resort was built after it was discovered that the island had the best salt water fly fishing in the world, but to call this resort a fishing lodge would be to do it a great injustice. Visitors here come not just for the fly fishing but also for the best diving in Seychelles, deep sea fishing and for simply staying in a luxurious resort on a remote tropical island for a relaxing get-away-from-it-all break.

The island resort has 25 traditional thatched A-frame chalets, built on stilts for tropical coolness. Each individual chalet has air conditioning, a sumptuous bathroom with Jacuzzi and an outdoor but private shower. The bedroom/living room has a king size double bed, satellite TV with around five channels, telephone and mini bar. Each chalet has a verandah facing the ocean, including the five suites, which additionally have an outdoor Jacuzzi a multi function shower cabin and large living area with sofa beds for children.

The Bijoutier restaurant is a covered courtyard area overlooking the reef and hotel swimming pool. There are set menus for lunch and dinner with a choice of either seafood or meat as the main course. As in the rest of Seychelles the seafood is highly recommended. Although the menus and meal times are set there is a great flexibility on offer for individual needs, including dietary requirements or the alternative of taking a picnic lunch to the beach or being served dinner in your chalet.

The hotel also has an all-day bar, a conference room equipped for hosting a maximum of 20 people and a beauty salon with a Swiss Masseuse who offers a variety of relaxing body massages and facials.

(previous pages) *Praslin awaits the rising sun*

There is also a wide variety of water sports facilities on offer such as canoes, windsurfers, sailing boats and pedalos. Excursions to nearby islands are available by boat, including the island of Bijoutier and St Francois where the bird watching is tremendous: Alphonse's eco guide, Francis Payet, accompanies the tour and can explain the many sea birds on the islands, including, if you are lucky, some rare migrant species. Francis also conducts walks on the reef, where guests can view the many colourful fish and shells, including good views of sharks and manta rays. For those that wish to see the marine life under the waves, there is a PADI 5* Dive Centre here which can take beginners to advanced divers out in the lagoon to view the myriads of ocean life here including a large number of green turtles. All dives here are drift dives, but suitable for beginners. There is also a wreck dive: the remains of a French coal steamer *Doile*, who sank on the reef in 1873. Other dive sites include wall dives of up to 35 metres where divers can see coral hideaways, and fish such as huge groupers, turtles, stingrays, and sharks. Dive instructors on Alphonse have recorded over 600 species of fish in these waters, a higher number of fish than any other dive site in Seychelles. Diving here has unfortunately been overshadowed by the fact that the waters around Alphonse offer the world's best salt water fly fishing, but the diving here too is the best in Seychelles and probably one of the best dive sites in the world for the abundance of corals and unspoiled marine life. Divers should note too, that the 'bleaching' effect of the weather system El Nino on the coral reefs of Seychelles did not affect the corals off Alphonse.

Each guest on Alphonse is given their own mountain bike for the duration of their stay, so they can explore the island more easily, lazily cycling down the sandy paths and across the island runway to explore deserted beaches, an old cemetery complete with pirate grave, and green tropical forest full of strange sounding medicinal plants like the Fish Poison Tree, otherwise known as the Yam Yam. Island tours, including a tour of medicinal plants, pre-breakfast island walks and moonlit walks to see turtles hatching on the beaches, can all be arranged with the resort's eco guide. The turtle hatching season is from December to late March.

Alphonse, unlike some of the other luxury hotels in Seychelles, does not try to impress with oriental styling: it is unashamedly a Seychelles style resort, and is all the better for it. This is the place for the ultimate tropical island getaway for those that enjoy deserted, pristinely white beaches, nature walks, diving and fishing. The best time to visit the island is from mid September to mid June. Alphonse is situated on the edge of the cyclone belt, and although tropical storms are infrequent, when they do occur they are spectacular.

Alphonse has the ultimate outer-island resort, combining luxurious accommodation with superb diving and fly-fishing in and around its spectacular lagoon

BIRD ISLAND LODGE
Tel: 224925. Fax: 225074. Website: www.birdislandseychelles.com

Bird Island Lodge is a comfortable, relaxed small hotel set on a Robinson Crusoe island whose bird population is vastly greater than its human inhabitants. From May to October, part of the island is home to millions of nesting sooty terns and with a year-round population of at least 20 other bird species; it is an ornithologist's heaven. It is also an important nesting site for turtles and boasts the world's largest land tortoise, Esmerelda who is in fact a he, not a she (but is probably too old to care).

The lodge has 24 large fan-cooled wooden bungalows: there are no locks on the doors here and no outside lights, for fear of disturbing the many nesting turtles (guests must find their way around outside by torchlight in the evenings). On arrival, guests are given guidelines on how to holiday on Bird Island without disturbing the wildlife.

The bungalows have four-poster beds surrounded by mosquito nets, with ceiling fans inside the canopy. Each bungalow has a living area, private verandah, large bathroom and shower. The island's natural water is slightly saline and, while safe to drink, is not particularly good to taste and leaves the skin feeling slightly sticky after washing. Flasks can be filled with spring water from the bar for drinking, teeth cleaning and face washing.

The food here is an unpretentious blend of Kreol and International fare, usually served as a buffet. This is the island for bird lovers, turtle watchers and for those who enjoy simply relaxing on a true desert island. Its beaches are whiter than white and so dazzling that sunglasses are an absolute necessity. Bird Island, situated on the Seychelles Bank, also offers excellent big-game fishing and bottom fishing excursions. A lounge with billiard table and a library serve for the very occasional wet afternoon.

Bird Island Lodge remains a true Seychelles treasure: a simple, tranquil, desert-island holiday escape

BIRD ISLAND
SEYCHELLES

SAINTE ANNE'S RESORT AND SPA

Saint Anne Island. Tel: (248) 292000. Fax: (248) 292002. Email: res.sa@bchot.com

The Sainte Anne's Resort has 87 rooms set in beachfront villas, spread along the small island's two main beaches, which form part of the Marine National Park and are an excellent starting place for snorkelling on the coral reefs.

Each spacious villa has a bedroom, lounge, bathroom and walk-in wardrobe. They also each have an outside shower and private garden. The 3-bedroom Royal Villa also has a private pool and terrace.

Sainte Anne's Resort has a private wharf on the island and transfer from the airport on Mahé is by a 15-minute boat transfer, or by helicopter. A transfer service on and off the island for guests is available and there are bicycle and electric cart hire at the resort to enable guests to easily explore Ste Anne island.

There are two restaurants, a boutique, business centre and a conference room. Water sport facilities are available, including diving, glass bottom boat trips, windsurfing and fishing. The resort also has two tennis courts. This resort also features a Clarins health spa.

COUSINE ISLAND RESORT

Registered address: PO Box 67404, Bryanton, 2021, South Africa
Tel: 27 11 463 3702. Fax: 27 11 463 1225
Email: info@indianoceanislands.net. Website: www.indianoceanislands.net

Sustainable, eco-friendly tourism, where guests can stay on a private nature retreat is what Cousine is all about. With four individual Old French Colonial style villas, there is a maximum of only ten guests on the island at any one time, which gives the hotel a very private and personal atmosphere.

Each villa is positioned to ensure maximum privacy, just 30m from the island's main beach. The villas are much larger than suites at other luxury resorts and have a small kitchen with tea and coffee making facilities, fridge with complimentary soft drinks, and an ice making machine. The living area has a dining table, so that guests can have the option of being served some meals in the privacy of their own villa rather than at the hotel's dining room. There is a large screen TV with full satellite service and French windows that open to a sundeck and sea views. The bedroom has a king size double bed with mosquito netting, a writing desk and a dressing area. The bathroom is huge with a Jacuzzi, twin head shower and a private outdoor shower. Guests have an option of using air conditioning or just ceiling fans in each villa.

Arrival is by helicopter transfer only, which gives a panoramic view of the island before touching down on a small grassy helipad close to the beach. Guests are taken to the hotel by buggy and there is no formal registration process, as most of the details will have already been taken care of when booking. The island's Environmental Manager greets guests as they arrive and briefs them on the island and it's wildlife. Nature walks can be arranged by request, particularly to view the daily feeding of the rare Magpie Robins and turtle hatchings when they occur. On arrival at the villa, guets will find a complimentary bottle of champagne on ice and a bowl of tropical fruits.

The hotel staff here are exceptionally hospitable and enjoy evening drinks with the guests in the bar in the evening, as well as hosting occasional soirees on the northern ridge of the island where guests can enjoy a drink and watch the magnificent sunsets on the horizon behind the island of Mahé. The food here is exceptionally good, and although there are set meals, guests can fill in a questionnaire in advance to notify the hotel about their individual likes and dislikes and any dietary needs which will be taken into consideration by the chef. The service is very personal and there are no fixed meal times—guests here can choose what where and how they wish to take their meals with impunity.

From each villa there is a small path and wooden steps down to the beach, which you are asked to keep to, in order to protect turtle nesting sites. The beach is a fine coral sand and although the sea can be rough along the coast, it is safe for swimming. There is also a swimming pool beside the restaurant and bar. Binoculars are placed in each villa, together with a bird watching guide, to enable guests to walk along the beach and around the island, and enjoy some rare bird watching. There is also a library with internet facilities and a collection of films on video for rainy days. Beyond this, Cousine is not about recreational activities—it is simply about peace, privacy, tranquility and nature. There is no dive centre, beauty salon or arranged excursions (although trips to other islands can be arranged if guests wish to go). A holiday experience on Cousine is mostly for the experience of living on a tropical nature reserve; sunbathing or walking on the beach, listening only to the sound of the sea and the calls of the birds. Total relaxation.

(opposite page) *Ste Anne's Resort lies within a national marine park and is close to the main island of Mahé*
(this page) *Ste Anne's chalets are set within palm gardens overlooking the marine park*

Cousin and Cousine islands lie off the coast of Praslin

Cousine Island Resort's bungalows are well spread out across the island's wide sandy beach (left middle & bottom) *Each of Cousine's bungalows offers privacy and comfort on this nature-reserve island*

CERF ISLAND RESORT
PO Box 1071, Victoria, Mahe, Seychelles
Tel: (248) 294500. Fax: (248) 294511. Email: info@cerf-resort.com. Website: www.cerf.sc
This small elegant 5 star resort offers just 12 private lodges on the small island of Cerf, a ten minute boat trip from the main island of Mahé. The lodges have three distinct room types: there are five Timber Lodges, four Hillside Lodges and three Hideaway Lodges.

Each air-conditioned lodge offers a large living space, bedroom, two large bathrooms, dining table and chairs on the balcony for in-room dining, a sun deck with loungers, satellite TV and DVD players, tea and coffee making facilities and a mini bar. In addition the Hideaway Lodges have four-poster beds, a half open-air bathroom and a private sun garden.

24 hour in-room dining is available but there is also the '1756' restaurant at the resort that has a commanding view of the ocean and marine park. There is a cocktail bar and a pool bar that also serves daytime snacks. Picnic lunches can be requested.

Facilities at the resort include a private mini spa which offers massages and beauty treatments, an outside Jacuzzi; an internet room, business facilities and a wide range of water sports equipment including kayaks, pedal boats, windsurfers and snorkelling equipment. Excursions to other islands, big game fishing trips, sailing and diving can also be arranged through the resort.

The lodges are close to the beach but surrounded by lush tropical vegetation. A pathway from the lodges leads guests to a panoramic Marine Park viewpoint and a stream crosses the resort, ending in a small private lake.

This is high glamour, romantic island luxury; a resort ideal for weddings and honeymoons. It does not have a strict 'couples only' policy, however children are only accepted over the age of seven when staying with parents.

Cerf Island Resort is hidden within the lush vegetation of this small island, situated within the Ste Anne's National Marine Park, off the eastern coast of Mahé

TAJ DENIS ISLAND RESORT

PO Box 404, Victoria, Seychelles. Tel: (248) 321143. Fax: (248) 321010.
Email: denis@seychelles.net

Taj Denis Island has 24 wooden roofed air-conditioned 'cottages' (too big to be called 'chalets') with sea facing verandahs and private courtyards, and one suite. Each cottage has a large bedroom, with romantic four-poster beds surrounded by tropical netting and a living area. There is a giant sized bathroom with a shower for two and in each private courtyard is a further shower for washing sand off from the beach or simply to enjoy the experience of showering under the stars. Each of the cottages are spread out along the beach, close to the main reception area and dining room of the hotel, in gardens of coconut palms and casuarinas trees, where fairy terns and brown noddys are so tame visitors can walk right under their nesting places.

The resort offers 'barefoot luxury': the décor throughout is tropical and relaxed, with wicker furniture and driftwood forming natural pieces of art; the tall roof and ceiling fans in the main lobby make it a cool, elegant meeting place. The restaurant serves a wide range of cuisine including a mix of Kreol and gourmet food.

There are a wide range of facilities on offer including tennis, water sports, diving, Big game fishing, fly fishing, sunset cruises and day trips to neighbouring islands. Plans to develop a gym and beauty salon are underway as well as Internet and telephone facilities in every cottage, which can be optional according to client request.

The 100 strong island resort staff (about four staff per cottage) are friendly and helpful and the service here is exceptional: the fact that more than 60 per cent of bookings to the resort comes from repeat visitors, including many celebrities, speaks for itself.

Denis Island is at its best from mid October to mid December, where there is little wind, the sea is calm and the temperature is around 26 to 29 degrees Celsius. The island can be reached from Mahé by an Air Seychelles charter flight four times a week, taking approximately 35 minutes. Private plane and helicopter charter can also be arranged by request.

Taj Denis Island is now being managed by Indian Hotel chain Taj Resorts and improvements to the resort facilities are likely in the future.

DESROCHES ISLAND LODGE
PO Box 356, Victoria, Seychelles. Tel: 229003. Fax: 229002.
Email: 7south@seychelles.net

The Desroches island resort, which re-opened in mid 2003 after an extensive renovation, has 20 junior suites in double sea-facing chalets on this stunningly beautiful island at the heart of the Amirantes group.

Two restaurants provide gourmet cuisine using fresh ingredients from the ocean and from the hotel's own vegetable garden on the island. There is also an informal eating area underneath thatched tables in a sandy area between the swimming pool and the beach where guests can enjoy evening barbecues or an informal lunch. The resort features a large swimming pool, floodlit tennis court, petanque (bowls) and a golf practice range. There is also an indoor games room with a snooker table and a business centre with fax and internet facilities. Canoes, pedalos and laser mini sails are available to hire and excursions to nearby islands in the Amirantes group, as well as deep sea fishing trips and fly fishing for bone fish can be arranged by request.

Many visitors to Desroches go for the excellent scuba diving: there is a PADI 5* certified dive centre at the hotel, with experienced guides who can take you to the superb dive sites to be discovered in the waters around the island including the famous 'Desroches Drop'. The centre also offers PADI dive courses for beginners, and even those new to diving can experience the thrill of seeing a huge variety of underwater life at the stretch of sea known as 'The Aquarium' which can be reached either by boat or from the beach close to the lighthouse. This area is also excellent for snorkelling trips. There are no real roads on Desroches, just tracks, and the island can easily be explored on bicycle, which can be hired from the hotel.

The beach by the hotel is at its best during the northwest monsoon, while the beaches on the other side of the island are better for swimming during the southeast monsoon, in particular the fabulous Bombe Bay beach.

Desroches can be reached by taking a one hour flight from Mahé, which departs five times a week. This is an island for those that wish to dive and fish or just enjoy the exquisite lassitude of a remote tropical island. A holiday combining Desroches with Alphonse island can be arranged through booking agent 7 Degrees South. Their website with full details of the package is at www.7degreessouth.net.

Desroches Island Resort is centred around the pool and beach

FÉLICITÉ ISLAND
C/o La Digue Island Lodge, La Digue
Tel: (248) 234233/234232. Fax: (248) 234100. Website: www.ladigue.sc
Located 4km from La Digue, this island can be reached either by taking a 20 minute boat trip from La Digue, or by 25 minute helicopter transfer from Mahé.

The private island lodge caters exclusively for a minimum of two to a maximum of eight guests in two old colonial bungalows, beautifully and elegantly restored from the original French plantation days of the 18th century, with air-conditioning and staff on hand.

The lodge has a reputation for excellent service and cuisine and guests here can enjoy pampered privacy and comfort. Félicité's beautiful beach at La Penice is superb for both swimming and snorkelling and other facilities on offer include water sports, fishing and sailing.

Félicité Private Lodge is associated with La Digue Island Lodge, which handles all reservations for this exclusive island paradise.

Felicité Island offers the rare privilege of a 'castaway' holiday experience:
an untouched island experience all to yourself

(top) *The shallows surrounding Coco Island are perfect for a relaxed snorkel*
(bottom) *Taking in Coco Island's grandeur from Felicite Island*

FRÉGATE ISLAND PRIVATE

PO Box 330, Victoria, Mahé. Tel: (248) 282282. Fax: (248) 282285
Reservations: Egerlanderstrabe 47. D-63069 Offenbach, Germany
Tel: 00 49 69 83 83 76 35. Fax: 00 49 69 83 83 76 36
Email: unique.experience@debitel.net   Website: www.frégate.com.

This resort came about from a German millionaire's dreams of owning an island and building one of the world's most exclusive resorts incorporating the highest facilities with the natural wild beauty of the island. His dream became a reality with the opening of Frégate Island Private. This is a 'Swiss Family Robinson Win the Lottery' holiday experience, and is listed as being one of the world's most expensive hotels, with rates from around $1,800 per night. Celebrity guests who have stayed here include Madonna, Bill and Melinda Gates, Brad Pitt and Jennifer Aniston.

There are 16 exclusive villas, for a maximum of 40 guests, built along the cliff top overlooking the Indian Ocean. Each villa has a bedroom and separate living room with a wooden decked terrace in between the two rooms. Inside the décor is hand carved wood, Thai silk and Egyptian cotton. Rare antiques and Asian artwork are included to give each villa it's own distinctive atmosphere. Each villa also has its own outside jacuzzi and day bed as well as a petrol driven buggy to explore the island.

The Frégate House restaurant serves the highest quality à la carte gourmet cuisine, using freshly caught seafood and fruit and vegetables grown from the island's own plantation. Once or twice a week a more informal Creole and East African Buffet is served from the Plantation House Restaurant and occasionally there are also barbecues served at the marina. Guests can also order a picnic lunch if they wish to spend a day on one of Frégate's breathtaking beaches: staff from the hotel will bring the picnic and serve to the guests wherever they wish. There is also 24-hour room service.

Frégate Island can be reached from Mahé either by taking a 25 minute helicopter ride, or just 12 minutes by light plane. As the helicopter lands on the island's grassy airstrip, first impressions are of the natural beauty of Frégate: a green hilly island, surrounded by clear blue sea and with dozens of white fairy terns and tropic birds circling above and around the coconut palms. On arrival guests are taken from the airstrip by buggy to the reception for a welcome drink and registration. The décor of the Frégate House reception and restaurant is one of tropical Asian elegance with carved mahogany and rattan furniture and water gardens. All the buildings are beautifully thatched and there are hand carved and pained screens and tropical flowers everywhere. I loved the Indonesian puppets in the ladies loo!

The swimming pool is sculptured around granite boulders above the beach with water cascading from the main pool to a small children's pool set in the rocks below. The beach below the hotel, accessed by a number of steps, has sun loungers and chairs with staff on hand to serve drinks or snacks throughout the day. Villas 1 to 6 are closer to the beach, and more suited to families with children, but there is no direct beach access from any of the villas. This is a resort for people who want more from a holiday than just sun and sea; it is designed with nature walks, sailing and water sports in mind. Above all it is a place of complete privacy and celebrities come here knowing they will not be hounded by the paparazzi.

Every morning at breakfast, guests can read the 'Frégate News', which give details of weather forecasts, tides and any activities planned for the day. There are excursions to nearby islands, nature walks to see Frégate's rare birds, or turtle hatchings from the beach at night. The island has a fully equipped 5-star PADI dive centre and three boats which can be chartered for fishing or sailing trips. There is also a gym, a library with internet facilities, a children playroom and each villa has a wide screen TV with satellite channels, DVD and CD player for occasional wet days. Most of the main beaches have sun loungers or hammocks provided for relaxation, and Anse Victorin has a ready supply of cool water in a cool box, much needed when there are over a hundred steps to reach the beach from the main path!

Guests here are encouraged to explore the island for themselves. There are 150 staff living on the island from 17 countries, working at the resort and the plantation, and they will be pleased to give guided tours of the plantation and hydroponic farm there. The resorts Eco Guide, South African Steve Hill, who has been actively involved with the wildlife conservation on Frégate for several years, also gives tours of the island and can explain the unique island eco-system, as well as tell a few tall pirate stories.

Frégate Island Private is the holiday hideaway for wealthy nature lovers who enjoy all the luxuries of a five star resort and fine food and service in a location that combines tropical nature with totally pristine coral beaches for a sublime island experience.

Please note that bookings to Frégate Island Private should not be made directly from the island: all enquiries and reservations should be made through their booking office in Germany.

(above) *A tropic bird flies down to its ground-level nest on Bird Island*
(right) *On Desroches Island, visitors can explore the many palm-lined paths by bicycle or on foot*

NORTH ISLAND RESORT
PO Box 1176, Victoria, Seychelles.
South African headquarters: PO Box 5219. Rivonia 2128. South Africa
Tel: (248) 293100. Fax: (248) 293150
Email: info@north-island.com Website: www.north-island.com
This resort is just so exclusive it would not deign to invite a mere guidebook writer such as myself to take a look! However, according to information provided by the resort, it has eleven 'handcrafted' reed thatched villas in a South African style. Each villa has two air-conditioned bedrooms, bathrooms with a marble bath, a living area, kitchen, study and private whirlpool. There is a central dining room at the resort, a library, pool and gym as well as a health spa. A full butler service offers optional in-villa dining and picnics on secluded beaches.

Facilities available on this very private island resort include diving, fishing, kayaking and yacht charter. A dive centre also offers all facilities for novice and experienced divers to experience the many superb dive-sites close to the island. Each villa has its own island buggy, designed to look like a miniature 4X4. Mountain bikes are also available for hire.

The North Island Resort is committed to nature conservation on the island and guests can read about their programmes within the library as well as attending slide shows and talks offered on a wide range of ecological topics.

An eco-friendly and luxurious resort, for the very rich, and the very private.

LA RESERVE
Anse Petite Cour, Praslin
Tel: 248 232211. Fax: 248 232166
Email: lrmk@seychelles.net
Website: www.lareserve-seychelles.com
This hotel gained some notoriety in the past, when the late rebel-rousing actor Oliver Reid stayed here while filming Castaway. In a later court case it was alleged that he pushed a crew member over the hotel jetty, which houses the restaurant, and into the shallow water (and corals) below. Sadly, Oliver Reid is no longer with us, but the jetty and restaurant is still there, and it is a beautiful place to sit, eat, drink and watch the sun set over the ocean. The hotel has 32 rooms and a swimming pool with swim-up bar and grill.

La Reserve nestles between the rocks and forests of Praslin, with a dining area that stretches out into the sea

North Island has an African back-to-nature approach that blends rustic safari-style architecture with modern luxury

North Island chalets blend well into their exotic backdrop in this eco-luxury resort

Silhouette Island Lodge has a romantic back-to-nature feel, with timber-framed chalets stretched along the quiet sandy bay; (main picture) *Tranquil Anse Mondon, at the northern tip of Silhouette, is just a few kilometres hike from the lodge along the island's well-worn footpaths*

The Wharf Hotel is close to the airport and overlooks its own marina on the east coast of Mahé

SILHOUETTE ISLAND LODGE

PO Box 608, Victoria. Tel: 224003. Website: www.silhouette-seychelles.com

A 15-minute helicopter flight from Mahé, Silhouette island dominates Mahé's north western horizon, but is home to a quiet resort best suited to nature lovers.

The lodge has 12 spacious and fully equipped timber bungalows set within gardens of unspoiled beauty. The setting is simple but elegant along a wide stretch of sandy beach edged by swaying casuarinas. The reception, bar and restaurant also overlook the ocean.

The lodge has recently been purchased by a hotel group from the Maldives, so improvements and upgrades to this resort are likely to follow. Facilities currently on offer include scuba diving, fishing, hiking, boat excursions and snorkelling. Silhouette is a nature lovers' retreat with awe inspiring mountain trails, unique flora and fauna and home to a tortoise conservation project.

Transfers to the hotel from Mahé are by Helicopter Seychelles and can be arranged when booking accommodation.

THE WHARF HOTEL AND MARINA

Providence, Mahé. Tel: 248 670700. Fax: 248 601700. Email: prodive@seychelles.net

A popular hotel for business visitors, diplomats and airport transfer guests, this hotel is conveniently located a five-minute drive away from both the airport and the capital, Victoria. It is no more functional-but-bland business hotel, but offers elegant and

spacious rooms, in a modern hotel, built in 2002, with stunning views of the marina and the small islands that are scattered around the Ste Anne National Marine Park.

There is a four-bedroom penthouse suite and 15 luxury rooms, two restaurants, swimming pool and a PADI dive centre. The marina has berthing facilities for 60 boats.

Marrying in Seychelles

Seychelles is very popular for honeymoons and package wedding holidays. While it may seem terribly romantic to be 'married in paradise', combining wedding and honeymoon amidst the lush beauty of the Tropics, the reality can be less idyllic. For the bride, stumbling out into the bright sunshine, sweating out photographs on the beach in full white wedding gear, surrounded by curious tourists in bikinis, it can seem somewhat absurd.

However, by being selective about the marriage package you choose it can work well. The trick is to opt for the more expensive hotels and make sure that you are not just one of many weddings on one particular day, to avoid that conveyor belt feeling. Some tour operators actually block book the registrar on a particular afternoon to avoid just that. This worked better when there was just one registrar, but as the popularity of weddings has increased, there are now several registrars. But you can check at your hotel, through your tour operator, to make sure yours is the only ceremony that afternoon.

Try to chose a secluded spot for the ceremony and photographs, avoiding the crowds around the hotel swimming pool or on Beau Vallon beach. L'Islette is popular, offering

Just married on La Digue

the necessary privacy and charm, but you will need suitable clothing to climb in and out of the small boat that takes you across to the island. Otherwise Praslin and La Digue on the whole offer better wedding deals than Mahé, mainly because they are smaller.

Clothing is important. A synthetic or even satin type wedding dress with all the trimmings will be uncomfortable and feel out of place. Opt for something cool, loose fitting and simple. Cotton is best and, if the wedding is to be on the beach, a short dress is far more practical. If travelling on Air Seychelles, wedding dresses can be hung in the cabin if placed in a special suit carrier and handed to the stewardess when boarding the plane.

The bride's hair can be done by the hotel hairdresser or by any of the hairdressers in Victoria. If you have long hair, it can be plaited very prettily and interwoven with frangipani flowers, which are the traditional decorations for weddings. For the groom a lightweight suit is best; something that will be cool but special enough for the occasion.

The wedding itself is a simple civil ceremony, usually taking place in the open air, weather permitting. The registrar will conduct the marriage, which will be recognised under British and European laws. Sometimes local musicians will serenade you on your way and the venue for the ceremony and reception is always beautifully decorated with palm leaves and tropical flowers.

If you require a church wedding, a service of blessing in addition to the civil ceremony can be arranged, although most travel operators may try to put you off the idea, because it involves extra paperwork without any extra profit for them. It is not possible to simply have a church wedding ceremony, as this is not recognised under Seychelles law. Anglican churches on the island will happily conduct a blessing service, which is free, although they do ask for a small donation. It is also possible to have a blessing service in one of the Roman Catholic churches, but this will need to be arranged well in advance.

To visit Seychelles on a wedding package, it is recommended to book at least 12 weeks in advance (or longer if you want a church service). You will also need to organise the legal part of the wedding in advance and to do this certain legal documents are needed, such as birth certificates, passports, details of name, address and occupation of both parties and their parents and, if previously married, the decree absolute or death certificate of the former spouse.

In addition, Seychelles has a minimum residency requirement of three days, which must be met before the wedding can take place. You must come prepared to spend at least one day of your holiday finalising arrangements: meeting the registrar, choosing flowers or the location for your wedding.

There is a supplementary cost for wedding packages which can be arranged through the travel agent you book with. The supplementary cost varies with the package you choose, but will pay for extras such as the registrar's fee; marriage licence; services of the best man, if required; a simple wedding cake and administration changes. Extras, such as bridal bouquet, buttonholes, photographs or video recording can cost more. It is wise to check thoroughly when booking your holiday about which details are included.

Many of the larger hotels offer special incentives for honeymooners, so if you are travelling to Seychelles on your honeymoon be sure to mention it when booking.

Newlyweds adopt Seychelles style with their choice of wedding car, Mahé

Restaurant Guide

Mahé is the island with the best choice of restaurants—some will serve traditional Kreol food, but most will offer a curious mixture of Kreol-influenced 'international cuisine'. Vegetarians be warned: if you can't eat fish you could be in for a hard time, as most Seychellois have never even heard of vegetarianism, let alone sympathise with it. Restaurants are usually open from 19.00 until 23.00 Monday to Saturday. Some, especially beach restaurants, will open for lunch as well. At weekends it is best to book in advance.

Lunchtime in Victoria, Mahé

KAZ ZANANA, Revolution Avenue
Tel: 324150
On the outskirts of Victoria on the road leading to Beau Vallon is a restored traditional wooden Kreol house which is a charming setting for a cafe and art gallery. Open daily except Sundays it offers tea, coffee and patisseries and a lunchtime menu of meals and snacks. In the evening it has a bar service and often has live music and other entertainment specials. Art exhibitions are also frequently held here.

THE PIRATES ARMS, Independence Avenue

Tel: 225001

This is still the best known watering hole in town. The Pirates Arms offers drinks, snacks and meals during the day and evenings. It is a popular meeting spot, offering a cooling place to sit under the ceiling fans on its wide, shaded verandah overlooking the street. It can get busy, particularly on a Saturday morning and service can be on the slow side. As well as the main restaurant there is a small bar and an amusement centre.

THE NEWS CAFÉ, Trinity House, Albert Street

On the first floor of Trinity House, this daytime café offers a good selection of lunchtime meals and snacks, including a wide range of salads and sandwiches. The balcony tables offer a good view of the hustle and bustle of one of Victoria's busiest streets below.

SAM'S PIZZERIA, Francis Rachel Street, Victoria

This Pizzeria can be found by taking the road past the petrol station from the clock tower, and then taking the first flight of stairs on the right. Sam's Pizzeria is next door to the SPACE Internet Café. Sam's is open for daytime and evening meals and has a nice selection of freshly baked pizzas, salads and pasta dishes.

Eating Out on a Budget—Mahé

At most restaurants in Seychelles you can expect to pay around SR200 to SR400 per person for an evening meal with wine. But below are the few places on Mahé where a meal can be bought for less.

THE BAOBAB PIZZERIA, Beau Vallon

Tel: 247167

The pizzeria is on Beau Vallon beach, where two robust Seychelloise mamas bake the pizzas in an open flame fire. The pizzas are huge and the pasta dishes are also good

(left) *A romantic table for two at Desroches Island Resort*
(above) *Creative cocktails at Desroches Island*

value for money. On some Friday and Saturday nights there is live music. An average meal of a starter (smoked sail fish is recommended), pizza or pasta and a soft drink or a Seybrew would cost around SR100 per person.

THE BOAT HOUSE, Beau Vallon
Tel: 247898
Every evening the Boat House at Beau Vallon offers what must be the best value three course fish buffet on the island, serving a selection of freshly caught fish (during the day The Boat House organises big game fishing and excursions), salads and pasta dishes. An extremely popular eating place, booking is advisable to avoid disappointment.

LE CANTON CHINESE RESTAURANT, Berjaya Beau Vallon Beach Resort
Tel: 257141
One of the three restaurants at the Berjaya Beau Vallon Beach resort, Le Canton offers lunchtime and evening à la carte and set menus at reasonable prices. There is a wide assortment of Chinese cuisine, specialising in dishes from the Szechuan region of China.

MARIE-ANTOINETTE, St Louis
Tel: 266222
A traditional Kreol restaurant, set in a colourfully refurbished wooden plantation style house just outside Victoria, on the St Louis road leading to Beau Vallon. Marie-Antoinette's offers a set evening menu for around SR150 per person. This is a good introduction to traditional Seychelles cuisine, including tec tec soup, parrot fish fritters, Kreol fish curry and tropical fruit for dessert. Often busy at weekends, it is best to reserve a table in advance.

THE MAHEK INDIAN RESTAURANT
The Coral Strand Hotel, Beau Vallon.
Tel: (248) 247036
The best Indian restaurant in Seychelles—actually the only Indian restaurant in Seychelles, but the food is excellent! Housed in the Coral Strand Hotel on the edge of Beau Vallon Beach, the Mahek is air conditioned with plenty of Indian ambience. It has a good selection of mainly north Indian cuisine, combining chicken, lamb, vegetable and seafood dishes. The tandoori dishes here are a particular speciality. At weekends The Mahek does get busy, so it is best to book a table in advance.

Catch of the day

Restaurants on Mahé

Most of the high-quality restaurants on Mahé offer a selection of both fish and meat dishes cooked in Kreol and continental styles. Italians seem to be cornering the restaurant market: the two eateries I visit most frequently are both Italian run—La Scala at D'Anzilles and La Perle Noire at Beau Vallon. There is not a huge choice of restaurants on Mahé, but most of the large hotels are open for dinner to non-residents. Hotels with the best culinary reputations are the Plantation Club at Baie Lazare, the Berjaya Beau Vallon Beach Resort (which has three restaurants) and the Berjaya Mahé Beach Hotel. In addition, the Reef Hotel and Golf Club has a rather nice pizzeria and bistro overlooking the swimming pool which is open for lunch and evening meals.

AUBERGE LOUIS XVII, La Louise
Tel: 344411
Situated on the La Misère road, overlooking the St Anne National Marine Park, Auberge Louis XVII is named after the son of King Louis XVI and Queen Marie Antionette of France, who is rumoured to have escaped death during the French revolution to live in Seychelles under an assumed name. The menu is extensive and includes a good selection of seasonal seafood.

AU CAPITAINE ROUGE, Anse à la Mouche
Tel: 371224
This luxurious French restaurant is practically on the beach at Anse à la Mouche, within earshot of the waves lapping the beach in the moonlight. The food is good, although expensive. A typical three course meal on offer would include a shellfish or prawn starter, chicken, steak or fish main course, followed by a good selection of desserts. The cost is about SR250 per person for a three course meal with wine.

LA PERLE NOIRE, Beau Vallon
Tel: 247046
Recommended for its steak and pasta dishes, La Perle Noire is open every evening from 7.00 p.m. This restaurant is run by Italians, and has a good selection of Italian fare but also serves some Kreol dishes. The atmosphere is friendly and unassuming and the service is usually excellent. Reservations are recommended, particularly at weekends.

POMME CANNELLE, Anse aux Pins
Tel: 376155
Pomme Cannelle is situated in the Craft Village on the east coast. The restaurant is in a restored plantation house, with a magical atmosphere and traditional Kreol food. The menu consists largely of fish and shellfish dishes, such as ginger crab and grilled fish in a lime sauce. More unusual Kreol delicacies are also served, like fruit bat

casseroled in red wine and breadfruit soup. The price of a typical three course meal should be about SR200 per person.

LA SCALA, Bel Ombre
Tel: 247535
Another high quality, expensive restaurant with a good reputation. The food is an unusual mixture of Kreol and Italian—try the crab stuffed with home made pasta, the fish soup or the stuffed clams. The restaurant also serves quality steaks, if you are tiring of seafood.

LE CORSAIRE, Bel Ombre
Tel: (248) 247171
For pirates with a taste for the high life: this restaurant is housed in what looks like an olde worlde large pirate boat shed overlooking the sea at the small fishing village of Bel Ombre on the northwest coast of Mahé. It has plenty of romantic atmosphere and the food too is of a very high quality, with the local lobster, when in season, highly recommended. The style of the food is unmistakeably French (even though it is Italian owned) with plenty of seafood in pernod sauces. My particular favourite dish is the lobster in vanilla sauce, but you will have to visit between November and February to eat local lobsters here.

THE ROSE GARDEN, Sans Soucis
Tel: (248) 225308
This small hotel high up on the mountain road of Sans Soucis has an excellent restaurant with an unusual mix of seafood and Thai style cuisine. A very romantic setting, the hotel has extensive rose gardens around the restaurant area and each lady is presented with a single rose at the end of the meal. The Rose Garden also hosts Sunday lunch buffets, but the evening meals are worth driving up the long winding road from Victoria for, particularly for the Thai style duckling.

Restaurants on Praslin

Aside from the many hotels, independent restaurants are few and far between on Praslin, although this may change as the island becomes increasingly popular. Most hotels, however, do open their restaurants to non-residents. There is a pizzeria at the Berjaya Praslin Beach hotel, Maison des Palmes at Grand Anse offers a very reasonably priced set evening menu, the food at La Reserve at Anse Petite Cour is more expensive and usually a la carte, as is the restaurants at L'Archipel and, the most expensive of them all, The Lemuria Resort.

BON BON PLUME, Anse Lazio
Tel: 232136
Another isolated eatery, Bon Bon Plume is by the beach at Anse Lazio, but the setting is full of romantic atmosphere and the mainly seafood menu is of an excellent standard. House specials include fish, lobster and a variety of fruit sorbets. An evening meal for two with wine would cost around SR300, but it is more attractive and less expensive as a lunchtime venue.

LA GOULUE RESTAURANT, Cote d'Or, Praslin
Tel: 232232
This small restaurant in the main resort area of Praslin is open for evening Kreol meals with plenty of fish and curries.

CAFE DES ARTS, Côte d'Or
Tel: 232131
This highly recommended restaurant is in the middle of the Côte d'Or stretch of coast, easily accessible from most of the hotels on Praslin. The style of food is 'gourmet Kreol' with a heavy French influence, but is sensibly priced. An evening meal for two will cost around SR200 per person. The menu changes according to the fresh produce available, but usually includes plenty of fresh fish dishes with rice, crêpes or pasta. Starters include crab bisque or crêpes stuffed with smoked fish; main dishes include a creamy crab curry with coconut milk or a seafood spaghetti.

CAPRI RESTAURANT, Hotel Marechiaro, Praslin
Tel: 233337.
Highly regarded Italian gourmet restaurant at Grand Anse, Praslin. The restaurant menu includes Italian and Kreol cuisine and has been presented with the gastronomic award of the Chaine de Rotisseurs. Lunch is served from 12.00 to 15.00 and dinner from 19.00 to 22.00.

LES ROCHERS, Grosse Roche
Tel: 233034.
A bit off the beaten track, but the excellent menu is worth the extra effort. Les Rochers is at Grosse Roche on the south coast of the island, down a rough potholed road, a 15 minute drive from the Valleé de Mai/Anse Consolation signpost at Grande Anse. The menu offers daily seafood specialities and has an extensive wine list, open for lunch and evening meals. It is best booked in advance, to avoid a disappointing and bumpy drive back on an empty stomach!

TANTE MIMI, Casino des Isles, Praslin
Tel: 232500.
A high quality gourmet restaurant in an impressive colonial style mansion on the outskirts of the Cote d'Or beach resort. Open evenings only the restaurant is on the first floor of the building, above the casino and games room. The menu offers a wide selection of international gourmet dishes with a local seafood flavour. Once a month the restaurant hosts speciality dinner dance evenings with live music. Advance booking is recommended.

Restaurant on La Digue

Zerof Bar and Restaurant, *La Digue. Tel: 234439*
A small friendly eatery in the centre of the island, Zerof specialises in high quality Kreol food. One of the few eating places on the island apart from the hotels, and all the more welcome for that.

Nightlife

By any standards, nightlife in Seychelles is limited. There are a few nightclubs on Mahé and a couple of casinos in hotels. Some hotels put on their own entertainment including live local bands and displays of Sega dancing. There is just one cinema in Seychelles; Deepam's in Albert Street, Victoria which has recently been renovated and upgraded to include air conditioning comfort. This one screen small cinema often shows films at around the same time as they are on general release in Europe as well as the latest Bollywood films from India. There are also a number of video and DVD rental shops around Mahé and Praslin, the best being GR Video at Mare Anglais, near Beau Vallon. Most of the larger hotels have satellite television and a DVD or video film library.

Dancing

Katiolo's nightclub (Tel 375453) is at Anse Faure, on the main eastern coastal road between the International Airport and Anse Royale. Recently renovated, the beachside club now boasts air-conditioning and a large dance floor. As it is the only sizeable nightclub on Mahé it is very popular and always crowded at weekends. There is a strict dress code: no shorts, beachwear or trainers allowed (when pop star Shaggy visited Seychelles he was not allowed in on account of his footwear).

On Praslin there are two nightclubs: **The Dome** at Baie Ste Anne (Tel 232800) and **The Jungle** at Grand Anse (Tel 512683). Both are open for air-conditioned late night dancing at weekends and on public holidays.

Additionally, some hotels have nightclub facilities, including the **Berjaya Beau Vallon Bay Hotel**, and Saturday night dinner dances. However, for most resorts and most certainly for the smaller islands, it is really a question of 'early to bed and early to rise'. Seychelles is most of all a holiday destination where guests will not be woken up by thumping music or by other guests returning in the small hours of the morning. In general, Seychelles remains a fairly sleepy little paradise: the only night noises tend to be dogs barking and the high-pitched call of the fruit bats.

Casinos

There are two casinos on Mahé and one on Praslin. The two Mahé casinos are at the *Plantation Club Hotel* at Baie Lazare on the southeastern side of the island, and the *Berjaya Beau Vallon Beach Resort* in northwestern Mahé. On Praslin the *Casino des Isles* is situated in a colonial neo-classical mansion at Cote d'Or. All three casinos offer rooms designed for classical games, Salon Privé and gaming rooms with slot machines. In Victoria there is also an amusement centre and bar at Oceangate House which is open every day and evening between 10.00 and 2.00 in the morning. *The Pirates Arms* in Victoria also has a smaller games room at the rear of the restaurant.

Romantic Evenings

Sunsets can be spectacular, so for the dedicated romantics a trip to a cocktail bar to watch the sky turn into a riot of tropical colours is an apt choice to begin the evening. The sun sets at around 18.30, whatever time of year, and goes down fast, so make sure you arrive at your chosen sunset venue on time or you will miss it!

Sit on the beach at Beau Vallon as the sun slips down to the west and watch the sky turn red behind the island of Silhouette on the horizon. Cocktails and other drinks can be bought at the beach bar at the Coral Strand Hotel or from the Beach Bar at the Berjaya Beau Vallon Bay Hotel. The cocktail served in a green coconut husk has good novelty value.

The Sunset Beach Hotel, at Glacis on Mahé is, as its name suggests, a good location for sundowners.

On Praslin the hotels along Grand Anse enjoy the best sunsets, along with The Lemuria Resort at Anse Kerlan. Small island resorts often organise champagne sundowners at impressive sunset viewpoints.

Sport

Sport in Seychelles really means water sports, as there is little else, apart from a magnificent golf course on Praslin and the occasional tennis court at some resorts. But there is a huge choice of facilities for scuba diving, snorkelling, sailing, deep sea fishing and, more recently developed as a sport in Seychelles, fly fishing. In order to make the most of the beaches, some safety precautions should be taken.

Careful Swimming

On most beaches in Seychelles, swimming is very safe—you will not need to wear anything to protect your feet, unless you are snorkelling over corals or sharp rocks, and there are very few things to be found in the water that could harm you. The most likely hazard you could come across, especially if you snorkel, are sea urchins. These will only hurt you if you accidentally put your hand (or bare foot) on one; the spines are sharp and will break apart very easily, so are difficult to remove. Stone fish can be deadly—sharp spines on their back can paralyse and even kill, but these are rarely encountered, as they are so good at camouflage they can remain undetected in the rocks or corals. However, if you are snorkelling or diving, or even walking on coral banks exposed by the tide, always wear flippers or plimsolls with thick rubber soles.

Occasionally tiny, newly-hatched jellyfish can be found in calm sea water off Beau Vallon, Anse Royale and Anse Lazio. Some people react more strongly to these than others—although you cannot see the jellyfish, some can feel them as tiny pinpricks on their arms and legs, causing a rash. Other people remain totally impervious to their presence. Usually jellyfish are not around for very long—just a few days, often in April and May. The other fish that can harm you is the lion fish. If you antagonise him—by poking and prodding and generally being unpleasant—he will sting you, which will probably mean a trip to the hospital. It is best to observe quietly from a distance and move away slowly.

Sand flies on some beaches can be unbearable. The main beaches on Mahé and Praslin are regularly sprayed to keep the sand flies at bay, but on some of the smaller islands this is not the case and, if you are allergic to their bites, you can erupt into an angry red rash on your arms and legs. The beaches at Cerf Island are often infested with them and, once they start biting, there's not much you can do about it, other than jump into the water!

Each year in Seychelles there are a number of unnecessary fatalities—mainly due to people swimming when drunk or not paying attention to the warnings against strong currents, which are displayed on some of the beaches. There is only a limited lifeguard service in Seychelles, so you do need to take special care, especially if you are with children or nervous swimmers. Below is a guide to the beaches that are unsafe for swimming at certain times of the year:

Grand Anse, Mahé: Strong southeasterly winds and powerful currents between May and October.

Anse Takamaka, Mahé: Fierce waves and strong currents between May and October.

Intendance, Mahé: Fierce waves make swimming virtually impossible between May and October—do not attempt to go out of your depth because of the strong undertow.

Anse Cocos, La Digue: Strong southeasterly winds and powerful currents between May and October.

Grand and Petite Anse, La Digue: Strong southeasterly winds and powerful currents between May and October.

Anse Kerlan, Praslin: Strong northwesterly winds and powerful currents may be experienced during December and January.

Safe Sunbathing

While on the subject of taking caution, a note on sunbathing. Remember that Seychelles is only four degrees south of the Equator, so the sun is much stronger than most Europeans are used to. Even if you hardly ever burn when on holiday closer to home, it is wise to use high factor sunscreens, especially in the morning and midday sun. When snorkelling or windsurfing always wear a T-shirt to protect your back. On the beach try to stay in the shade for the first few days at least. Overdoing things the first week will simply mean your tan peels off in the second week and taking too much sun on the first day can lead to sunstroke. By taking things slowly, using sunscreens and moisturisers or aftersun lotion, your tan will be darker and last much longer.

(left top) *Anse Cocos, La Digue;* (left bottom) *Anse Source d'Argent, La Digue*
(below) *Anonyme Island*

Diving

The coral reefs surrounding many of the islands in Seychelles contain over 300 species of fish and more than a 100 varieties of coral. The water, particularly in the northwest monsoon season, is calm and clear, offering good constant visibility—often up to 50 yards at average depths of between 60 and 90 feet. The vivid colours of the corals and fish also make for excellent underwater photography.

There are scuba diving schools on Mahé and Praslin, as well as on some of the smaller islands like La Digue and Desroches. On Mahé there is a school at the Coral Strand Hotel on Beau Vallon Bay and at the Northholme Hotel in Glacis. On Praslin, the Praslin Beach Hotel has a diving school, as does the Paradise Hotel.

Most diving schools in Seychelles offer PADI (Professional Association of Diving Instructors) diving courses, from beginners to advanced. This is the American-style course, which is designed to get you out into the water as quickly as possible. All the necessary equipment is provided and the first lesson teaches breathing and safety measures in a hotel swimming pool. An instructor will always be with you and will take you out to the reef in waters that are safe, but enable you to see as much as possible.

A basic PADI session will cost about SR400, including equipment rental. Subsequent accompanied dives will cost about SR250 each. For about SR2,200 you can take a full course for an International PADI Open Water Certificate, which is a four day intensive course, including five theory tutorials, five pool training sessions and four qualifying dives. To apply for a course you must be at least 16, fit, able to swim and have experience of snorkelling. First time divers must complete a medical questionnaire. Pregnant women, epileptics and those on certain medications will not be permitted to dive. If you are unsure, visit your doctor and ask for a fitness certificate before your holiday.

You can book up for a diving course after arriving in Seychelles, either through your hotel or guest house or by visiting or phoning the diving school direct. Experienced divers can rent all the necessary equipment from most of the dive centres. Although the water temperature in the Indian Ocean frequently reaches 29C/84F, wetsuits are worn on deeper dives.

If you are bringing your own equipment, it must work properly and you must dive with a BCD or similar power inflation mechanism. You must also use a contents gauge and bring your log book.

DIVE CENTRES

Most of the Dive Centres in Seychelles offer a PADI 5* service and are members of the Association of Professional Divers Seychelles. All the small island resort Dive Centres, such as Frégate, Alphonse, Desroches and Denis are PADI 5*. In addition to these there are a number of diving schools on Mahé, Praslin and La Digue.

Island Ventures Dive Seychelles. PADI 5* Gold Palm resort. This is the first top PADI dive school rating to be awarded in Seychelles. Highly recommended, Island Ventures welcomes both experienced divers and complete beginners. Offering a variety of dive options and packages as well as PADI and NAUI courses, their multi-lingual staff are all qualified Dive Masters or Instructors. Island Ventures are based at the Berjaya Beau Vallon Bay Hotel. *Tel: 247845. Fax: 247433*

Seychelles Underwater Centre, PADI 5* Centre, Coral Strand Hotel, Beau Vallon, Mahé. *Tel: 247357.* Head Office: *Tel: 345445*

One the best dive centres on Mahé run by British dive veterans in Seychelles, David and Glynnis Rowatt. The main centre is based beside the Coral Strand Hotel on Beau Vallon and offers dives off Mahé and also to the outer islands in the dive boat Indian Ocean Explorer. The Underwater Centre also manages dive centres at the Paradise Sun Hotel on Praslin and at the Northolme Hotel on Mahé.

Big Blue Divers, PADI 5* Centre, Vacoa Village, Mare Anglais.
Tel: 247854/ 248046/ 378121

Le Diable Des Mer, Beau Vallon Beach. *Tel: 247104*

Le Meridien Diving Centre, Barbarons Hotel. *Tel : 378253. Fax: 247433*

The Seashell and Silhouette Cruise Ships also offer diving charter trips and holidays.

Seashell Silhouette Cruises, Shipping House, Victoria. *Tel: 324026*

The following centres also provide diving facilities, but are not members of the APDS and may not operate to their standards:

La Digue Lodge Dive Centre, La Digue Island Lodge, La Digue.
Tel: 234232/3 or 234339.

Pro Diving Seychelles (Pty) Ltd, Plantation Club Hotel, Mahé. *Tel: 361361.*

DIVE CENTRES ON PRASLIN
Cote D'or Octopus Diving, Anse Volbert, Praslin. *Tel: 232350. Fax: 232350*
Savuka Dive/Fishing Centre, Anse bois de Rose, Praslin. *Tel: 233900. Fax: 233919*
Scubamania Diving Centre, Hotel Marechiaro, Grand Anse, Praslin. *Tel: 233875*

DIVING SITES
For experienced divers, probably the best diving in Seychelles is off the outer island of **Desroches.** Shallow dives of 10 metres can be made on the inshore reefs, but there are also several wonderful deeper dives and a superb area for underwater photography. Desroches is famous for the Desroches Drop, the edge of a huge limestone coralline

A school of Emperor Fish virtually take over a reef

Fish, including a bright red grouper, leisurely graze about the coral reef

(left) *Aldabra boasts a vast lagoon*

Waves crashing on Bird Island

plateau, deeply sliced into gullies, undercuts and caves. Under safe supervision from the guides at the Desroches Dive Centre, it is possible to see an array of large fish, including sharks and stingrays. But it is the background scenery that is superb: a mysterious cavernous world of plinths and pillars, canyons and crypts. Diving is also superb off the island of **Alphonse**, which again has amazing coral scenery, large drops and a quantity of coral and deep-sea fish to see.

Many of the hard corals around the more northerly islands of Seychelles were severely damaged by bleaching, caused by the sharp rise in sea temperatures which formed as part of the El Nîno effect, and it will take many years for these reefs to fully regenerate. However the soft corals have grown back, particularly around the inner island reefs, and the numbers of fish and other sea-life that live there are just as abundant. Visibility in the Seychelles' waters is extremely good, exceeding 30 metres, with water temperatures reaching 28C. The best diving conditions are seen between March to May and September to November, when the sea is calm and warm, and visibility is at its best. During July and August underwater visibility is reduced, by plankton and choppier seas, but these conditions do encourage the arrival of the magnificent whale shark.

Most visitors to Seychelles will visit dive sites around the inner islands of Mahé, Praslin and La Digue. Here, there are a great many dive sites to choose from, to suit beginners to advanced level scuba-divers, including wrecks, night-dive sites and coral gardens.

MAIN DIVE SITES OFF MAHÉ
Aquarium Depth 6–14m: Coral reef. Experience level: All divers
This has two huge coral heads on either side, with a large low-lying patchwork reef. Novice divers are often taken here by diving centres on Mahé, and it is a superb site for safe, easy diving that offers the opportunity to see a large variety of sea-life.

Bay Ternay Marine Park Depth 5–18m: Coral reef. Experience level: All divers
An easy dive in this unspoilt marine park, with superb coral formations, among the best to be seen around Mahé. A variety of reef fish can be viewed here, including Moray eels, turtles and schools of jackfish.

Sand, sea, sun and kites: what more could a child want?

Brissare Rocks Depth 12–18m: Granite and coral reef. Experience level: Qualified divers
Midway between Mahé and Praslin, this rock is one of the best-known dive sites because of its huge array of sea-life. The submerged granite massive and surrounding rocks create protected surroundings for schools of snappers and a multitude of reef fish. Some of the largest brown morays can be seen here as well as a lot of invertebrates. The currents here also bring in schooling pelagics, stingrays, turtles, sharks and Whale Sharks.

Cap Ternay Depth 10–20m: Granite and coral reef. Experience level: Qualified divers
This site is at the base of the granite cliffs of Cap Ternay, which descend into the deep-water channel running along the west coast of Mahé. The sheer sides drop down steeply to a sandy bed and a hard coral reef. The current flow here encourages visits from turtles, sharks and pelagic fish.

Small fishing boat at La Digue harbour

Cerf Depth 6–11m: Coral reef. Experience level: All divers
Just off Cerf island in the Ste Anne National Marine Park, this site is an easy dive onto a shallow gently sloping shelf of granite and coral reef. It is a particularly good site for beginners and underwater photographers, with a good selection of reef fish.

Chuckles Depth 12–18m: Granite and coral reef. Experience level: All divers
Close to the north western end of Beau Vallon Bay, this reef is a single granite massive, deeply ingrained with gullies and surrounded by a field of submerged granite boulders. The rocks are heavily

encrusted with soft corals, including many fan corals. The steep sided gullies shelter a wealth of reef fish and invertebrate life. This site can be subject to strong currents, but under the right sea conditions it makes a superb site for night dives.

Conception Depth 15–30m: Granite and coral reef. Experience level: Qualified divers
Just west of Conception island off the south western coast of Mahé is a submerged granite reef forming a natural arena. There are swim-throughs through deep gullies and in-between granite boulders, with a shelving sandy bottom dropping away from 30m. The site attracts larger fish species including stingrays, sharks and turtles. Whale sharks can also be spotted here in season. Off to the south of Conception is a further dive site with similarly steep walls, gullies and boulders.

Dragon's Teeth Depth 12–20m: Granite and coral reef. Experience level: Qualified divers
Close to Brissare rocks, this site is recognisable by the group of sharp-looking rocks jutting out over the surface of the sea, resembling teeth (hence the name). This site has good numbers of reef fish, sharks and eels. There are occasional strong currents in the area and it is also possible to spot whale sharks from here in the right season.

Dredger Wreck Depth 18–26m: wreck. Experience level: Qualified divers
This wreck was purposely sunk by the Association of Professional Divers Seychelles, and is now a superb site for viewing a wealth of marine life including a lot of invertebrates. Often visited by large pelagic fish, large black groupers and red snappers can sometimes be seen here.

Snorkelling the pristine waters around Alphonse Island

Espadron fishing boat, St Pierre

Ennerdale Wreck Depth 18–30m: Wreck. Experience level: Qualified divers
The Ennerdale was a British tanker, which floundered here in 1970 on an unmarked rock. When it sank it had already discharged its cargo of oil and did not pose any risk of pollution, so the British navy just blasted the ship apart to make it safe for shipping, and let it lie. It is now home to a huge range of reef fish, snappers, large groupers, moray eels and some large scorpion fish. The currents here also attract schools of pelagic fish, stingrays, sharks and sometimes whale sharks.

Grouper Point Depth 7–20m: Granite and coral reef. Experience level: All divers
This dive site can experience strong currents and is suitable for a drift dive. Here there are large, dramatic granite boulders and masses of coral dropping to sand at 28-30m. There are many large groupers, moray eels and turtles. Sharks are sometimes seen here as well as whale sharks in season.

Harrison Rocks Depth 5–18m: Granite and coral reef. Experience level: All divers
Just outside the Ste Anne National Marine Park, these huge granite boulders are encrusted with coral and home to a wide variety of reef fish. The site is also sometimes visited by turtles, some pelagic fish and reef sharks.

Horseshoe Rocks Depth 8–14m: Granite and coral reef. Experience level: All divers
Horseshoe rocks are in fact one large granite massive off the northern coast of Mahé with spur and groove formations on the off-shore side. The site occasionally picks up a long-shore current. This is a good spot for reef fish, moray eel and invertebrates. Turtles and stingrays can be seen and octopus dens are often discovered at the base of the granite walls.

L'Ilôt Depth 5–20m: Granite and coral reef. Experience level: All divers
L'Ilôt is a tiny granite island off the north eastern tip of Beau Vallon Bay. Above the water there is not much more to see than rocks and a couple of palm trees, but below the waves is an array of colourful marine life. The island's steep sides and grooved with gullies and surrounded by large granite boulders that provide underwater archways and swim-throughs. This is a particularly good spot for night-dives for torchlight views of the colourful soft corals that have formed on the rocks around the island.

Shark Bank Depth 18–30m: Granite and coral reef. Experience level: Qualified divers
Shark Bank is consistently voted the top dive site in Seychelles by visitors; halfway between Mahé and Silhouette, is the shallowest area for hundreds of kilometres and a natural focus for marine life, especially pelagic fish. Granite boulders protect a resident population of reef fish and invertebrates, with schools of snappers and big eyes. Barracuda, stingrays, sharks and whale sharks can also be seen at certain times of the year.

Trois Bancs Depth 5–25m: Granite and coral reef. Experience level: Qualified divers
Several miles from the western coast of Mahé, this site is made up of three large submerged granite reefs, with steep walls, deep gullies and large boulders forming a maze of swim-throughs and small caves. There is an impressive number of large reef fish and schools of snappers. The site suffers occasionally from strong currents but attracts schooling pelagic fish, barracudas, stingrays, sharks, turtles and, sometimes, whale sharks. A good site for night dives in the right sea conditions.

Twin Barges Wreck Depth 12–24m: Wreck. Experience level: Qualified divers
These two wrecks were purchased and sunk at the foot of the Corsair reef in 1989 by the Association of Professional Divers Seychelles, and have since become heavily encrusted with corals and sponges. There are large numbers of reef fish including resident lion fish and invertebrates. Although a slightly deeper dive, this is a popular night dive site.

Whale Rock Depth 8–14m: Granite and coral reef. Experience level: All divers
This is an easy dive onto a reef of large granite boulders stacked together to form archways, swim-throughs and corridors. Here there are many reef fish, moray eels, some turtles and stingrays. The site is especially good for night dives when the coral studded rocks become a blaze of colour in torchlight.

Willy's Rock Depth 5–16m: Granite and coral reef. Experience level: All divers
This is a shallow dive within a bay exploring a large granite massive which descends to the sandy seabed. Reef fish, moray eels and occasional turtles can be found here.

MAIN DIVE SITES OFF PRASLIN AND LA DIGUE

Anse Marron Bank Depth 10–26m: Granite and coral reef. Experience level: Qualified divers
This ridge of granite is really an extension of the southern tip of La Digue and a favourite gathering point for reef sharks and other large pelagic fish. Constant currents here make this a good site for drift dives.

Anse Severe Depth 8–16m: Granite and coral reef. Experience level: All divers
North of La Digue, this granitic outcrop is perfect for photographers, with colourful soft corals and reef fish. There are also overhangs and crevices to explore.

Aride Bank Depth 8–20m: Granite and coral reef. Experience level: All divers
Part of the Aride island nature reserve, this site has a huge array of fish, including sharks, Napoleon wrasse and barracuda. Dolphins are also often seen in the area.

Ave Maria Depth 6–20m: Granite and coral reef. Experience level: All divers
This small island between Praslin and La Digue is one of the best dive sites in the inner islands, particularly for beginners. The reefs surrounding the island are home to small sharks, turtles, rays and moray eels.

Booby Rock Depth 12–25m: Granite and coral reef. Experience level: Qualified divers
A drift dive around this rock, which is north west of Praslin, is a good place to view eagle rays, Napoleon wrasse, turtles and dolphins. Whale sharks are also a possibility in season.

Caiman Rocks Depth 10–18m: Granite and coral reef. Experience level: All divers
Corals and rocks make up pretty underwater scenery, a good spot for underwater photography. Shoals of fusiliers swim overhead, and white-tip sharks, turtles and some barracudas can be seen.

Channel Rocks Depth 8–16m: Granite and coral reef. Experience level: All divers
Drift along this granite ridge, situated between Praslin and La Digue, to see shoaling fusiliers, snappers and reef fish. Small reef sharks and some friendly turtles also live here.

East Sister Bank Depth 12–20m: Granite and coral reef. Experience level: Qualified divers
Off Grande Soeur island, this is a drift dive over dramatic rock formations with swim-throughs and coral gardens. A variety of reef fish can be seen here including parrot fish and the colourful clown triggerfish; hawksbill turtles are also regularly seen.

Red Point Depth 10–16m. Experience level: Qualified divers
This red granite headlands juts out from Curieuse island, and is surrounded by rocks and coral reef. There are lots of gullies and overhangs for divers to explore. The point itself is a meeting place for jackfish and barracuda. Part of the Curieuse National Marine Park.

Renomee Rock Depth 10–30m: Granite and coral reef. Experience level: Qualified divers
South of La Digue island, this rock is an excellent site for drift dives with spectacular coral formations. Marine life seen here includes wrasse, sharks, turtles and shoaling fish which gather at either end of the rock

Roche en Bas Depth 8–14m: Granite and coral reef. Experience level: All divers
These underwater rocks form a circular pattern, encrusted with corals, with swim-throughs for divers to explore. A good location for finding bumphead parrotfish, turtles and eagle rays. Small stingrays and white tip sharks sleep under the corals.

Roche Marianne Depth 12–24m: Granite and coral reef. Experience level: Qualified divers
Roche Marianne is a submerged pinnacle of rock close to Felicité island. Here reef sharks and stingrays can be found resting at the base of the rock. Turtles, batfish and snappers are found in the shallower waters where there are some swim-throughs in the rocks.

Round Island Depth 10–14m: Granite and coral reef. Experience level: All divers
This small island east of Praslin offers gentle drift dives along its side. Stingrays, parrotfish and other reef fish can be seen in abundance as well as some species of large grouper, often concealed under overhangs.

Sister Rocks Depth 8–22m: Granite and coral reef. Experience level:
South of Grande Soeur island, this site offers a pretty collection of corals and granite ridges. Large lobsters can be seen in depths of about 18 metres, with Napoleon wrasse and eagle rays. Whale sharks have been spotted in season.

South Cousine Depth 14–18m: Granite and coral reef. Experience level: Qualified divers
Part of the nature reserve of Cousine island, this site is full of marine life. Turtles, Napoleon wrasse and shoals of snappers can be seen swimming along the granite ridge, while lionfish, scorpion fish and morays hide away in the nooks and crannies of the rocks.

South Marianne Depth 10–16m: Granite and coral reef. Experience level: Qualified divers
Marianne island drops steeply into the sea forming dramatic underwater cathedral size structures. This is a particularly good spot for seeing several species of shark.

Trompeuse Rocks Depth 12–26m: Granite and coral reef. Experience level: Qualified divers
This is a series of dramatic pinnacles of granite, which break the surface of the sea northwest of Cousine island. Underneath the waves is home for numbers of stingrays, sharks and large coral formations. Turtles are often seen in the shallows.

Wolfgang's Wall Depth 8–14m: Granite an coral reef
West of Curieuse island, this amazing granite wall drops vertically to 14 metres then opens up into a pretty coral garden. The crevices in the wall are full of invertebrates and eels, while the reef is home to a colourful variety of fish.

Night Diving
Most of the Diving Centres in Seychelles will offer night dives, an experience not to be missed. The artificial lights used for the dive will throw up a whole new colour spectrum. Striped fusiliers, blue and yellow during the day, appear purple and green. Many of the corals, which look a dull grey-green in the sunlight, are spectacularly yellow or bright pink. On night dives discover how parrot fish sleep and look out for the occasional lobster ambling along on the sea bed, something you don't see during the day.

Diving Sites from Mahé

	Site	km	Season	Exp.	Depth	Terrain	Features	Marine Life
1	Ternay Bluff	S	Feb–Nov	A	6–19m	GR		
2	Grouper Point	S	Feb–Nov	A	6–30m	GR		
3	Baie Ternay M. Park	S	Feb–Nov	A	6–18m	GR		
4	Ray's Point	S	Feb–Nov	A	>15m	GR		
5	Willy's Rock	S	Feb–Nov	A	6–12m	GR		
6	Whale Rock	S	Feb–Nov	A	>12m	GR		
7	Horseshoe Rocks	S	Feb–Nov	A	6–12m	GR		
8	Danzille Rocks	S	Feb–Nov	A	>11m	GR		
9	Danzille Reef	S	Feb–Nov	A	8–14m	COR		
10	Auberge Reef	S	Feb–Nov	A	6–15m	COR		
11	Dredger Wreck	S	Feb–Nov	X	27m	WR		
12	Scala Reef	S	Feb–Nov	A	6–15m	COR		
13	Corsair Reef	S	Feb–Nov	A	6–15m	COR		
14	Twin Barges Wreck	S	Feb–Nov	E	14–25m	WR		
15	Fisherman's Cove	S	Feb–Nov	A	6–12m	COR		
16	Beau Vallon Reef	S	Feb–Nov	A	12–20m	COR		
17	Aquarium	S	Feb–Nov	A	5–12m	COR		
18	Vacoa Reef	S	Feb–Nov	A	10–16m	COR		
19	Coral Gardens	S	Feb–Nov	A	9–15m	COR		
20	Sunset Rocks	S	Feb–Nov	A	>12m	GR		
21	Vista Bay Rocks	S	Feb–Nov	A	14m	GR		
22	Chuckles	S	Feb–Nov	A	8–15m	GR		
23	L'Ilot	S	Feb–Nov	E	>16m	GR		
24	Cap Ternay	L	Feb–Nov	X	12–20m	GR		
25	Beacon Island	S	Dec–Jan	A	>15m	GR		
26	Pinnacle Point	S	Dec–Jan	A	>17m	GR		
27	Cerf Island	S	Dec–Jan	A	6–11m	COR		
28	Harrison Rocks	S	Dec–Jan	A	>14m	GR		
29	Turtle Rocks	S	Dec–Jan	A	>15m	GR		
30	Cheedle Rocks	S	Dec–Jan	X	15–25m	GR		
31	Conception Arena	L	*	X	15–30m	GR		
32	Conception Point	L	*	X	>18m	GR		
33	Thérèse Island	L	*	X	>20m	GR		
34	Trois Dames	L	*	X	>22m	GR		
35	Iles Vaches	L	*	X	>20m	GR		
36	Trois Bancs	L	*	X	>25m	GR		
37	Shark Bank	L	*	X	18–30m	GR		
38	Brissare	L	*	X	>18m	GR		
39	Dragon's Teeth	L	*	X	>18m	GR		
40	Ennerdale Wreck	L	*	X	18–30m	WR		
41	Ennerdale Rocks	L	*	X	18–25m	GR		

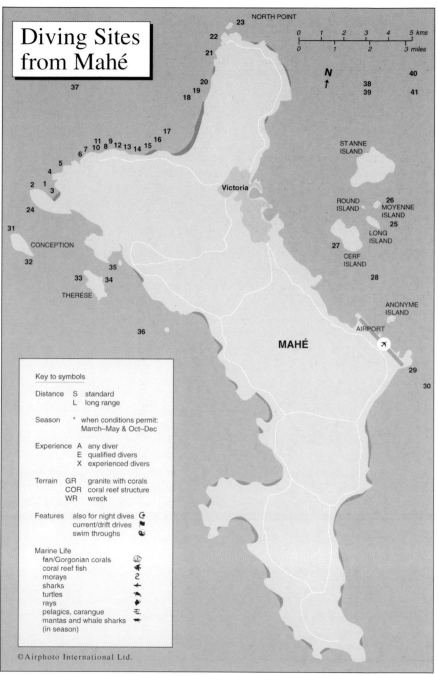

Diving Sites from Mahé

NORTH POINT

23
22
21
20
19
18
37
17
16
11 9 12 13 14 15
7 10 8
6
5
4
2 1
3
24
31
CONCEPTION
32
35
33 34
THÉRÈSE
36

Victoria

ST ANNE
ISLAND

ROUND
ISLAND
MOYENNE
ISLAND 26
25
LONG
ISLAND
27
CERF
ISLAND
28

38
39
40
41

N

0 1 2 3 4 5 kms
0 1 2 3 miles

ANONYME
ISLAND

AIRPORT

MAHÉ
29
30

Key to symbols

Distance   S   standard
           L   long range

Season   *   when conditions permit:
               March–May & Oct–Dec

Experience A   any diver
           E   qualified divers
           X   experienced divers

Terrain   GR   granite with corals
           COR coral reef structure
           WR   wreck

Features   also for night dives
           current/drift drives
           swim throughs

Marine Life
    fan/Gorgonian corals
    coral reef fish
    morays
    sharks
    turtles
    rays
    pelagics, carangue
    mantas and whale sharks
    (in season)

© Airphoto International Ltd.

Recent reclamation of Mahé not shown here

DIVING HOLIDAYS

For the committed diver there are travel companies that specialise in diving holidays to Seychelles, offering diving and cruising holidays around some of the more remote islands. More details on diving in Seychelles can been obtained from the websites: www.aspureasitgets.com or on www.diveseychelles.com

SUBIOS FESTIVALS

SUBIOS (Sub-Indian Ocean Seychelles) is an annual underwater festival on Mahé, usually held in November or December. Activities include marine conservation workshops, underwater photography lessons and competitions, plus various presentations by international guest speakers. Further information on this festival can be obtained from the Seychelles Tourist Offices.

> *Please note that it is forbidden to take spear-fishing guns or harpoons with you when you dive in Seychelles waters. It is illegal to bring them into the country and customs officials will confiscate any found on yachts sailing into Seychelles, while staying in the country. It is also illegal to fish or take corals or shells from any of the areas designated as national marine parks.*

Snorkelling

Those not inclined to take up scuba diving need not miss out on the wonders that the coral reefs around Seychelles have to offer. Snorkelling is a must; it is easy, fun and free.

It is not difficult to adapt to breathing through a snorkel. Spit on the mask before putting it over your face, to prevent it from misting up; thread the snorkel through the mask strap on the side of your head to keep the snorkel upright (make sure it doesn't have any water in it first, by blowing though the mouthpiece); put your flippers on when you are standing on the edge of the water and walk backwards until you can swim—it is easier than waddling penguin-like down the beach.

It is best to wear flippers, as they make swimming much easier. If these are not available then wear rubber soled shoes, as the corals and rocks can be razor sharp and a cut could easily become infected. Also wear a T-shirt to prevent your back from getting sunburnt.

Once in the water make for the nearest reef or rocks and observe! You will not need to swim out very far or to keep swimming around. Just simply float above the reef and the fish will come to you.

SNORKELLING SITES

ANSE ROYALE, Mahé

The very best snorkelling spot on Mahé for the beginner. Head out by the rocks towards the small island and you will see myriads of bright coral fish. The water here is enclosed behind a reef, which keeps out the large fish and is fairly shallow, so you will not need to go very much out of your depth. The currents can be fairly strong, so make sure you don't drift away. This is best during the northwest monsoon, between October and April. During the rest of the year the water tends to be cloudy and seaweed-prone, so it is best avoided.

SAINTE ANNE NATIONAL MARINE PARK

To snorkel here you will either need a boat or to join an organised tour of the inner islands and marine park. The tours take you over the reef in a semi-submersible boat, so you can view the fish and corals without even getting wet. For the best view put on the snorkel and mask provided and flip over the side of the boat. The corals here are amazing: all shapes, sizes and colours from white to purple and there are always plenty of fish to admire. A guide on the semi-submersible will tell you the names of the main species.

SUNSET BEACH, Glacis, Mahé.

Sadly, this beach by the side of the Sunset Beach Hotel is now not accessible to anyone apart from guests at the hotel. If you are staying here, do make the most of this good snorkelling spot by the rocks to the side of the hotel restaurant, which gives a good cross sectional view of small and large marine life, including manta rays, turtles and shoals of mackerel. This swim is only for the confident as it is a good way out, with occasional strong currents. It is a good spot for scuba diving too. I once saw an enormous hammerhead shark here, chasing a shoal of mackerel very close to the rocks by the side of the hotel—but don't let this put you off swimming!

ANSE SOLEIL, Mahé.

This beautiful beach is somewhat remote, but it provides calm clear waters for snorkelling around the rocks at either end of the bay. The marine life here combines small and larger fish, all living around the corals which have formed near the rocks. You will not need to swim much out of your depth to see a wide variety of colourful fish.

ANSE KERLAN, Praslin.

The two small rocky coves of Anse Kerlan and Petite Anse Kerlan are home to a wide variety of fish species. There are strong currents here and the rocks are sharp, but the views in the water below are worth the slight risk. Sadly, these coves are now only accessible to guests staying at the Lemuria Resort.

CÔTE D'OR and the CURIEUSE NATIONAL MARINE PARK, Praslin.
The best snorkelling along this stretch of the coast is towards the northern end of the bay and the island of **Chauve Souris**. There is also good snorkelling to be found at the small stretch of beach known as **Anse Matelot**, beyond the L'Archipel hotel. Organised snorkelling trips can be arranged through the Praslin Beach Hotel, which will take you out to the islet of St Pierre to the rich waters and beautiful corals of the Curieuse National Marine Park, also a good spot for scuba diving. Among the rocks and corals of St Pierre there lives a large, solitary hawksbill turtle who will be happy to make your acquaintance.

Sailing and Boat Charter

To explore the many islands of Seychelles at your own pace there is no better way than chartering a boat. Sailing weather is better during the northwest monsoon, between October and May, when the seas are generally calmer. This is particularly true if you wish to sail to the outer islands, which are not accessible during the high trade winds during the south eastern monsoon in July and August.

The Amirantes are just 24 hours sailing time from Mahé, while nearer islands like Bird, Denis, Praslin and La Digue are just a few hours sail. Navigating around the inner islands is easy and safe, with distances of lesss than 32 miles between mooring sites. The outer islands, however, are much more difficult and hazardous to navigate, with more unpredictable currents, sea-depths and weather conditions as well as dangerous low-lying reefs.

Anchoring on coral is strictly forbidden. Mooring buoys are provided around north-west Mahé and around the north-eastern side of Praslin. Other areas provide a soft sandy bed suitable for anchorage and are clearly marked on Seychelles' shipping charts.

The ocean around Seychelles is subject to currents with speeds of between 0.5 knots up to 1.5 knots during windier

(above) *Ferry from Praslin to La Digue*; (right) *Local fishing boat at Port Launay Beach, Mahé*

conditions. The prevailing currents around the Seychelles bank, around the inner islands, averages at between 0.4 to 0.8 knots.

Tides in Seychelles are semi-diurnal and asymmetrical, with around 6 hours between high and low tides. Swells are generally moderate, with waves of up to 1 to 2 metres, becoming higher only in strong winds and open seas.

Yachtsmen should note that access to some areas and islands is restricted. The National Marine Parks and private nature reserves require either permission or payment on arrival. Fees levied include landing or entry fees, and overnight mooring fees. Within the National Marine Parks, prior permission is not necessary: yachts can arrive and anchor in the demarcated zones and marine park officials will visit the boat to collect the necessary fees, which start at US$ 10 per person.

The National Marine Parks are: Curieuse, Ile Cocos, Ste Anne, Ste Pierre, Port Launay and Baie Ternay.

Private nature reserves are around: Aride and Cousin.

The following islands are privately owned with access strictly controlled by the owners. Permission to land or moor is not always granted and requests to moor must be made to the owners well in advance: Anonyme; Bird; Chauvre Souris; Cousine; D'Arros and St Joseph Atoll; Denis; Félicité; Frégate; Grande Soeur and Petite Soeur; Moyenne; North and Round Islands off Mahé.

The following islands are managed by the Island Development Corporation and permission to access must be granted by the IDC prior to arrival. Landing fees start from around US$20 per person: Alphonse; Bijoutier; Coetivy; Desroches; Farquar; Poivre; Platte; Providence; Rémire; Silhouette; St François.

A full guide to the access and fees for islands in Seychelles can be downloaded from the official Seychelles tourist information *website: www.seychelles.com*

Sailing vessels wishing to make use of the facilities at the jetties on Praslin and La Digue need to contact the Pier Masters at least 24 hours in advance.

Pier Master, Baie Ste Anne Jetty, Praslin. *Tel: (248) 232434*

Pier Master, La Passe Jetty, La Digue. *Tel: (248) 224300*

There are a number of yacht charter companies operating on Mahé and Praslin. Some, like Sunsail, VPM and The Moorings, offer all-inclusive sailing package holidays, while other small companies can also offer day or weekend charters.

Sailing holidays can be pre-booked from the following companies:

Sunsail Seychelles, Inter Island Quay, Mahé, Seychelles. *Tel: (248) 225700*
Email: ssseychel@seychelles.net Website: www.sunsail.com

The Moorings, The Wharf, Providence, Mahé. *Tel: (248) 601060*
Email: moorings@seychelles.et. Website: www.moorings.com

VPM Yacht Charter, Roche Caiman Marina, Mahé. PO Box 960. *Tel: (248) 344719*
Email: vpm@seychelles.net Website: www.vpm.fr

Day or weekend charters can also be booked locally through the following:
Angel Fish Ltd, Roche Caiman Marina, PO Box 1079, Victoria, Mahé
Tel: (248) 344644. Email: angelfish@seychelles-charter.com
Website: www.seychelles-charter.com
The Marine Charter Association, Victoria, Mahé. PO Box 469
Tel: (248) 322126. Email: m.c.a@seychelles.net Website: www.seychelles.net/mca
The Boat House, Beau Vallon Bay, Mahé. *Tel: (248) 247898*
Island Charters Ltd, Victoria, Mahé. PO Box 100. *Tel: (248) 323790*
Email: island@seychelles.net Website: www.seychelles.net/islandcharters
High Aspect, PO Box 911. Mahé
Tel: (248) 513911. Email: hiaspect@seychelles.net Website: www.highaspect.sc
Inter Island Cruising, Hotel Maison des Palmes, Amitie, Praslin
Tel : (248) 233411. Email: maisondp@seychelles.net
Website: www.hotelmaisondespalmes.com
Dream Yacht Seychelles, Baie Ste Anne, Praslin. *Tel: (248) 232681*
Email: dream@seychelles.net Website: www.dream-yacht-seychelles.com
Voyage Charters, Baie Ste Anne, Praslin. *Tel: (248) 232829/512378*
Email: info@voyagecharters.com Website: www.voyagecharters.com
Sagittarius Taxi Boat Charter, Cote d'Or, Praslin. *Tel: 512137/ 711987, or 570454*

Visiting Yachts

Seychelles is a popular destination for visiting yachts. Port Victoria on Mahé is the sole official point of entry and exit in Seychelles and all vessels arriving from a foreign country, or about to depart Seychelles for foreign waters, must call at the port first to obtain a one month visitor's permit. At the port, customs, health, immigration and security checks are carried out by the authorities.

On arrival, foreign vessels must submit the following documentation to the customs officials:

(1) A valid outward clearance from their last port of call.

(2) Full crew and passenger lists. (3) Consumables list.

(4) Arms and ammunitions list.

A comprehensive guide for visiting yachts is available at the Seychelles official tourist website: www.seychelles.com

Visiting yachts can also contact the Port Victoria Harbour Master:

Harbour Master, Port and Marine Services
New Port, PO Box 47, Port Victoria, Mahé
Tel: (248) 224701. Email: marineservices@seychellesports.sc/ hm@seychellesports.sc
Shipping agents can also handle all the formalities for visiting yachts:

La Digue's rocks attract photographers from around the globe

Anse Marron, La Digue: sculpture by Mother Nature

Bijoutier, an unwinking emerald eye in the face of the Alphonse group

Cousin Island, owned by Birdlife International, is home to many rare and endangered species

Mahé Shipping Agency, PO Box 336
Maritime House, Laurier Avenue, Victoria, Mahé
Tel: (248) 380500. Email: maheship@seychelles.net
Hunt Deltel, PO Box 14
Trinity House, Albert Street, Victoria, Mahé
Tel: (248) 380300. Email: hundel@seychelles.net
Visiting yachties can also enjoy temporary membership of the Victoria Yacht Club.
The yacht club has a subsidised cafeteria (offering excellent fish and chips), a bar and
a cruising yacht notice board. Tel: (248) 222126.

Cruises in Seychelles

A number of cruise lines visit Seychelles as part of longer Indian Ocean voyages. There
are, however some cruises that operate solely in Seychelles, including a luxury
catamaran, old-fashioned schooners, and a marine research vessel.

Le Meridien Pearl of Seychelles is a 34-cabin catamaran, that sails from Mahé and
Praslin for 3 or 7 night cruises around the inner islands. Islands visited include La
Digue, Grand Soeur, Mahé, Curieuse, Cousin, Praslin, Therese and Silhouette. The
ship moors alongside the islands, giving guests time to explore ashore. Activities
available on the cruise include snorkelling, kayaking and windsurfing.

The catamaran is 177 feet long and 49 feet wide; it has a swimming pool, lounges,
restaurant and open-air bar. The 34 cabins are classified as either deluxe or superior
deluxe, all have sea views, air conditioning and en-suite facilities. The Superior Deluxe
rooms are larger and have sleeping accommodation for two adults and one child.

Cruises on Le Meriden Pearl of Seychelles can be booked with travel agents or
through Le Meridien Fisherman's Cove Hotel on Mahé.

Two schooners offer romantic cruises in the waters of Seychelles: the SV Sea Shell
and the S.V. Sea Pearl are both 2 mast top sail Dutch-built schooners. Both schooners
have been modernised and re-fitted with modern-day luxuries such as air-conditioned
cabins (there are eight cabins on each ship), with TV, video, washing machine, hair
dryer and ice-machine.

Both ships offer seven night cruises around the inner islands between November and
April, and six night cruises between May and October. Personalised cruises can also be
organised. These cruises are particularly recommended for diving enthusiasts as they
offer the opportunity to reach some of the best dive sites around the inner islands and
the crew includes PADI dive instructors. Other facilities on board include windsurfing,
banana boat rides, kayaking, surfing, fishing and snorkelling equipment.

Reservations can be made through Silhouette Cruises, at 7° South Tour Operator, Victoria. Tel: (248) 322682 Email: 7south@seychelles.net

The Indian Ocean Explorer is far less glamorous, but offers diving and research trips to the outer islands for those interested in studying the environment both above and below the waves. This converted oceanographic research ship built to Lloyd's exacting standards is outfitted for diving. Facilities on board include seven air conditioned double cabins all with en suite bathrooms.

Itineraries range from 3 to 15 days, with some expeditions designed to offer alternative Indian Ocean thrills to non-diving companions. The ship can also be custom chartered for diving, snorkelling, fishing and bird watching holidays.

Specialist cruises include the Whale Shark Expeditions around the inner islands. In conjunction with the Shark Research Institute, the programme includes tagging and whale shark encounters. Using a light aircraft, whale sharks are spotted from the air and the boat is then guided so divers can experience the thrill of diving with these huge fish.

The Indian Ocean Explorer offers cruises around the Amirantes, where there are some spectacular dive sites including the Desroches Drop. The itinerary covers the southerly Alphonse group where six wrecks lie around the reef of St. Françoise. The trip includes diving on the Alphonse wall, which is reckoned to be among the best in the Indian Ocean, and the Gorgonian fan forest is a must for photographers hunting the Long Nosed Hawkfish.

One expedition run only once a year is the Indian Ocean Explorer voyage to Aldabra and Madagascar. The expedition starts with a charter flight from Mahé to Assumption where passengers join the ship. Diving expeditions are arranged off the outer islands of Assumption, Cosmoledo and Astove before heading to Nosy Be and the island of Nosy Komba on the North West of Madagascar. Visits are arranged to the lemur sanctuary on Nosy Komba, the old French colonial port of Helville, and dives on reefs off Madagascar that are seldom visited.

The ship then sails back to Aldabra, with the chance to dive on Aldabra's terraced walls, which are dramatic, but the diving highlight of this atoll is the stunning drift diving through the channels into Aldabra's vast lagoon: with shoals of snappers, surgeon-fish and stingrays as they drift into the lagoon following the strong currents at speeds of up to six knots.

The Indian Ocean Explorer can be booked through its American office.

Tel : + (1) 352 4015678. Email: info4@ioexplorer.com

A fine bonefish catch off Alphonse Island

Customers wait on the beach at Beau Vallon, hoping to get first pick of the day's fishing catch

(above) *Catamaran fishing trips from Praslin can be booked at the Maison des Palmes hotel*

Dinghy Sailing, Waterskiing, Windsurfing and Paragliding

All four water sports are offered along Beau Vallon Beach on Mahé at an hourly hire rate. Windsurfing is a popular choice here, as well as at a number of other hotels and guest houses on Mahé and the other islands. Most of the larger resorts will offer windsurfing and other water sports free of hire to guests. For experienced windsurfers there is an annual race between Mahé and Praslin (around 40km). The record time is just under one hour twenty minutes.

Dinghies and small catamarans can be hired hourly from Beau Vallon, Côte d'Or on Praslin and at most large resorts. On Alphonse island there are also paddle boats. Paragliding is also available at Beau Vallon.

Fly Fishing in Shangri-La

For a few of us, the dream goes like this: big uneducated bonefish in a perfect setting, no people or jet skis on an endless hard gleaming white flat. Punctuate this scene with beautiful hawksbill turtles, fairy terns and blue crabs the size of a dinner plate. Imagine the bonefish to be so naïve that they would eat a bare hook. Picture giant black and silver fish the size of a semi truck tire so intent on eating that you can't swim in the water. Visualize grouper and snapper so plentiful that a fly in the water is eaten within twenty seconds. Grouper on poppers? Yes! Bonefish to twenty pounds? Sure! Giant Trevally over one hundred pounds? Better have a big stick!
(Taken from 'Bonefish Dreams in the Seychelles', an article by Brad Wolfe.)

The sport of salt-water fly fishing for bonefish was only really discovered some fifty years ago, largely in the Florida Keys. As the popularity of fly fishing grew in the 1970s and 80s, many American anglers began to look beyond the Keys, where often the flat boats were practically outnumbering the fish. New hot spots were discovered and opened up, including Yucatan, where the fish were plentiful but on the small side, or Christmas Island in the Pacific where the fish were good but living conditions on the island were extremely spartan.

The Bahamas was, and still is, a popular spot, but good as all these places were, there was still speculation among anglers that there was somewhere else in the world which would be the perfect spot for landing plentiful and large bonefish; somewhere totally unspoilt, where the fish could be there for the taking, and even perhaps a place which could offer anglers some comfortable accommodation? The fly fisherman's Shangri-la.

It was not until the 1990s that rumours started to circulate. Such a place indeed existed. Fly fishing heaven was indeed on earth—and in Seychelles.

The outer island of Alphonse is this heaven: it offers undisputedly the world's finest salt water fly fishing. On the lagoon at St Françoise island, just across the ominously named 'Channel of Death' from Alphonse, there is a natural reservoir which is virtually unexploited. In the flats around the island there is about a mile long stretch of bonefish, and according to fly fishing guides, the numbers there are so vast that at certain times of the tide it seems to be wall-to-wall bonefish.

Bonefish between 5–7 kg may be caught there, and fly fishermen with experience can catch over 40 a day. Even beginners have caught 20 on their first day.

Fly fishing on Alphonse was developed in the mid 1990s, when the huge numbers of bonefish were discovered and anglers were able to fish the flats from a chartered catamaran. Following the discovery, the Alphonse island resort was developed, not as some humble fishing lodge, but as a luxurious five star resort, an attractive tropical island holiday getaway in its own right. The fly fishing season runs from the second week in September to the first week of June.

As a conservation measure to protect the flats around St Françoise, the number of clients fishing at any one time is limited to a maximum of six. A Catch and Release policy is strictly adhered to, and only barbless hooks are used. Fishing here makes visitors part of a very small set, privileged to have the fly fishing experience of a lifetime.

Bonefish are hard to see: their backs are the same green shade as the warm shallows where they live and their sides are silver like the sand below them. Anglers say they have to look often not for the shape of a fish, but for something that looks like unusually dense water. Slowly, as the angler squints his eyes against the sun, the shape of the bonefish begins to emerge from its camouflage.

A fly is cast, the fish bites and the big chase begins. This is what makes fly fishing for bonefish so exciting for the angler: the bonefish may be a humble-looking fish and relatively small, but it is a superb fighter. Some of the bonefish seen at Alphonse have also not exactly been minnows either: bonefish in the range of 19 to 20 lbs have been seen here, hooked and lost, with many anglers having broken their rods in the process. One of the largest bonefish hooked was weighed in at around 20lbs and was caught be angler Larry Dahlberg. He recalled: "It took off like a Sherman tank, did three right-angled turns and cut off. I still have nightmares!"

Another angler, Geoffrey Norman, describes his bonefishing experience in Seychelles as essentially an aural one:

"You hear that line peeling off your reel and slicing through the water and the sensation is one of power translated into speed, like watching a Formula One car up close, lapping a track. That first run, along with its exceeding wariness, makes the bonefish one of angling's three or four greatest prizes and accounts why one travels more than 8,000 miles to experience the newest and perhaps, ultimate, hot spot."

ENCOUNTERS WITH WHALE SHARKS

Whale Sharks are regular visitors to the waters around Seychelles during the months of July and August, and again from October to January, when it is often possible to swim with these amazing giants of the deep.

The Marine Conservation Society, Seychelles, runs a research and tagging programme and can supply details on how visitors can see and swim with a whale shark, who despite being the largest of all the fish in the sea, is a placid, docile creature who seems pretty much unaware of any dangers as it has no natural predators. Its huge mouth gathers up and filters-in small fish and plankton in much the same way as baleen whales.

The whale sharks swim at a stately pace of 2 to 3 miles per hour, never far from the surface of the water, which is where they feed. Their bodies can measure up to 18 metres long and normally provide a home to numerous shark suckers (*remoras*), some of which can be an impressive size in themselves.

Sometimes kobias follow whale sharks around: these large fish act as bodyguards to the whale sharks, and can occasionally get quite aggressive on the whale shark's behalf.

Whale sharks, or sagren, as they are called in Kreol, are unique among sharks and are the only member of their family, *Rhinocodonidae*. They have swum in Seychelles waters for centuries, but little has been known about their behaviour until recently. Indeed it is still not known how many whale sharks there are or whether they are already endangered.

English marine biologist David Rowatt has lived in Seychelles for many years and he is the Chairman of the Marine Conservation Society of Seychelles (MCSS) and the whale shark specialist for the

Remoras hitch a ride with a whale shark in hope of a free lunch

region. David and his partner Glynnis operate a dive centre on Beau Vallon, and together they have sighted whale sharks in Seychelles' waters over a long time.

When very few sharks were sighted in the 1998–9 El Nino season, David was worried that the whale shark population in the region might be declining before anyone had the chance to uncover even the most basic information about them. This spurred David to act, and as a result he formed his own NGO, the MCSS. One of the major achievements of the MCSS was the decision by the government of Seychelles, in 2002, to declare the whale shark a protected species in Seychelles territorial waters.

Much of the work of this organisation is dedicated to monitoring whale sharks and it receives funding for this from the World Bank. The funding has allowed David and his team to purchase tagging and survey equipment to gather more comprehensive data on the population status and migration patterns of the Indian Ocean whale sharks.

"We tag with marker tags, which is just a big placard with a registration number on, so that we can see that the shark has been tagged by us. Whenever it's re-sighted again, it's very easy for even an average snorkeller to say—"well it was shark S230".

The MCSS also uses two types of satellite tag: one type tracks the sharks' movements while the other records the depths that whale sharks dive to. All the information from these tags is put in a database, to help scientists research this large but little-known fish.

The Marine Conservation Society, Seychelles (MCSS) incorporating the Shark Research Institute, Seychelles (SRIS) is a local not-for-profit NGO formed in 1997, focusing purely on marine research and management.

The MCSS has undertaken pioneering research on the whale shark and effectively lobbied the Seychelles Government to declare the species protected in January 2003.

MCSS has been monitoring whale sharks in Seychelles since 1996, following a pilot project to tag whale sharks. Aerial surveys with the MCSS micro-light are used to local whale sharks in the coastal waters around Mahé. The pilot is better able to direct the tagging team onto the shark via VHF radio.

Over a hundred tags have been deployed, which include visual tags for identifying sharks as well as satellite and acoustic tags to track shark movements.

The majority of sharks that have been identified in Seychelles are juvenile males ranging in size from three to eight metres. This suggests that whale sharks come to Seychelles to feed rather than breed.

You can participate in the following activities to help fund the MCSS Whale Shark Monitoring Programme:

Whale Shark Encounters: learn about the sharks and participate in the tagging project.

Aerial Surveys in the MCSS micro-light: assist with monitoring whale shark distribution and movements.

Whale Shark Monitoring Network: report sightings to the MCSS hotline on 590772

Adopt a Whale Shark. By becoming a whale shark foster parent for one year you can ensure that research on whale sharks is continued. The cost of adoption is US$50, payable to MCSS.

The Marine Conservation Society Seychelles, PO Box 1299, Victoria, Mahé, Seychelles.

As well as bonefish, the St Françoise lagoon has exceptionally good trevally fishing: giant and other trevally species can be found here in large numbers during the fishing season. Other species of fish caught include triggerfish; groupers; emperors; sharks; rays; pursemouths; milkfish (although for a 'legal' catch you have to be "both lucky and a damn good angler," says one fishing expert); three species of needlefish—many over world record size have been sighted—and huge barracudas of up to 70lbs.

While commited enthusiasts will fly from the United States to Alphonse for the fishing, there are also other sites in Seychelles that do have some fly fishing facilities; maybe not so good that they deserve a half-way-around-the-world-pilgrimage for, but they could be included within a more general island hopping holiday to Seychelles.

Denis Island has some bonefishing around the island flats, which can be reached on foot, but the numbers are much fewer than off Alphonse. There is some limited fly fishing off Mahé, Praslin and La Digue, and tour operators on those islands can put anglers in touch with local guides who can advise on the best locations.

Fly fishing is also available from Desroches Island Resort, which runs trips to the waters around Poivre and St Joseph, where the fishing is certainly better than that on the inner islands. Some charter boats additionally offer trips to other outer islands of Cosmoledo and Astove.

It has to be said though, that fly fishing heaven can only be found off Alphonse, and thanks to conservation efforts and the exclusivity of the resort, it is likely to remain an angler's perfect bonefishing Shangri-la for many years to come.

Big Game Fishing

Big game fishing in Seychelles is fast becoming a popular attraction for beginners and more experienced fishermen. Many record-breaking dog tooth tuna have been caught in Seychelles waters (off Denis Island, which is a popular holiday venue for the serious big game fisherman), as well as huge marlin, sail fish and sharks.

The best big game fishing grounds are at the edge of the Seychelles Bank, where the ocean suddenly drops to over 1,000 fathoms. Denis and Bird are the nearest, but boats can take you out to the area from Mahé and can be chartered from the Marine Charter (*Tel: 322126*) or through tour operators in Victoria. Some hotels will also offer trips, which include the hire of all necessary equipment, bait and tuition. Minimum half-day/full-day charter rates for big game fishing start at around SR1,700 to SR2,800. The best time of year for big game fishing is between the months of November and April. There is a sponsored national fishing competition each year in March—contact the Marine Charter Association for details.

Land-Based Sports

There is a magnificent 18 hole championship Golf Course at the Lemuria Resort on Praslin. Non residents at the hotel can play for daily green fees. Golf buggies are available for players to use and much needed as the course twists and turns around the steep hillside. There is also a golf pro on hand who can provide lessons and plans are underway for the course to host major regional championships in the future. (Tel 281281). On Mahé there is at present a small 9 hole course, The Reef Golf Course. It has a small clubhouse and caddies are available if you book in advance. Visitors are welcome (Tel: 376251). There are plans to improve the golf facilities on Mahé in the future.

Riding is not widely available: there is no harrier in Seychelles so the few horses in the country are unshod and so cannot be ridden on the roads. There are short beach rides available at Chateau d'Eau at Barbarons in southern Mahé (Tel: 378177) and at the Union Estate on La Digue, booking through La Digue Island Lodge (Tel: 234232).

Tennis is available at many of the larger hotels on floodlit courts, for play during the cooler evenings and The Lemuria Resort on Praslin also has a resident tennis pro. The Plantation Club Resort on Mahé usually hosts an annual local tennis tournament.

Rock climbing is a sport which should be more developed in Seychelles. The granite mountains of the inner islands, especially the block and cliff faces on Praslin and La Digue, offer experienced climbers a fine challenge. There are no rock climbing centres in Seychelles to exploit this natural resource at present, so climbers will need to bring their own equipment and insurance. The best climbing spots on Praslin are behind Anse Lazio and at the end of the Anse Kerlan road at Pointe Ste Marie. For cliff climbs, try near La Reserve Hotel at Anse Possession or the rocks between Anse Gouvernment and Anse Matelot. On La Digue there are wonderful rocks at Source d'Argent and many of the other beaches offer good climbing, as do the cliffs at Pointe Jacques.

Mountain Walks and Nature Trails

There are a number of well marked mountain walks on Mahé, Praslin and La Digue. Trail guide booklets are available from the Tourist Office on the best known nature trail walks. Guides are also available for some walks and can be booked through the main tour operators, at a cost of around SR300 per person.

Booklets have been published by the Seychelles Ministry of Tourism on the following trails and are available from the Tourist Office in Victoria:

Anse Royale–Anse à la Mouche: The trail follows minor roads and tracks across the southern hills of Mahé. There are two optional detours to a small valley lined with native palms and to an old chapel and two cemeteries. Towards the end of the trail there is a choice of routes—one finishing at Anse à la Mouche bay and the other finishing close to Anse Boileau. *Graded as EASY. Three–four hours.*

Danzil–Anse Major: A walk which follows the rocky coastline of northwest Mahé and leads to the secluded beach of Anse Major. *Graded as EASY. Three hours.*

La Digue: La Passe–Grand Anse: This trail can be followed on foot or bicycle. It follows the coastline road south from the jetty at La Passe, then turns inland through the La Digue Veuve Reserve to the large bay of Grand Anse on the other side of the island. *Graded as EASY. Two hours.*

Glacis–Anse Étoile: The trail follows minor roads across the northern hills of Mahé to the picturesque reservoir of La Gogue and downhill to the coast at Anse Étoile. *Graded as EASY. Three hours.*

La Reserve and Brulee: La Reserve contains one of the best areas of palm forest remaining on Mahé against a backdrop of granite cliffs and boulders. *Graded as MEDIUM. Two–three hours.*

Tea Factory–Morne Blanc: Apart from a short steep section at the start of the trail, this is a shaded and steady climb through forest of the Morne Seychellois National Park. Spectacular views of the west coast of Mahé from the summit of Morne Blanc and walks through the mistforests, which contain many unique species of flora and fauna. *Graded as MEDIUM. Two hours.*

The Trois Frères Trail: The Trois Frères path leads through a section of the Morne Seychellois National Park to the summit of the mountain overlooking Victoria. Spectacular views of Mahé from the summit and a chance to see the unique Seychelles pitcher plants. *Graded as HARD. Three and a half hours.*

Val Riche–Copolia: A fairly shady walk through forest of the Morne Seychelles National Park. Provides views of the east coast of Mahé and other islands. Pitcher plants and other flora and fauna unique to Seychelles can be seen. *Graded as MEDIUM. Two hours.*

Enjoying a hike in the forests on Curieuse

Victoria–Beau Vallon: A climb over the low ridge of hills between Victoria and Beau Vallon Bay, on the west coast of Mahé. The trail can be walked in either direction, following the main road for part of the way and minor roads for the rest. Passes through the historical part of Victoria. *Graded as EASY. One and a half hours each way.*

Whether the walk you choose has been listed as easy, medium or hard, it is advisable to take a few minor precautions; take a hat, sunscreen, sunglasses and something cool to drink. Try to avoid walking at midday. Inform your hotel where you are going and what time you intend to return. Always make sure you have ample time to complete your walk before the sun sets. Do not stray from the paths; above 500m cloud can descend with remarkable speed and it is surprisingly easy to become disorientated. Take care to stub out cigarettes properly; the forest floor is highly flammable and fire has caused terrible destruction in the past. Wear shoes which provide a good grip; flipflops are not suitable. Please do not pick plants or take animals. Carry all your litter home.

The road from Beau Vallon Bay to Glacis 1939

Recommended Reading

While a number of well-known authors have visited Seychelles over the years, such as Somerset Maugham and Ian Fleming, and while popular author Wilbur Smith has a second home on Cerf Island, few authors have been inspired to weave the islands into their fiction. Most of the published material tends to be factual.

TRAVEL GUIDES

Mauritius and Seychelles Insight Guide (APA, Hong Kong, 2002).
Takes readers on a number of different tours, guiding them around the main sights to see on Mahé, Praslin, La Digue and some of the smaller inner islands.

Seychelles in Your Pocket, by *Antonio Rolfini*. (Le Guide del Leone Viola Explorer; under patronage of Seychelles Milan Consulate, 1997). Updated annually, a hefty pocket sized book, pretty Michael Adams print cover and with lots of adverts but a little confusing to use with its mix of English and Italian text on each page.

Bradt Guide to Seychelles, by *Lyn Mair*, Lynnath Beckley (2001).

NATURAL HISTORY

Birds of the Indian Ocean Islands, by *Ian Sinclair and Olivier Lagrand (US) Bellegrande (UK)*. (1998) Struik, South Africa.

Birds of Seychelles by *Adrian Skerrett* et al. (Princeton University Press, 2003).
Large and comprehensive guide to the many birds to be seen in the archipelago.

A Birdwatcher's Guide to Seychelles, by *A Skerrett and Ian Bullock* (Prion, 1989).
A useful tool for serious bird watchers.

The Beautiful Plants of Seychelles. *A and J Skerrett* (Camerapix, Nairobi, 1995).
A small simple collection of photographs.

A Fragile Eden, *Rosemary Wise* (Princeton University Press, USA, 1999).
A beautiful record of the endemic plants of Seychelles, with full colour plates of Rosemary Wise' intricately detailed botanical paintings.
Horribly expensive but a work of art.

The Flora of Mauritius and Seychelles, by *JG Baker*,
(Asian Educational Services, 1999)

Marine Shells of the Seychelles by *Alan G Jarrett*, (Carole Green Publishing, 2000)

DIVING

Diving and Snorkeling Guide to Seychelles (Pisces Diving and Snorkeling Guides),
by *Lawson Wood* (Lonely Planet Publications, 1997).
Tropical Marine Life by *Dieter Eichler* (Immel Publications Ltd, 1995).
Neutral Buoyancy: Adventures in a Liquid World, by *Tim Ecott* (Penguin, 2002).
Seychelles is included in this anecdotal book describing the raptures of diving.

HISTORY

Rivals in Eden: A History of Seychelles from 1740–1827 by *William McAteer*
(2nd edition, Pristine Books, Seychelles, 2002). A detailed account of the early
history of Seychelles, chronicling the discovery and early settlement of the islands,
to the end of French rule.
Hard Times in Paradise: A History of Seychelles from 1827–1919,
by *William McAteer*, (Pristine Books, Seychelles, 2000).
The second volume in William McAteers fascinating studies on the history of
Seychelles: this covers much of the English rule.

Desroches Island Beach

Seychelles Since 1770 by *Deryck Scarr* (C. Hurst & Co., 2000). An ambitious book, which despite its wide historical sweep is full of detail and especially interesting for those with family connections in Seychelles as it makes constant reference to well known families in the islands.

Sunshine and Shadows by *Maxime Ferrari* (Minerva Press, 1999). An interesting glimpse, through one man's memoirs, of the political intrigues in Seychelles since independence.

GIFT BOOKS

Aldabra, World Heritage Site, by *Amin, Willetts and Skerrett* Camerapix, Nairobi, 1995. Visually stunning record of Seychelles' remote atoll.

Island Homes, Seychelles by local authors *Maryse Eichler de Saint Jorre, Ardill and Bossu-Picat* (Artistic Productions, Seychelles, 1989). A charming record of traditional architecture.

Journey Through Seychelles by *Amin, Willets and Skerret.* (Camerapix, Published by Nairobi 1999). Large format glossy photographic record of the many islands in Seychelles.

Seychelles by *Norbert Frich*. A large format glossy by the German photographer.
The Seychelles Archipelago by *Claude Pavard* (Richer/Hoa Qui, Paris, 1990).
Coffee table book strong on aerial views of outer islands.

TRAVEL WRITERS

A Vision of Eden by *Marianne North* (The stationary Office Books, 1993).
The views of the Victorian artist and traveller, this attractive book also contains many of her paintings of Seychelles and the many other countries she visited.
Marianne North at Kew Gardens by *L Ponsonby*, (Webb and Bower, 1990)
Seychelles: Beyond the Reefs by *William Travis* (Arrow Books, London 1990).
A racy account of his adventures trying to make a living fishing. Written some 30 years ago but still in print today and remains the most entertaining travel writing in print on Seychelles.
Voices: Seychelles Short Stories by *Glynn Burridge*.
(Nighthue Publications, Seychelles, 2000)
A collection of fiction and fact based on the author's experiences of living on D'Arros island in Seychelles and the many 'outer island tales' he heard there.

Useful Websites

www.seychelles.uk.com—official tourist board site with lots of very useful information on planning a holiday to Seychelles.
www.sey.net—Seychelles super site
www.airseychelles.com—Airline information and timetables
www.helicopterseychelles.com—helicopter charter and flight schedule information
www.pps.gov.sc/meteo—Seychelles Meteorological Service weather site
www.diveseychelles.com—Site for the Underwater Centre, Seychelles
www.the-seychelles.com/sha—Seychelles Hotel Association site, includes all hotel listings.
www.yellowpages.sc—telephone business directory

Index

Anse Lazio, Praslin

Woman with Calou bottle, La Digue

Shopping for souvenirs on La Digue